Pelican Books
Politics in France

Advisory Editor: Jean Blondel

Pierre Avril is a political journalist who was born
in 1930 at Pau in the south west of France. After
studying law and economics at Toulouse, then in
Paris, he involved himself in politics and became an
associate of Pierre Mendès-France. He was
editor-in-chief of *Cahiers de la République*, a
political journal founded by Mendès-France, until
1962, when he submitted his doctoral thesis to the
faculty of law in Paris; published under the title
Le Régime politique de la Ve République (with a
second edition in 1966), it is an extremely critical
study of the Gaullist constitutional machinery. He
has also published, in 1965, an essay on French
institutions called *Un Président pour quoi faire?*
Pierre Avril is married and has a son.

Pierre Avril

Politics in France

Translated
from the French
by John Ross

Penguin Books
Baltimore, Maryland

Penguin Books Ltd, Harmondsworth,
Middlesex, England
Penguin Books Inc., 7110 Ambassador Road,
Baltimore, Maryland 21207, U S A
Penguin Books Australia Ltd, Ringwood,
Victoria, Australia

This translation first published 1969
Copyright © Pierre Avril, 1969

Made and printed in Great Britain by
Hazell Watson & Viney Ltd
Aylesbury, Bucks
Set in Monotype Times

Contents

Contents

Preface to the Penguin Politics Series

One of the most striking developments of the last decade has been the growth in the academic study of politics: but this growth has also coincided with a marked increase in the popular demand for books which attempt to study political life in a systematic fashion. Many still do not admit that 'political science' is a true science, but those who believe that political events are the product of fortuitous circumstances have become much less numerous. Studies of elections, of parties, of the role of the military, of administrations, of international relations are part of the modern 'culture': they are now recognized to be as important an object of study as other aspects of social, literary or artistic life.

The Penguin politics series aims at presenting a picture of political life in its various facets to the reader who is concerned with understanding the patterns which lie behind the surface of political events. It is geared to describing the problems, explaining the theories and accounting for the happenings which are most characteristic of the modern political world and which are of equal interest to the politician, the student of politics and the public at large. The subject of the series is therefore as broad as the subject of politics itself – that of this 'political animal' which man is when it applies itself to ordering the society in which it lives.

Jean Blondel

Introduction

There are more than two hundred varieties of cheese in France.[1] Sir Winston Churchill is reputed to have said once that this range and diversity might well reflect more than the importance the French attach to the pleasures of the table, important as this is. . . . And indeed the political history of the country turns out to be almost as varied, whether we take constitutions (fifteen or so since the fall of the Bastille on 14 July 1789) or Governments (over 140 Cabinets since the definitive foundation of the Republic in 1871). We might even be tempted into drawing parallels between cheeses and Governments, on the grounds that both belong to the same cultural reality, one which we must come to know fully if we are to understand French politics.

On the other hand, we could take the opposite approach, and consider the attempts that have been made to reduce this diversity, in particular those aimed at an ideal form of government supposedly embodied by the British parliamentary system. This line of attack presents added advantages in view of the fact that French theorists and politicians, from Benjamin Constant to Michel Debré,[2] have been fascinated by the British model, which they have tried to reproduce. In this, however, they can scarcely be said to have succeeded, since for the most part they have a rather special conception of the British system, which turns out

1. Exactly 289, according to Advocate-General Raymond Lindon, the foremost contemporary authority.
2. Benjamin Constant (1767–1830) worked on the theory of constitutional liberalism, but is best remembered for his *Adolphe*, one of the earliest and finest psychological novels in French. Michel Debré, as Minister of Justice, was a prominent member of the team who drafted the 1958 Constitution; he served as Prime Minister from January 1959 to April 1962, and as Minister of Finance from January 1966.

in the end to be an idealized form of the traditional French model: unconscious projection is a phenomenon familiar to psychologists, who are well aware of the fact that it is difficult to know others except through oneself.

Our task is rendered more difficult by the fact that the terms *Government*, *State*, *Parliament* and *Party* refer to political elements which are only apparently constant; while in many countries the words designate closely related forms of institutions, it is impossible to say that they have exactly the same meaning everywhere. Up to a point, these words – and institutions – play the same role in all countries, but at the same time they are designed to meet the needs of the individual societies in which they function.

In short, the way a given country is governed defines a system of relationships between State and society; it does not necessarily localize power, nor need it specify *who* wields this power at any one moment, for the answer to such a question is bound to vary with circumstances. The intervention of individuals or groups, which may appear of fundamental importance for explaining a particular event or decision, can generally be fitted into a relatively stable structure: this structure is the subject of the present book.

We therefore propose to examine the relationships established between State power (which in France has been an autonomous decision-making centre since the Middle Ages) and society, in order to set out certain characteristic traits. Naturally, these factors have developed in varying ways, but none the less they still seem to group themselves round three main ideas, corresponding to three historical turning-points.

The Solution of a Problem: Conflicts of Legitimacy

The French political system can be looked on first of all as the solution to a problem: the crisis that dates from the fall of the monarchy at the end of the eighteenth century. The ensuing hundred years were spent in search of a solution which began to emerge only in 1871, with the establishment of the Third Republic. In fact, the crisis resulted from a clash between two conflicting legitimacies, in which the monarchical order, based on divine right, was challenged by the democratic principles laid down in 1789 in the Declaration of the Rights of Man. The two doctrines were completely incompatible and, most important of all, this fact was recognized. The execution of Louis XVI on 21 January 1793 represented a deliberate, tragic break with what at that very instant automatically became the Old Regime. But society does not progress by leaps and bounds. The new principle was introduced too abruptly for it to take the place of the old without a period of transition to allow the turbulence to calm down so that a regime acceptable to every citizen could emerge. The Republic, which met with attack and resistance both inside and outside France, was soon forced to give way to Napoleon Bonaparte who, by having himself crowned Emperor of the French, took the first tentative step towards a reconciliation of the two orders. He tried to marry the inheritance of the Revolution, to which the masses were passionately attached, and the prestige and customs of the monarchy, which were still somehow missed. This attempt collapsed when challenged by the European coalition which in 1815 restored Louis XVI's brother to the throne; thereafter it became evident that while the Republic was not yet viable, the monarchy had completely ceased to be so. In spite of this, it lasted until 1848, sometimes in a position of resistance (the 1830 Revolution swept away the Bourbon dynasty) and sometimes allying itself with Parliament. However, the clash of principles was so complete that this second reconciliation was merely tolerated, and Louis-Philippe[3] stepped down without protest as soon as the first barricades rose in the streets of Paris.

The Second Republic was fated to be even more short-lived than its predecessor. It was proclaimed at a moment when the decline of royal power was complete, but the idea of a Republic was still very abstract and as yet it lacked the broad social support indispensable for its survival. When Napoleon's nephew presented himself in the December 1848 elections (it had been decided to elect the President of the Republic by universal

3. A cousin of Charles X, he reigned from 1830 to 1848.

suffrage) he won a triumphal victory. Hostility towards the idea of having the head of State appointed directly by the electorate can be traced back to this experience, which turned out to have unfortunate results; the new President never managed to come to terms with his Deputies and, above all, he could not be re-elected. Consequently, a few months before his mandate expired he engineered himself undivided power with the *coup d'état* of 2 December 1851. In the following year the Empire was re-established and Louis-Napoleon Bonaparte became Napoleon III. His reign lasted until 1870; on the eve of the Franco-Prussian War a constitutional plebiscite produced seven million votes in favour of the regime, as against one and a half million hostile voters. But at the end of the summer France's defeat at Sedan led to the collapse of the Empire, and on 4 September 1870 the Republic was proclaimed. This time it was here to stay.

At this point one man, himself almost a personification of the period, came forward. Adolphe Thiers, then aged seventy-three, had been in the forefront of political action almost without interruption since 1830.[4] After contributing to the fall of the Bourbons and the installation of Louis-Philippe, under whom he served six times as Minister and twice as Prime Minister, he supported Louis-Napoleon Bonaparte, but moved over to the Opposition after the 1851 *coup d'état*. He was called on to negotiate the armistice with Prussia in February 1871, while Gambetta[5] and the radical wing of the Republicans wanted to carry on with the war. The bulk of the country longed for peace, and was grateful to Thiers for bringing the war to an end, just as it approved the savage repressive measures he took against the left-wing insurrection, known as the Paris Commune, which immediately followed. Despite the Armistice, Paris refused to stop fighting, and proclaimed the 'Commune' on 26 March 1871, an act of patriotic revolt which was soon to turn into a social revolution.

4. cf. Jacques Chastenet, *Histoire de la Troisième République*, Paris, 1952, vol. I, p. 54.

5. Born in 1838, Lèon Gambetta was elected deputy for Paris in 1869. He was the main Republican leader, and served in the National Defence Government in 1870, becoming President of the Council in 1881; he died the following year.

Thiers crushed the rebellion, thus breaking the extreme Left and reassuring the country population and the urban bourgeoisie, and then cleverly evaded the constitutional question raised by the Royalists, who had made a striking comeback at the February 1871 elections. Once he had been recognized as 'head of the executive of the French *Republic*' by a largely monarchist majority, he gradually accustomed his fellow countrymen to life in a Republic – which he presented as 'the regime that divides us least'. He thus forestalled the plans of the left-wing leaders, who had had plenty of time under the Empire to think over their past mistakes; the principal figure among these, Gambetta, wrote in 1869: 'The Left must be seen to be the reassuring, logical consequence of what is and of what is ending.'

Despite the unostentatious way in which the Republic was founded, it still met with resistance in some quarters; however, the new regime's opponents tended to be looked on as irresponsible trouble-makers, since for the first time the Republic was associated in people's minds with the ideas of security and peace. At the price of a tendency towards conservatism in social matters and some undeniable inconsistencies (which were later to weigh heavily on the Third Republic), the regime was soon equipped with institutions by the three constitutional laws passed in 1875. These laws were the result of a compromise between the moderate Republicans and the supporters of constitutional monarchy, and in a pragmatic way provided the blueprint for a parliamentary system of government, the republican nature of which was to be affirmed only after several years of conflict. The outcome of these struggles was a tacitly agreed attitude towards the regime, giving rise to what later became known as the 'Republican tradition'. The most serious incident occurred in 1877. The President of the Republic of the time, Marshal MacMahon, whom the Royalists had, after much argument and deliberation, decided to elect to the office symbolizing the new regime, decided to dismiss the Cabinet and dissolve the Chamber. The grounds he gave were that the Cabinet was not taking a firm enough line with the Deputies, the majority of whom were by then, as a result of the 1876 elections, Republicans. In the election campaign which followed dissolution, Gambetta and Thiers joined forces. The consequences of this *rapprochement* and the resulting Republican victory were to be far-reaching.

Dissolution was branded from then on as the weapon of the authoritarian Right used to crush the people's elected representatives; although the power to dissolve Parliament was written into the constitution, no other President dared take advantage of it during the Third Republic. Moreover, it became a fundamental tenet of the regime that the President should play only a minor, unobtrusive role in politics; the corollary of this was, clearly, the supremacy of Parliament.

It is significant that the arguments that surrounded the birth of the Third Republic were frequently quoted eighty years later, when the Fifth Republic was being established. Interpreted in the broad sense, as not merely a set of legal arrangements, but also as a body of conventions and values, the French political system has remained profoundly marked by the tradition that crystallized in the early 1870s and still influences the modern interpretation of several key ideas in politics; the characteristic features of the Presidency of the Republic, the Government and Parliament are all related to this past, and the transformations taking place today acquire their full meaning when we consider them in terms of an almost century-old model, and not merely in the context of the contemporary world.

The Antagonism between Democracy and Government

The second basic idea, one which is familiar to British historians,[6] is the contradiction which in France appears to oppose democracy and government. The French political system has developed around a split between power and society which, far from being eliminated by the democratic form of the State, has been assimilated by the Republic. The Republic tried to preserve a zone of authority communicating with, but independent of, the electorate, the aim being to enable the country's inhabitants to live in peace

6. e.g., David Thomson, *Democracy in France*, Oxford University Press, 1958.

despite the deep divisions caused by the conflict between the two forms of legitimacy (i.e. the divine right of kings *versus* the sovereignty of the people). The 1875 compromise manifested this preoccupation in so far as it removed the head of the administration (the President) from the hurly-burly of political life, while at the same time organizing a system of representation.

The institutions of the Third Republic largely met the requirements of a parliamentary regime, since the head of State was not politically responsible, and Ministers were answerable to the Chambers. However, they had some unusual features: First, although State authority was legitimized by universal suffrage, communication with the electorate took place only through a series of intermediaries which acted as filters; one of these was the President of the Republic himself, who was elected for seven years by a joint meeting of Deputies and Senators. Secondly, the influence of the electorate was limited by the Senate, whose members were elected for nine years by delegates of municipal and local councils, a third of them being replaced every three years. Unlike the House of Lords, the French Second Chamber strengthened its position between its creation in 1876 and the First World War; from 1896 onwards, it was accepted that the Senate could not only paralyse legislation, but even topple the Government. Throughout the Third Republic, the Senate did not hesitate to use this power whenever it felt that a Government had gone too far, whether towards the Right or to the Left.

Finally, the Prime Minister was not mentioned in the 1875 Acts; indeed, the head of the executive was the President of the Republic, who was not politically responsible. But the logic of governmental responsibility duly led to the emergence of a leader of the Cabinet: the President of the Council of Ministers, though for many years his exact position remained ambiguous (as can be seen from his official title itself, since the Council of Ministers was presided over by the President of the Republic).

The new regime succeeded in handling the problem of governing France until the Thirties. In particular, it managed to carry on the nation's business during the First World War without abdicating to others, and it later succeeded in overcoming the difficulties of national reconstruction. But it could not stand up to the two-pronged attack of the Great Depression and Hitler's ambitions, and its decline led to the loss of public confidence that has constantly bedevilled French institutions ever since. The 1940 *débâcle* finally toppled the by then half-rotten structure; the lessons learned during the decrepitude of the regime were borne in mind when, after the Second World War, attempts were made to reconstruct the political system. The Constitution of the Fourth Republic, adopted after a referendum in October 1946, reduced the powers of the Second Chamber, renamed 'Council of the Republic', to consultative status and gave total sovereignty to the National Assembly; it recognized the existence of the President of the Council, who became the head of the executive, and laid down new rules governing the relations between Government and Parliament with a view to streamlining the functioning of the system.

Despite uncontestable successes in the field of economic reconstruction, the Fourth Republic failed to live up to the high hopes which had been placed in it. The measures intended to ensure governmental stability soon proved to be inadequate, and although the need for reform was generally recognized, the regime seemed incapable of reforming itself. The death-blow came with the loss of the colonies; in June 1958, Parliament, fearing that the military rebellion in Algeria might spread to metropolitan France, empowered General de Gaulle, as President of Council, to revise the Constitution. De Gaulle was asked only to maintain the principle of governmental responsibility to Parliament and to submit the projected changes to the country in a referendum.

The revisions led in fact to the approval, by the referendum held on 28 September 1958, of a completely new Constitution. The main features of the Fifth Republic are the following. First, the position of the President is strengthened, not only because the Presidency regains powers granted in 1875 and abolished in 1946, but because decisions can now be taken without the counter-signature of a politically responsible Minister. As a result, he may call for a referendum on a bill, dissolve the National Assembly and, most important of all, apply Article 16 of the Constitution, which gives him virtually dictatorial powers in times of emergency. Second, the National Assembly no longer has full sovereignty; its activities are henceforth subject to direction by the Government; the Senate, which regains its old title and part of its former prerogatives, is once more empowered to stop legislation, as long as the Government does not see fit to step in and ensure that the last word rests with the Deputies. Finally, the procedure of Parliament is streamlined; in this context the new Constitution goes beyond the experiments of 1946 and the measures envisaged in the last years of the Fourth Republic, particularly in relation to the exercise of cabinet responsibility through the use of the motion of censure.

Thus, as far as the functioning of Parliament is concerned, the Fifth Republic simply continues and develops the tendencies already present in the Fourth Republic, and the system of Cabinet leadership constitutes a reasonably faithful adaptation of the British model. But the other features are much more ambiguous. The limits imposed on the Assembly's sovereignty and the increased status of the Presidency can indeed be interpreted as a swing of the pendulum back towards the doctrine of a strong State whose basis is not universal suffrage – an idea which had been advanced without success in the Thirties. As long as the two organs flanking the Assembly, itself elected by universal suffrage, were chosen by a restricted electorate, this view was generally correct; the Senate, which continued to be elected in the same way as before, resumed its tutelary role, and the President of the Republic, who was no longer appointed by Senators and Deputies only, but chosen by a larger, though still restricted, electorate, acquired the status of a national arbiter placed above party politics. It was under these conditions that General de Gaulle was elected in December 1958.

Yet such a 'reactionary' (to borrow Raymond Aron's term) interpretation of the system does not correspond to reality. The Senate constantly opposed de Gaulle from the end of 1962; as a result, it came to be bypassed by the Government, which has regularly ignored the Upper House and sought support among the Gaullist majority of Deputies. Thus the Senate no longer forms part of the decision-making machinery, except to suggest technical modifications. In order to simplify an already sufficiently complex picture, we shall therefore pay little attention to the Second Chamber. Meanwhile the process for electing the President of the Republic has been brought in line with the actual role played by General de Gaulle, since the President is now elected by universal suffrage. This essential modification was decided by referendum in October 1962, but as this measure apparently affected only the means of selecting the head of State, other constitutional arrangements, particularly those concerning governmental responsibility to Parliament, remained unaffected.

The Fifth Republic is thus a fundamentally ambiguous regime, as it appears to constitute both the logical outcome of the crisis which destroyed the traditional model and an attempt to evolve a new system.

The Impact of Social Change

The third basic point is related to the startling transformations that have taken place in France since the end of the Second World War. Spectacular changes have taken place on every front; whether in terms of population increase or in relation to socio-economic structures, the imperative of growth has taken the place of the former ideal of peaceful equilibrium. This is indeed virtually a revolution, but a revolution which is peculiar in that, in general, it did not affect the political sector. Society as a whole has been shaken up and recast, profound changes have taken place in the public bureaucracy (which in many ways was at the root of this revolution); but for the most part the intervening sectors have remained unaffected.

Such a marked contrast is no doubt partly accounted for by the conditions in which the main political parties first emerged and by the ideological nature of party battles. The conflicts which characterized the old political system did take social issues and movements into account, but interpreted them in terms of the political system, using political forms and specialized, rather idiosyncratic language and images. In view of this we must not disregard the serious crises of the last two centuries, for the fundamental cleavages of the present are determined in relation to the issues disputed in the past; each subsequent crisis left a further scar, which can still be traced in the language of today. In the absence of other stimuli, the memory of these past events can, by itself, serve as an irritant. Thus political parties have kept their former differences, while present-day conflicts have been superimposed on these old quarrels.

The principal cause of debate, the one that lies at the root of all the others, is the regime itself. The Republic is not only a form of institutional organization but, as we have seen, it embodies a particular type of legitimacy. We start then from the Revolution of 1789, which represents the original and fundamental split, to such a degree that even in 1965, André Malraux could declare without hesitation that 'it would not be unreasonable to say that a right-winger is a man who, when he thinks of the Revolution, sees a guillotine, whereas a left-winger thinks of Fleurus'.[7] Although the reference may appear rather rhetorical today, it provided the background for the struggles of the end of the nineteenth century, as these cannot be separated from resistance to the secularized, egalitarian order of things that the Republicans were trying to impose. The part played by a concept such as that of the secular state illustrates the transformation of political conflicts into philosophical confrontations. Secularization implied the rejection by the State of all values not contained in the Declaration of the Rights of Man; it denied all the principles on which the Old Regime had been built, thereby striking a blow at the Church's claims to influence, if not actually to direct, the temporal order. The first attacks against the Church were launched in 1877 by the Republicans on the occasion of campaigns in favour of the Pope, who was at loggerheads with the new Italian State; it was then that Gambetta first uttered the battle-cry that was to echo

7. The guillotine (named after its alleged inventor Dr Guillotin) has been used for executing criminals since the Revolution, and was used on Louis XVI. Fleurus was a victory won by the Revolutionary armies in 1794.

André Malraux, author of novels and essays, became Minister of Culture in 1958.

for over thirty years: 'Our true enemy is clericalism!' After a short lull, anti-clericalism flared up again violently with the Dreyfus Case. Among all the opponents of the regime who banded together to oppose the appeal against the first anti-Dreyfus verdict[8] the most hot-headed were members of religious congregations; often extremely rich, with access to an important sector of the press, the religious orders took on the character of organized cadres of a party hostile to the Republic.

Attachment to the principle of the secular State thus led to political anti-clericalism, since 'reaction' and the Church came to be looked on as the two faces of one and the same enemy against which the Republicans had to defend themselves. Electoral anti-clericalism followed naturally, as it provided a simple and convenient means of maintaining discipline among the Republican forces. After the 1905 Act which established the separation of Church and State, it often became no more than a conservative alibi.[9]

The main consequence of the spirit in the Republic, and the significance attached to it at the time, was that French political divisions developed along ideological lines, while other types of conflict took second place. Men who otherwise would have joined forces to form a conservative party continued to oppose one another, while the republican movement came to include men of widely diverse outlooks. But the less important conflicts (less important by comparison with the main division, that is) were to prove perfectly adequate replacements when the main arguments lost their sting, and the informal 'republican party' of the 1877–1900 period came to split into separate parliamentary groups and,

8. Accused of treason on the basis of documents which turned out to have been forged, Captain Dreyfus had been condemned to deportation to Devil's Island in 1894. The Dreyfus Case split France in two until the beginning of the twentieth century.

9. Although the issue had lost most of its sting, even in 1951 the question of secularism still touched off sufficiently strong reactions for the Gaullists to consider it worth using in an attempt to split the majority: it was enough to suggest subsidizing religious schools. The Christian Democrats could not oppose such a move, and duly broke away from their Socialist and Radical allies.

later, into organized parties (e.g., the Socialist Party, created in 1905, or the Radical Party which dates from 1901).

Other factors later came into play, such as the emergence of the Communist Party in 1920, and later the Resistance movement. In 1944 Christian Democrats who had served in the Resistance grouped together to form the MRP (Mouvement Républicain Populaire); the Liberation also led to the creation of various short-lived organizations, as well as of the Gaullist movement. With the success of General de Gaulle in 1958, the fragmented nature of French politics was further complicated by a new division of loyalties which still endangers the State: the present regime is challenged by avowedly republican parties, which are not prepared to concede their opponents any share in government.

Yet other conflicts arose alongside this division, though this still constitutes the main axis of French political life. Some, resulting from social struggles, were similar to those that resulted from industrialization elsewhere in Europe; they did, however, include a particular strain of resentment stemming from the violent repression of the Paris Commune, which beheaded the working-class movement in 1871. Others, focused on foreign policy, sometimes took an emotionally charged tone (the title of 'republican' was denied to the Conservatives, who in turn denied their opponents the right to call themselves 'patriots'). Yet during most of the period foreign policy remained surprisingly immune from controversy. Despite changes of government, French diplomacy was led over long periods by the same men: Delcassé directed the Ministry of Foreign Affairs for seven crucial years, from 1898 to 1905, as did Aristide Briand from 1925 to 1931. The Fourth Republic had only two Foreign Ministers between 1946 and 1954, both of whom belonged to the MRP: Robert Schuman, one of the 'fathers of Europe', and Georges Bidault. It is also worth remembering that M. Couve de Murville took office at the Quai d'Orsay in June 1958. . . . In such circumstances, decision-making in foreign affairs took place in an atmosphere of relative calm and dignity, disrupted only occasionally by violent polemic, as when the country was split down the middle over German

Introduction

rearmament and the proposed European Defence Community (rejected in August 1954).

This complex inheritance led to a political structure in which problems of present-day society are perceived through the fossilized remains of past confrontations. In an abstract fashion these battles express the profound movements of the time; behind the conflict between the two forms of legitimacy we can see the desire for social upgrading of the classes excluded from power, whose aspirations become sublimated into philosophical demands. The words have survived the realities that gave rise to these questions, but new demands have still to be expressed in similar language. Consequently French political parties are often criticized for failing to provide a political personnel in touch with modern society.

Adjustments have indeed been made, but these have managed to spare the persistent, strongly ideological biases of the political class. French political life is thus Janus-like: one of its faces is doctrinaire and intransigent, the other pragmatic and even opportunist. For instance, the French Socialist Party is the only one of its kind in Europe to have refused up to now to carry out the slightest revisions of its doctrine; it still proclaims its 1905 principles, whereas it actually behaves like a very moderate reformist party. In the same way Gaullism, which had assumed the defence of French greatness, had within four years of taking office completely liquidated its overseas possessions.

In 1815 Chateaubriand hoped to lead the French 'to face reality through dreams: which are the things they really love'.[10] This aim, according to the American political scientist Nicholas Wahl, is shared by General de Gaulle, but the intellectual or sentimental compensations brought by such an attitude are not without their drawbacks if the country is turned into a nation of sleepwalkers in the process. The Fifth Republic has been organized in such a way that it does not favour the political reawakening that should by rights have accompanied the transformation of

10. *Mémoires d'Outre-Tombe*, Book 28, Ch. 17. Chateaubriand (1768–1848), a monarchist writer, was Minister of Foreign Affairs from 1822 to 1824, after having served as French Ambassador in London.

France. The institutional changes which have taken place have helped direct communication between the head of State and the electorate, but left the intermediate bodies untouched. Organs of representation still exist, but they are virtually disconnected from the system, and no longer fulfil their true function of channelling information and ideas. Parties are well aware of the functional constraints of the new system, which force them into new groupings; but, so far, they have only timidly begun to face up to the question of France's future government. With de Gaulle in power, this sort of speculation seems rather academic. . . .

In an historical perspective, French government can be seen as the adaptation of a model; in political terms, it corresponds to the search for a new balance between authority and democracy. If we look at the consequences for the system as a whole of transformations affecting the nature of society, we can observe a pronounced change of direction in the development of the French regime. The object of this book is thus less to give a precise description of the present state of government than to attempt to locate it between a known past and a still uncertain future. We shall, therefore, not adopt the logical order, which would mean starting from social realities and the forces behind them, and moving towards institutions: this would be reasonable in relation to a stable political situation, but it would lead to endless contradictions and anomalies in the case of France. Marxist analyses of the Fifth Republic have not succeeded in pinning down the basic factors that must be examined if we are to move from the socio-economic infrastructure to the political superstructure. It therefore seems better to reverse the usual procedure and start from the traditional political framework. We shall then examine the administrative and social structures, and finally we shall attempt to describe the long-term considerations that will influence the French system of government in the future.[11]

11. In order to avoid overloading the main body of the text, each chapter is followed by appendices containing basic data to which the reader may refer.

Part One The Political Model

Part One The Political Model

According to a widely held belief, French public life is characterized by a permanent state of antagonism between democratic
forces and Government – and this interpretation, though clearly
an oversimplification, does correspond in many ways to the
reality. In brief, regimes based on popular representation seem to
lead to instability and disorder, whereas periods of effective
government apparently coincide with times when the representative system is limited or suspended. It is a commonplace to describe French history as a mere alternation between periods of
anonymous, confused parliamentary sovereignty and periods of
arbitrary personal power. But could it be that this pendulum
movement functions within one and the same model, a model
which makes allowance for such oscillations?

It would no doubt be possible to trace the development of this
model throughout the nineteenth century: in its contemporary
form, it crystallized a century ago with the establishment of the
Third Republic. Since then, all attempts at reform (including
those under de Gaulle) have followed the same pattern, which
reveals a particular collective way of facing up to and solving
problems. Thus it appears that this pattern stems from needs and
attitudes that go deeper than mere institutional arrangements;
indeed, one might even think of it as a significant feature of
French culture. If we limit ourselves to the strictly political
aspects of this phenomenon, we can say that there is a 'French
style of government' which is characterized by the importance of
a particular concept of crisis (notwithstanding the Gaullist
regime's efforts to impose a less spasmodic rhythm on public life),
and stems from an ancient, deep-rooted conception of representative democracy, which the journalist Roger Priouret christened

the 'Deputy-centred Republic'. Two other salient features are worth noting: the difficulty of integrating parties and the persistence of a quasi-monarchical element of tutelage. However, as we shall see, these different aspects have been modified over the last ten years.

1 'Government by Fits and Starts'

Apart from the short period between 1940 and 1945, France has lived continuously under a parliamentary system since the official birth of the Republic in 1875. But this parliamentary system was unusual in many ways: power was not distributed or exercised in accordance with the normal rules of this type of system. There was, it is true, a Government, but its authority was intermittent and incomplete.

It has been said that Racine's tragedies are the *dénouement* of a crisis situation. This definition also holds good for French politics, in which governmental action can be analysed in terms of periods of crisis rather than slow progressions. This jerky rhythm fits a national history which, for the last two centuries, can be described in terms of a series of dates which sum up the most important events, from 14 July 1789, the date of the storming of the Bastille and the beginning of the Revolution, to 13 May 1958, when the Fifth Republic made its appearance. The *coup d'état* managed by Napoleon I is remembered as 18 Brumaire, while the fall of the Bourbons is linked with the 'three glorious days' (the three days of rioting which led to the departure of Charles X in July 1830); an exception is Louis-Philippe's constitutional monarchy, which takes its name from a whole month and is known as the 'July Monarchy'. But we return to our historical calendar-entries with the *coup d'état* of 2 December 1851, which founded the Second Empire. Similarly, it is normal practice to refer to '16 May', without specifying the year, to denote the dissolution of the Chamber of Deputies pronounced in 1877 by Marshal MacMahon, which has since become a byword for anti-republican action, and, yet again, we have '18 June', evoking the beginnings of the Resistance in 1940. This has even inspired one publisher to

29

bring out a series of books under the general title of 'Thirty Days that Shaped France'.

This unusual rhythm can be traced further within each regime, as small-scale incidents repeat the alternating tension and *dénouement* that occur regularly throughout the country's history. Indeed, this rhythm seems to be so deeply engrained in French political life that General de Gaulle himself, who continually sings the praises of stability and continuity, is not above whipping up simulated tension when events deny him the opportunity of solving fresh crises. Circumstances had indeed imposed de Gaulle on the nation as 'one of these men who spring forth from events and are the spontaneously born children of danger', as the Prime Minister, Georges Pompidou, described him, with the not wholly felicitous help of a quotation from Chateaubriand; once the Algerian war was over, he tried to create a dramatic, emotionally charged climate around each electoral campaign in order to appear as the one and only man capable of bringing about a peaceful solution. The notion of 'stakes' reappears in each of these battles, which consequently come to resemble a game of double or quits in which the French people are invited to join. In this sense, Gaullism merely gives systematic form to a basic characteristic of French political life; and it tries to avoid the weaknesses inherent in society by pushing its more positive leanings to the limit.

The role of the notion of crisis in public life has been interpreted in many ways. Some theories refer to the numerous difficulties the country has had to face, both internally and externally, throughout its history. Others note the structure of French society (which the American political scientist Stanley Hoffmann called the 'Stalemate Society'), in which conflicts could not be resolved by pragmatic adjustments but only by splits and direct confrontations. Some refer to the French style of authority, which is hierarchical and formal, while others base their explanations on the national psychology, in which ideological extremism and abstract passions seem to play a major role. But whatever the cause, the mechanics of the system are clear enough: 'when events make themselves felt', de Gaulle once said, 'and we are in agreement over the substance procedures acquire a considerable degree of flexibility'. When the conditions for a crisis are combined, a sort of arbitration takes place in favour of the substance, and formal preferences, ideological or subjective considerations – in short, 'procedures' – go by the board.

From 'Functional Crisis' to 'Mechanical Crisis'

The French have always loved ideological battles, which sharpen political conflicts and favour the dramatic and the spectacular. Domestic politics may be irritating at times, but they are rarely boring, and governmental crises seem to act as the harmless but exciting projection of a far more dangerous drama. These crises are, in fact, a form of play-acting, at the end of which the dead and wounded stand up and dust themselves down, often to continue their roles in the following performance; their symbolic death is usually enough to calm the anger of their opponents and dispose of the original discontent.

If understood in this way, the governmental crisis had a 'functional' role in the Third and Fourth Republics. It is a well-known fact that Governments taking power after crises were almost always granted, sometimes on identical terms, the very powers that had been denied to their defeated predecessors. The fall of the latter provided an amusing but effective way of arbitrating between the contradictory claims of the parliamentary parties and forcing the Assembly to take a decision. The new Prime Minister led the Deputies to accept the idea of making the difficult choice which they had avoided by precipitating the fall of the previous Government, and made it clear that the problem could no longer be avoided. Having redistributed ministerial posts, and taken into account the demands of those responsible for the crisis, he put the original trouble-makers with their backs to the wall and thus associated them in the inevitable outcome. Sometimes the crisis was aimed at proving that a formula attracting a fraction of the majority was in fact impractical; a process which came to be known as 'clearing the mortgage'. Once it had been demonstrated, for instance, that a more daring or more

31

generous policy did not attract enough support in the Assembly, the left-wing Deputies on the fringe of the majority (i.e. the very Deputies whose votes were indispensable to any Government) had to resign themselves to supporting a moderate Cabinet. Since other constraints were absent, the crisis had thus brought about a necessary compromise between the desirable and the feasible; but in order for this to happen the crisis still had to take place. The history of the last forty years provides endless examples of such an evolution, though it sometimes went out of control when unusual difficulties cropped up, as when, between the May 1932 elections and the riots of 6 February 1934, a succession of five Cabinets attempted to resolve the nation's financial problems.

After 1950, decolonization triggered off a similar development in the cases of Indochina and, later, Algeria. This time, however, the weight of events proved stronger than the system, which could no longer stimulate the decisions and choices that were the one reason for its existence. 'The worrying thing is not the number of crises: far more serious is their complete uselessness,' as a former President of Council (Edgar Faure) remarked in 1953. 'The crisis is no longer the sanction of a policy, but the excuse for a concession. Stripped of its serious content and with its meaning distorted, it is becoming an alibi for government by fits and starts.' This downgrading of the 'functional' role of crises corresponded to the disintegration and contradictions then becoming evident in parliamentary circles. It was impossible to find solutions for even the most serious and urgent problems without once more raising the whole question of the fragile coalition on which the Government was based. Artificial pretexts were therefore found postponing decisions, as, for example, in the case of the famous 'foregoing considerations' which made it possible to keep the European Community Treaty in cold storage for two years until hypothetical conditions were met. This is the situation, characteristic of the Fourth Republic although it can be traced back to the nineteenth century, which has been termed 'immobilism'.

Undecided which line to adopt and exposed to the crossfire of Opposition attacks, Governments took to hibernation, in the hope that in the fullness of time solutions would emerge by themselves or, at least, the Opposition's energies would wane. As a result, creeping paralysis set in, spreading slowly through current affairs and literally petrifying Cabinet activity. Like a patient on the danger list, the Government was liable to expire at the slightest movement, and as it could hardly remain completely immobile, any shock was sufficient to bring its life to an end. In this way the 'functional' crisis, which had begun as a means of choosing between controversial alternatives, developed into the 'mechanical' crisis, which could be touched off by mere ill-temper or the most trivial parliamentary accident.

Crises could also have 'subjective' causes, as when they were caused by changes in the feelings of Deputies towards the Government, considering it too daring or excessively timid, too aggressive in periods of slackness, too lethargic in periods of tension. Sometimes, on the other hand, the crisis was 'objective', in that it resulted from a genuine challenge presented by events, one which had to be met. Power was then given to the candidate who appeared most suitable. But 'subjective' and 'objective' aspects could at times be combined: a timid Prime Minister would seem ill-equipped to deal with a situation calling for strong measures, or the fatigue of a legislature could show itself by unseating the moderate elements of the majority. This explains why the elections of 1924, 1932 and 1936, which returned largely left-wing Chambers, all led sooner or later to Centre-Right Governments.

Under the Fourth Republic, the origin of crises was clouded by the absence of a majority, a situation resulting logically from the electoral system of proportional representation, which in itself ruled out the possibility of a majority.[1] During the first legislature (1946–51) the elimination of the Communists by the Socialist Premier Paul Ramadier put an end in 1947 to 'tripartism', that is, the pact concluded between Christian Democrats, Socialists and Communists. Harried by Gaullists on the Right and Communists

1. The list of crises under the Fourth Republic is contained in an Appendix to this chapter. Where electoral systems are concerned, see Appendix to Chapter 2.

on the Left, most Cabinets fell victim to the Socialists' repugnance for the unpopular measures rendered inevitable by the nation's economic and financial plight. As a result, intrigues inside the Socialist Party forced Ramadier to resign without a vote, on 19 November 1947. A whole series of Cabinets was then defeated over financial difficulties. Each successive Government was obliged to pick up the problem where its predecessor had left off and, allowing for some form of transaction designed to save appearances, continue with the same policies as before. When the second Queuille Ministry was defeated as soon as it was formed, in July 1950, M. Pleven took over the succession, only to resign voluntarily on 28 February 1951, 'to avoid aggravating divisions within the majority', which was in disagreement over the electoral law – a law which Henri Queuille duly saw through Parliament shortly after. The second legislature (1951–5) was more conservative, particularly at first, as the controversy over subsidizing religious schools forced the Christian Democrats to move further to the Right. The Socialists, refusing any compromise, refused to serve in Governments, therefore alternating between positions of support and opposition. First René Pleven, then Edgar Faure, were overthrown, in January and February 1952 respectively, because of their financial plans; then Antoine Pinay achieved a measure of stabilization before being abandoned by the Christian Democrats, who had been irritated by his measures concerning family allowances. In May 1953 René Mayer fell in his turn, again over financial problems, and the powers he had requested were granted to Joseph Laniel. During this period, controversy over the planned European Defence Community and German rearmament remained permanently at the back of the Deputies' minds; they wanted to avoid taking a decision on these matters, and preferred to use taxation or social policies as an excuse for disposing of Prime Ministers whose intentions seemed suspect. But at the same time the war in Indochina was still raging, and as the Geneva Conference was unable to discover a solution, the Assembly overthrew Laniel and replaced him with Pierre Mendès-France, although Mendès-France's policies had been rejected a year previously. In February 1955, Mendès-France was duly displaced after a debate on North Africa (the Algerian war had begun on 1 November 1954) and his successor, Edgar Faure, was removed from office in December over a question of electoral reform, but not before he had pronounced the dissolution of the Assembly.

During the Fourth Republic's last Parliament (1956–8), the three successive Governments were all increasingly conservative variations on the same Cabinet: Guy Mollet, who inaugurated the return to power of the Socialists and presided over the longest-lived Ministry of the Fourth Republic, was defeated over a taxation issue in May 1957 (but uneasiness about the Algerian war was also lurking in the background); Maurice Bourgès-Maunoury fell victim, in September of the same year, to right-wing hostility to a projected outline law on Algeria, however timid in its content; and Félix Gaillard fell on 15 April 1958 over the issue of United States intervention in the Franco-Tunisian conflict. The crisis lasted until 13 May, and the new Prime Minister, Pierre Pflimlin, whose election took place on the very day of the Algeria rising, stepped down of his own accord on 28 May to make way for General de Gaulle.

The overall pattern followed by governmental crises reveals the main characteristics of the crisis process. Crises do not change the basic nature of the problems which lead to the fall of a Government any more than they transform the political composition of the Assembly; but they seem to justify the concessions made to the incoming leader. The defeated Premier becomes a scapegoat; his symbolic sacrifice marks the beginning of a new period during which for a short time Deputies reluctantly agree to the inevitable by granting a limited form of credit to the new head of the Government.

'Consuls' and Compromisers

In such circumstances, governing cannot be construed as a series of policy acts, but as the resolution of a crisis, and the statesman is the pilot who guides the nations through difficult straits. The function of the head of the Government can be summed up in terms of this 'steering' power, which may be exercised at different levels, according to the nature of the problems to be solved, and ranges from working out an ingenious compromise, to responsibility for carrying through the whole difficult process of reconstruction. Each of these extreme situations corresponds to a type of man.

The first type can be thought of as the compromiser. It is not essential that he should be able to win enthusiastic support and pursue the execution of a grand master-plan, but he must possess tact and skill with which to iron out disagreements, disarm threats and continue along his cautiously chosen path. Men of this type appeared spontaneously at the beginning of the Third Republic; an outstanding example is provided by Freycinet, 'the white mouse', Prime Minister four times between 1879 and 1890; another is Aristide Briand, who headed eleven Governments between 1909 and 1929. In the Fourth Republic, Queuille fits into this category, to which we can add a sub-species: men whose extreme flexibility and ability to discover compromises ensure success, but who, by virtue of their very promotion, mark the decay of a regime that depends on illusions for its survival. This was the case of Chautemps in the Third Republic, and of René Pleven in the Fourth. There is even a caricatural form of the compromiser, whose virtue is his almost inert neutrality: here the prototype is Sarrien, whom Clemenceau described as 'the dry dock where we put the ship of State from time to time'. Joseph Laniel served as the Fourth Republic's dry dock.

The compromiser often belongs to a small parliamentary group placed in a key position for the majority – i.e., in the Centre. Apart from this strategic position – which is tenable only if the support of his friends is forthcoming – he has less difficulty in obtaining concessions from the major parties than would one of their own representatives, who would appear as a rival for a share in influence.

The other governmental type is the 'consul'; he alone can resolve those crises which cannot be reduced to parliamentary or psychological elements, but constitute genuine fundamental challenges. The consul does not try to reconcile opposite viewpoints; what makes his intervention different is the fact that it results from an uneasiness in public opinion, so that authority does not come to him solely from the Deputies, but also from the people. The consul thus has a tacit mandate to deal with a question that the parties cannot solve – but naturally his stay in office seldom lasts long after a solution has been found. The consul-type is represented by Adolphe Thiers, who was elected in 1871 to negotiate a peace, liberate the national territory from Prussian occupation and safeguard social order; Waldeck-Rousseau,[2] who in 1899 was called on to clear up the Dreyfus Case; Clemenceau[3] during the First World War; Poincaré[4] during the financial panic of 1926, Pierre Mendès-France after the defeat of Dien-Bien-Phu in 1954, and lastly, of course, General de Gaulle.

These are characteristic examples of the consul and compromiser types, but history abounds in figures occupying positions between the extremes. The successes scored by France since the beginning of the Third Republic can be explained to a great extent by the quality of the upper strata of the political personnel; while these leaders may have provoked the impatience of Deputies, they generally managed to obtain time to implement the main aspects of their policy. Thiers, defeated by the Monarchists, would have returned to power at the head of the Republicans after the dissolution of 16 May 1877, had he not died suddenly. Waldeck-Rousseau stepped down of his own accord in 1902 after he had led the Left to victory at the polls. Poincaré withdrew a few weeks before his death. Among the consuls, only Clemenceau, who was kept out of the Presidency of the Republic in 1920 as a result of parliamentary intrigues, despite the support of public opinion,

2. Waldeck-Rousseau was a follower of Gambetta, under whom he served as Minister of the Interior in 1881, at the age of 34; he headed the longest Cabinet of the Third Republic, from 1899 to 1902.
3. Born in 1841, Clemenceau belonged initially to the extreme Left. He was Prime Minister from 1906 to 1909 and again from 1917 to 1920.
4. Poincaré belonged to the Centre-Right; in 1894, at the age of 33, he became Minister of Finance; he was elected President of Council in 1912 and President of the Republic in 1913. He returned as President of Council from 1922 to 1924, and again from 1926 to 1929.

and Mendès-France, the first victim of the Algerian war, were eventually subjected to the rules of the Deputy-centred Republic – which had been suspended in each case to allow them to take power. We should perhaps also add Caillaux,[5] who failed to reveal the whole extent of his foresight and energy at the eve of the First World War and, at a lower level, Antoine Pinay, whose programme of financial stabilization in 1952 won him a popularity that undoubtedly went beyond his real stature as a statesman. And finally, of course, de Gaulle, who gave up power in 1946, refusing to share it with parties, but who returned on his own terms, in 1958 at the height of the Algerian war.

The French Style of Government

The role played by the consuls throws some light on the particular way in which the system functioned; it could react only in spasms, by renouncing provisionally the principle of parliamentary sovereignty on which it was based. Instead of assimilating such customs as normal practice, the system developed along lines which continually took it farther away from them, but paradoxically the strengthening of political organization that emerged during the inter-war period and, even more, after 1946 undermined the basis of the traditional model without introducing any alternative arrangements.

Leadership defined in terms of crises and their resolution is bound by definition to operate above the party level. As Albert Thibaudet, one of the most clear-sighted commentators of the Third Republic, wrote: 'The head of a Government must not throw in his lot completely with any one party, but he can, indeed must, give himself over wholeheartedly to one idea.' In such conditions a Government leader could therefore never be a

5. Joseph Caillaux was a follower of Waldeck-Rousseau, under whom, at the age of thirty-six, he served as Minister of Finance. He became Prime Minister in 1911, and in 1913 was elected president of the 'Radical' Party. He was hostile to the idea of war with Germany, and in 1917 he proposed negotiation with the enemy; as a result of this he stood trial before the Supreme Court. He later returned to Parliament but moved towards financial conservatism.

party leader; rather, he had to identify himself with a programme specifically related to a given situation. To put the matter in philosophical language: in such a situation the leader's mode of action is existential, since it does not fit the traditional ideological classifications, but formulates its own responses to events. This predicament is unavoidable, since party doctrinal positions are conceived along narrow, restrictive lines, and parties always have to stress the features that distinguish them from their near neighbours. This explains why Governments headed by 'consuls' seem to fly in the face of the logic of party tactics; Waldeck-Rousseau's first Government included Millerand, the first Socialist Minister in French history, and, at the same time, General de Gallifet, who had played an active part in repressing the Paris Commune; the 1926 Poincaré Government, normally described as a conservative team, included a Foreign Minister committed to left-wing policies (Briand) and an anti-clerical Minister of Education (Herriot). Coming closer to our times, the 1954 Mendès-France Government included left-wingers like François Mitterrand, Gaullists like Christian Fouchet (later to become a Minister under de Gaulle) and Moderates such as Bettencourt (also to belong later to the Pompidou cabinet). De Gaulle always surrounds himself with men coming from a variety of party backgrounds, and thus turns the French Government into a microcosm of political opinion in France.

Under such conditions the party composition of Governments has little significance in itself, since the diversity of views may be brought together because of the influence of a strong personality or, alternatively, constitute a heterogeneous coalition. This is why Waldeck-Rousseau, a lucid observer of the Third Republic, opposed ideological regroupings under the leadership of one man – the type of political 'concentration' that took place in the 1890s; this concentration consisted in

bringing together men of very dissimilar opinions, with opposing views on almost every subject. The aim was to produce Governments that would worry nobody, taking every parliamentary group into account and weighing it in the balance; with this in view, a certain number of hostages was chosen from each group, in order to reassure the others.

The Political Model

Power was delegated only with considerable reservations and it was wielded with defiance, and in this way some progress was made towards the partial organization of the particular type of immobility that results from being pulled in opposite directions.

This description can be applied to the whole of the Third Republic and still held good for the Fourth.

After taking over leadership of the Government, Waldeck-Rousseau summed up the two ways of conceiving a Cabinet:

One: the Government in which the head dominates or absorbs all the others. Two: each member of the Government is a specialist in the field allotted to him. In this latter case, the Prime Minister does not embody Government policy; rather, the average arrived at by giving due weight to all parties is expressed through him. He is a responsible, respected interpreter of opinion, not a leader planning and executing as he wishes.

The trend towards a greater degree of organization within the parties favoured the second formula at the expense of the first, but by introducing an increasing rigidity into the 'weighting' mentioned by Waldeck-Rousseau. After 1946 the 'party regime' fairly soon led to an almost total paralysis from which it was possible to break free only by calling once more on somewhat marginal compromisers, who duly resurrected the style of government that had characterized the Third Republic. It had been hoped at the time to give France a system of government based on disciplined parties. But far from proving an element favouring progress, discipline turned out to be a stumbling-block: pressed into the service of rival, contradictory pretensions, in the end it effectively neutralized the Government. Everybody in Parliament was so angered by the immobilism now characteristic of the party regime that public opinion gave an enthusiastic welcome to Mendès-France when he announced his refusal to negotiate with parties and his intention of choosing his own Ministers independently.

To quote from his inaugural address:

There will be no more interminable negotiations like those of the past. I shall tolerate neither demands nor vetos. The choice of Ministers . . . belongs to the appointed Prime Minister and to him alone. I am not prepared to concede any of the rights you might, by your vote of investiture, give me.

In Waldeck-Rousseau's doctrine, as in that of Mendès-France, the Prime Minister's complete freedom of action is the essential factor, for it alone opens up the possibility of escaping from a predicament which would end in deadlock at the level of party chiefs. Consequently the French style of government appears doubly in contradiction with basic parliamentary principles. Firstly, it is contradictory to the notion of party organization, which it undermines; secondly, since power comes to be vested in the consul, it also contradicts the principle of parliamentary sovereignty. This political model masquerades as a parliamentary system, but in reality it is diametrically opposed to its very idea, at least in the contemporary version of the model in which power is in the hands of an organized majority. The functioning of government is a permanent exception to the rules of the system; it represents a concession to the need for action, but this concession is precarious and uncertain and it may be revoked from one moment to the next.

The rise of the Fifth Republic in 1958 was the logical outcome of this process. Indeed, de Gaulle's return presented all the characteristic features of a consular situation, since it was provoked by a crisis which the Fourth Republic had shown itself incapable of solving, and accordingly the Deputies voted the General full powers so that he might bring the Algerian conflict to an end. But the first use de Gaulle made of his newly acquired powers was to place his own authority above parliamentary control, before he even began to tackle the Algerian problem. He was granted the power to prepare a new Constitution, which was to be approved by the referendum of 28 September 1958, while his first direct action concerning the Algerian question was to be his 'self-determination' speech of 16 September 1959. In other words, he made a point of beginning by neutralizing the institutional crisis mechanism by placing his power beyond the Deputies' reach; once the war was over, the Deputies wanted to close the constitutional parenthesis opened in June 1958, but then de Gaulle completed his new constitutional structure and thereby made it impossible to return to the old state of affairs; this he achieved mainly by getting approval, in the referendum of 28 October 1962, for the principle that the President should be elected by universal suffrage, and by dissolving the National Assembly. The Fifth Republic is the last manifestation of 'government by fits and starts' – is it also the beginning of a new era? We shall return to the question in the last section of this book.

Appendix 1 Crises under the Fourth Republic

First Parliament (November 1946–June 1951)

The majority was formed by a tripartite alliance (Socialists, Communists and the Christian Democrats of the MRP) until the exclusion of Communist Ministers in spring 1947; after this, the 'Radicals' (Liberals) came back into the coalition, which became known as the 'Third Force'.

19 November 1947   Paul Ramadier (Socialist) resigned without a vote after Guy Mollet leaked the information that Léon Blum was willing to take over as President. In any case the MRP was hoping for a change of Cabinet.

19 July 1948   Robert Schuman (MRP) had made the rejection of an amendment reducing military spending an issue of confidence; the amendment was adopted by 297 votes to 214 and Schuman resigned.

27 August 1948   The André Marie (Radical) Cabinet broke up without a vote after a meeting of the Council of Ministers in the course of which divergences over economic and financial questions appeared irreconcilable.

7 September 1948   After taking power on 31 August, Robert Schuman (MRP) formed his second Cabinet, which was defeated by 295 votes to 289 as soon as it was presented to the Assembly.

6 October 1949   The Cabinet headed by Henri Queuille (Radical) broke up after the resignation of the Minister of Labour, Daniel Mayer (Socialist), and resigned without a vote.

24 June 1950   Georges Bidault (MRP) sought a vote of confidence over the application of a law limiting the right of the

Assembly to increase public expenditure; the vote of confidence was refused for the first time by an *absolute* majority (352 votes to 230).

4 July 1950   Elected on 30 June, Henri Queuille (Radical) was questioned over the composition of his second Cabinet and the vote of confidence was refused him by an absolute majority of 334 votes to 221.

28 February 1951   René Pleven (Centre-Left UDSR) resigned, without a vote of confidence, to avoid deepening the divisions within the majority over the new electoral law.

10 July 1951   According to custom, Henri Queuille (Radical) gave in his resignation after the general elections.

Second Parliament (July 1951–December 1955)

As a result of the electoral alliances designed to resist Communist and Gaullist pressure, this became known as the 'hexagonal' Chamber, as it was composed of six groups of roughly the same strength: Communists, Socialists, 'Radicals' (or Liberals), MRP, Conservatives and Gaullists. The 'third force' was replaced by a fourth, with the entry of the Conservatives into the Government, replacing the Socialists, who from then on oscillated between support and opposition.

7 January 1952   René Pleven (UDSR) asked for the confidence of the Assembly eight times concerning the budget, and was defeated by an absolute majority at the first vote (341 votes to 243).

29 February 1952   Edgar Faure (Radical) asked for twenty votes of confidence over financial projects and after the second vote, confidence was refused by a relative majority (309 votes to 283, with 26 abstentions).

23 December 1952   Antoine Pinay (Moderate), on learning that the MRP would vote against his budget because of the family allowance question, resigned without a vote.

21 May 1953   René Mayer (Radical) asked for a vote of confidence over financial policy; confidence was refused by an absolute majority of 328 votes to 244.

12 June 1954   Joseph Laniel (Conservative) asked for the confidence of the Chamber over his Government's policy concerning Indochina. He was defeated by a relative majority of 306 votes to 273.

6 February 1955   Pierre Mendès-France (Radical) asked for confidence over his North African policy. Confidence was refused by an absolute majority of 319 votes to 273.

29 November 1955   Edgar Faure (Radical) asked for a vote of confidence over a procedural matter relating to a reform of the electoral system. Confidence was refused by an absolute majority of 318 votes to 218. This enabled the Prime Minister to dissolve the Assembly (according to a procedure which we shall examine later).

Third Parliament (January 1956–June 1958)

Two parties dominated this Parliament: the Socialists, controlling the Government, and the Conservatives, who gave the Government its intermittent support. At first the Communists voted for the Mollet Cabinet, but repressive measures in Algeria sent them back into opposition, as was also to be the case for the section of the Radicals headed by Mendès-France.

21 May 1957   Guy Mollet (Socialist) was defeated by 250 votes to 213 at the thirty-first vote of confidence over the Government's financial policy.

30 September 1957   Maurice Bourgès-Maunoury (Radical) was defeated by 279 votes to 253 after having asked for the confidence of the Chamber over an outline law on Algeria.

15 April 1958   Félix Gaillard (Radical) asked the Chamber to defer discussing the question of the use of American 'good offices'

in the Franco–Tunisian conflict. This was refused by 321 votes to 255. Gaillard resigned.

28 May 1958   Pierre Pflimlin (MRP) resigned to make way for de Gaulle.

2 A Deputy-centred Republic

The basic antagonism between the forces of democracy and those of authority manifests itself most clearly in the functioning of the French Parliament, which seems not to have moved beyond the first stage of development of representative institutions, namely that when Deputies acted as spokesmen for their constituents and defended their interests. They then won the right to vote taxes and thereafter, as a result of their financial powers, their influence spread to cover running the nation's business. As Ministers became accountable to the elected representatives, authority shifted from Crown to Cabinet, and the latter acted in the name of the parliamentary majority.

The French system seems to have stopped developing before power was completely transferred to the responsible Ministers. Deputies have never ceased to treat the Government as opponents to be kept under constant watch since, even after the disappearance of the monarchy, its influence was felt to rival their own. This general feeling was lucidly analysed by Waldeck-Rousseau in 1883:

We have an almost instinctive aversion to the executive branch. Our feelings about it are hedged round by a whole string of prejudices and reservations, as if we were still reacting against some past enslavement. We have been its opponents for so long that we appear to have failed to notice the not insignificant fact that in 1791 executive power was otherwise known as Louis XVI, whereas today it goes under the title of President of the Republic.

A general distrust of governmental power, established during the period when the Republic opposed first the monarchy, then the Empire, has outlived these regimes in the minds of Deputies and in the procedure of the Assembly. French political parties have never moved beyond a negative conception of their role, in terms of which they are first and foremost the spokesmen of interests and ideologies and the channels through which demands of a doctrinal or material kind are brought to the notice of authority. In this respect the system has failed to evolve: it has in fact deteriorated, as it has become obliged to deny its own principles in order to function.

The Agora

The critical, negatively oriented image inherited by Parliament did not preclude its claiming exclusive sovereignty – not only in relation to the rival legitimacy (the monarchy) but, which is stranger, also in relation to public opinion. This attitude is founded on two elements that back each other up: theoretical doctrine and practical experience. The element of practical experience dates from the first Assemblies, during the Revolution. The 1789 Constituent Assembly had barely won its independence from the King when it lost it again under public pressure, literally besieged by the Paris mob. Threatened with physical violence and pestered by delegations with claims and counterclaims, the Deputies acquired a sort of siege mentality which was kept alive and intensified by the various revolutionary 'days' of the nineteenth century.

The doctrine, on the other hand, can be traced to one of Montesquieu's ideas, according to which the mass of the people is well equipped for designating the men best fitted to represent it, but incapable of choosing the policy these representatives must follow. The Third Republic's parliamentarians considered the truth of this proposition amply demonstrated by their own experience of disorders in Paris. Following on this belief, which gradually acquired the status of an institutional theory, the nation came to be thought of as a person who gave Parliament a full mandate to act on its behalf. Each Member of Parliament is the representative of the whole nation and his mission is to play his part in expressing the will of the people. To quote a theorist: 'The Deputies are called on to decide freely and arbitrarily in the name of the people, which is deemed to think and speak through its representatives.'

Thus the people expresses its opinions exclusively through its representatives, who, once designated, take the place of the electorate, which ceases to exist as an active element until the following elections.

At the time of the change from limited to universal suffrage, when the main part of political activity was still in the hands of the citizens, this conception was no doubt a realistic assessment of the state of society, but the particular feature of the French parliamentary system is that it has survived unchanged since then. When General de Gaulle proposed that the President of the Republic be elected by universal suffrage, thereby intentionally taking liberties with constitutional forms according to which Parliament intervened in the process, Paul Reynaud[1] gave a clear expression of the parliamentary orthodoxy in significant terms: 'When the assembled elected representatives deliberate and vote,' he declared on 4 October 1962 in the Assembly, 'they act in their full capacity as representatives of the nation. *For us Republicans, France is here and nowhere else. To admit anything else implies the end of the Republic.*'

Consequently, representatives are granted a complete sovereignty; a direct appeal to the people is a limitation of their power, for it amounts to an attempt to make the people disown its representatives. The obsession with the Bonapartist practice of 'appealing to the people' against Deputies has exacerbated the extreme consequences of the French theory of representation. Napoleon I and, later, his nephew Napoleon III had indeed used plebiscites to consolidate their position. Memories of these plebiscites die hard: hence the paradoxical position in which a democracy is suspicious of universal suffrage unmediated by Parliament.

1. Paul Reynaud was Minister of Finance in 1938, then President of Council in 1940, when he opposed the 1940 Armistice but none the less was forced to hand over office to Marshal Pétain. A brilliant, nonconformist mind, he had defended the military theories of Charles de Gaulle (whom he had taken into his Cabinet in 1940); he was one of the few representatives of intelligent conservatism.

The Political Model

In order to have a better understanding of the ideal Republic as imagined by French politicians, we should probably think of Athenian democracy. Assembled together in the Agora, the people listened to orators, then came to a decision; the Deputies gathered together in the Palais-Bourbon's semi-circular chamber re-create the Agora as if the Deputies were the people. Through the fiction of representation, the Chamber becomes the stage on which the Deputies enact the workings of a perfect democracy in which the people listen to orators and decide as a sovereign body. The Government vanishes in this interpretation of a 'direct' democracy, which paradoxically enough is based on the most extreme form of government, since the rules of the game assume the silence of the 'real' population until the curtain falls.

We may well ask how this conception, which could be explained and even justified to a certain extent at the time of the first railways and illiterate masses, came to be maintained. An inheritance of bitter memories and the inertia of ideas can hardly provide a complete explanation. On the strictly institutional level, it seems that democratic development was halted at a very early stage: two accidents in particular have steered French parliamentary life on to the path it has since followed.

The first confirmed the elected representatives' independence of their constituents by neutralizing the right of dissolution. Ever since the time when this procedure was used by Marshal Mac-Mahon with a view to intimidating the Republicans and hindering the spread of their ideas, France has associated dissolution with authoritarianism. In this context, the 1877 episode constituted a decisive turning-point. It did not create the general suspicion surrounding dissolution, which manifestly went against all the basic tenets of parliamentary sovereignty in any case, but it provided an excuse and a justification for this mistrust. The Assembly was never dissolved again under the Third Republic. When, in politically debatable circumstances, Edgar Faure dissolved the Assembly in December 1955, institutional structures and behavioural patterns had become so ossified that the dissolution procedure turned out to be inoperative and merely added to the general confusion.

The second of these 'accidents' underlined the lack of any direct relationship between election and Government – a basic feature of a Deputy-centred Republic. The oligarchical tendencies of the French parliamentary system prevailed only because the parliamentary system was flouted right from the beginning and at the end of the nineteenth century there emerged a practice which no reform has managed to correct. Historically the crystallization of this tendency dates back to January 1879, when Marshal MacMahon resigned from the post of President of the Republic and his successor, Jules Grévy, appointed as Prime Minister a Senator of limited fame by the name of Waddington, instead of calling on the unchallenged leader of the Republican forces, Gambetta. Indeed, since the Republicans had gained control of all State organs, a tradition began to grow up, according to which the Government could be given to any one of a number of leaders, providing his political leanings did not conflict with the average feeling of the Assembly. The fact that the leader of the political majority was not necessarily the head of the Government led first and foremost to the disintegration of parliamentary parties which were no longer united with a view to governing, but came to be divided into competing factions, centred around the most prominent members of the Chamber. The pattern of government formation launched and continued by Grévy thus encouraged rivalry and introduced personal jealousies instead of political confrontations as the main basis for action in French public life. The result of this was the recognition of the divisions within the Republican camp, and the groups which emerged did not correspond in any clear way to parties organized in the country, but simply expressed the independence of parliamentary factions. Some of these groups, such as the *'Gauche radicale'* (or liberals) under the Third Republic, had been created to exploit the privileged strategic position of border-line groups, whose support was essential for the success of any majority coalition and who were thus endowed with an influence out of all proportion to their size. Each group ensured automatic participation in parliamentary events for its leader and gave him certain privileges. In this way the Agora developed into a sort of feudal system.

The Three Characteristics of the French Parliamentary System

From the very beginning of the Third Republic it is possible to observe the main features of a system which was to undergo no further development, except perhaps to acquire greater rigidity: these features are *anonymity*, *lack of accountability* and *instability*.

Anonymity results from the lack of any close relationship between the Government and the political leaders. The most popular figures are not necessarily those who will lead the Government. It is striking to note, running down the list of Prime Ministers, the number of unknowns whose names recur persistently, while statesmen appear only sporadically. Sometimes, of course, a leader became Prime Minister after an election – Herriot[2] in 1924, Poincaré in 1928 and Blum[3] in 1936 – but the parliamentary plums were normally shared among a restricted group of influential people who succeeded one another in power without their promotion being affected by universal suffrage; the same was true of their various downfalls.

Anonymity also tended to lead to *lack of accountability*, as no political organization existed to counteract this 'depersonalization' of power. The main cleavages in public opinion became fragmented at parliamentary level where centrifugal forces came into action.

This situation was further aggravated by the electoral system. The single-member two-ballot system was at first opposed by the Republicans as it tended to favour established local notables; but their attitude changed as they acquired and consolidated positions in local politics.[4] They then used the system to put a

2. The head of the Radical Party, Édouard Herriot (1872–1957) was President of Council from 1924 to 1932; he presided over the Chamber of Deputies from 1936 to 1940; and the National Assembly from 1947 to 1954.
3. Léon Blum (1872–1950), the head of the Socialist Party, was President of Council in 1936, and again in 1938 and in December 1946.
4. The electoral system is discussed more fully in Appendix 4 to this chapter.

stop to the progress of subversive movements such as that led by General Boulanger in 1889. 'Defence of the Republic' replaced the theme of the 'Republic Triumphant' as a battle-cry, which was spread through the nation by grass-roots organizations such as constituency committees and masonic lodges, which constituted a series of bastions against which the attacks of the Right broke; however, this also tended to give public opinion trends a less national turn. Later attempts at setting up more effective communications between electorate and Government were no more successful. The system of proportional representation introduced after the Second World War intended to deparochialize the competition, to the benefit of the organized parties; in fact, its sole achievement was to transfer influence to the party executives, which thus acquired the power to negotiate over the composition of Cabinets. Indeed, proportional representation, combined with the discipline of the main political parties, strengthened the influence of the parties at the expense of the electorate. The result was a return to a more flexible system, which, however, proved unworkable because the system was blocked. The 1956 election campaign, which Pierre Mendès-France fought on the theme of peace in Algeria, ended with the Radical leader's place being taken over by Guy Mollet, who duly introduced policies opposed to those he had defended while wooing the electorate.

This anonymous, non-accountable parliamentary system was also bound to be *unstable*. Once it became possible for any Member to hope to become Prime Minister without popular support, merely through personal acumen and an absence of controversial opinions, the mainspring of parliamentary government snapped. As the circle of potential Premiers broadened, the ranks of possible Ministers grew still further, and the slightest incident served as the pretext for a general reshuffling of portfolios to start a fresh governmental crisis. According to the rules, limits were set to gains and losses, and winners should not take unfair advantage of their victory; they were not supposed to stay on too long in positions of power, and it was considered bad play to brush aside the temporary losers completely.

The Lop-sided Relationship between Parliament and Government

Power was therefore wholly concentrated in the Assembly, instead of moving between the electorate and the Government. The Government merely implemented the will of the Deputies, who could end its life as freely as if the electorate had spoken.

Thus the relations between Government and Parliament were distinctly asymmetrical, as was noted by the French political scientist Georges Vedel[5]: the main split was between Government and Assembly, and not, as the logic of parliamentary system entails, between the Government majority and the Opposition. The prevailing behaviour patterns correspond to those of a system based on the separation of powers, as in the USA, but the executive branch did not have the independence and authority normally associated with separation of powers.

In this lop-sided model, the Government can act only as long as the Deputies continue to give it their confidence: in itself it has no means of influencing the Assembly, since it cannot appeal to the people, and holds its power from the Deputies and from them alone. From this stem the working characteristics of the Deputy-centred Republic, particularly the exercise of parliamentary control and ministerial responsibility.

In the French context, parliamentary control has a twofold significance, expressing the ambiguous nature of the relationship between Government and Parliament. It refers on the one hand to the preponderant influence that Deputies consider themselves entitled to exercise on policies, and on the other to the vigilant supervision they constantly exercise over the Government's actions.

A Deputy-centred Republic corresponded to a model of authority tempered by criticism; this required an autonomous, efficient civil service organization of the kind we shall discuss in the second part of this book. Throughout the system, the function

5. In his report to the Congress of the Internation Political Science Association: 'Les Rapports du législatif et de l'exécutif', in *Revue française de science politique*, December 1958.

of control, in a restrictive sense, is exercised by the superior body over its immediate subordinate. Citizens control Deputies, Deputies control the Ministers, who in turn control the bureaucracy. The cornerstone of the system is thus Parliament, the controlled controller. This ideal type is based on the belief that obedience is tolerable only when the citizen (or his representative) keeps a close watch over the actions of those in power and foster a healthy state of fear in all titular holders of even the slightest authority. Power is therefore constantly challenged and must justify itself; it must 'give account' (an expression which often appears in the writings of the 'Radical' philosopher Alain[6]), for the general suspicion is that any use of power naturally leans towards the arbitrary.

This rather sceptical type of wisdom was embodied in the organization of Parliament, where all the procedure was geared to force the Government to account both for its actions and for its intentions. A case in point was the committee system. Committees constituted a permanent anti-government, in which each Minister had his parliamentary shadow who specialized in supervising the appropriate department (Table 1). The influence wielded by these committees, the prestige enjoyed by their chairmen, and the minute, detailed control that was exercised, suggest an immediate comparison with American Congressional Committees; but this control resulted in fact in a real tutelage of the executive, in so far as the Government was the product of the Chamber itself and had no direct popular mandate to counteract pressures brought to bear by Deputies. The committees also provided an arena for effective action by pressure groups, and this combined with the influence and personal ambitions of members, dangerously weakened Government authority. A list of commissions under the Fourth Republic gives an idea of the attractive openings offered to the spokesmen for ex-soldiers (Pensions), wine-growers (Wines and Spirits) or wheat or beet producers

6. Alain, pen-name of Émile Chartier (1868–1951), was a teacher of philosophy. Every day from 1906 to 1914 *La Dépêche de Rouen* published one of his Socratic 'Propositions' which invited the reader to exercise his own judgement.

TABLE 1. Committees of the National Assembly at the End of the Fourth Republic

Committee for Economic Affairs
Committee for Foreign Affairs
Committee for Agriculture
Committee for Wines and Spirits
Committee for National Defence
Committee for Education
Committee for Family, Population and Health
Committee for Finance
Committee for the Interior
Committee for Justice and Legislation
Committee for Merchant Navy and Fishing Fleets
Committee for Communications and Tourism
Committee for Pensions
Committee for the Press
Committee for Industrial Output and Power
Committee for Reconstruction, War Damages and Housing
Committee for Universal Suffrage and Constitutional Law
Committee for Regulations and Petitions
Committee for Labour and Social Security
Committee for Parliamentary Privilege
Committee for Overseas Territories

(Agriculture), while leaders who did not belong to the Government normally sat on the Finance or Foreign Affairs committees.

Constantly under attack from the committees, the Government occupied an inferior position and possessed no procedural means of ensuring success for its policies. When a commission agreed to examine a Government Bill, the Assembly still had to agree to put it on the agenda and discussions then opened, but of the project as amended by the committee, not the original draft. From the beginning to the end of the legislative process, the Cabinet was thus forced to fight for its proposals, and quickly became worn out by this state of permanent guerrilla warfare.

On all these points, the Fifth Republic tried to learn from the experience of its predecessors. In particular, the regime has reacted against the spread of the committees' influence by placing their activity within strict limits, laid down in the Constitution so as to stress the importance of this measure; in order to avoid excessive specialization, the number of permanent commissions is now reduced to six[7], and their role is confined to handling bills and seeking information; they can no longer intrude into the functioning of the administration. Moreover, the Government has at its disposal standing orders that enable it to maintain an effective control over Parliamentary business. It has been given priority in arranging the agenda; Government Bills are programmed for dates chosen by the Government itself, and committees must submit their reports by the dates fixed on this timetable. Discussion on the floor is based not on the draft amended by the committee, as formerly, but on the original text; amendments liable to increase expenditure (or decrease revenue) or affecting the field of regulations[8] are automatically disallowed. Finally, the Constitution explicitly allows for Parliament to empower the Government to take decisions by ordinance (in fields normally covered by legislation) in accordance with a procedure which developed during the Third Republic, and which the Fourth tried in vain to abolish. Between 1959 and the summer of 1967, the Government fell back on this procedure eight times.

After the First World War, the equilibrium reached between parliamentary control and day-to-day administration of the country was questioned once more. Major ideological debates gave way to more concrete preoccupations: first and foremost, how to replenish the Treasury, then how to defend the currency

7. This is not without drawbacks, since each Deputy sits on one permanent committee; as a result, committees comprise between 60 and 120 members and are cumbersome bodies. At present the six standing committees of the National Assembly are: Cultural, Family and Social Affairs; Foreign Affairs; National Defence and Armed Forces; Finance, General Economy and Economic Planning; Constitutional, Legislative and Administrative Affairs; Production and Exchange. Furthermore, the Constitution also allows for special temporary committees (see Appendix 1 to this chapter).
8. The Constitution lays down the list of matters with which the law is concerned; everything else automatically counts as regulations, and is therefore subject to government decree (see Appendix 1 to this chapter).

and, finally, how to ensure the correct functioning of the national economy. But only the Government can achieve objectives of this kind, as a Parliament, while indispensable for establishing lasting legal relations, quickly becomes lost when dealing with technical controversies that do not lend themselves to political compromises. Thus, from 1926 on, the Assembly resigned itself to delegating legislative power in those fields to the Government: Poincaré was the first to benefit from these 'full powers', and after the onset of the Great Depression, the technique of decree-laws – once exceptional – had become the rule. It has been calculated that during the seventy-six months between 1 March 1934 and 1 July 1940, France lived for a total of thirty-four and a half months under a regime of legislation by decree, i.e. in a situation in which Parliament had abdicated its law-making powers. Parliament had, indeed, entrusted the Government with the responsibility for taking the unpopular steps demanded by the situation, but compensated itself for this sacrifice by defeating the Cabinet at regular intervals. Thereafter, attempts were made to rule out the possibility of such relinquishing of power, but the pressure of events was so strong that delegations of power began to reappear in 1948. The situation steadily worsened with the Algerian war and finally took on the character of a complete abdication of the Paris political authorities in favour of the army and the Algiers bureaucracy; the military revolt on 13 May 1958 was the logical conclusion of this trend.

One-way Accountability

A very special interpretation of the separation of powers led to the Cabinet being vested with a responsibility of its own, independent of that of the majority that had voted it to power: the Government was supposed to submit to the will of Parliament, but at the same time it was expected to play its full managerial role.

This subordinate position explains the importance of the processes of accountability in the French parliamentary system; in other parliamentary regimes (as in Great Britain) the choice of whether to retain or dismiss a Prime Minister ultimately rests with the people. In France, the cornerstone of the system had remained the vote of confidence given by the Deputies. But in this situation accountability functioned in one direction only, in that it applied to the Government, while Deputies who had voted for the Government when it first presented its programme did not feel obliged to maintain their support; they had not been elected with a mandate of this kind, and reserved the right to vote against the Government, even to vote it out of power, without being required to justify themselves to their electors.

Although considered permanently suspect, the French Cabinet had only one means of self-defence: its responsibility to the Assembly. By admitting that its existence depended entirely on the confidence of the Deputies, and virtually putting itself in their hands, the Government thus presented them with a clear-cut alternative: either they approved the project judged indispensable by the Government, or they overthrew it and started looking for a new team. . . . The question of confidence, originally used by Ministers to check whether their personal action was approved of by their colleagues, thus became transformed into a means by which the Government could bring pressure to bear on the Deputies. After 1946, it was regulated by the Constitution of the Fourth Republic, which incorporated a series of procedures intended to make sure the question of confidence was taken seriously and, hopefully, to limit the number of ministerial crises. It was decided that confidence would be refused only by an absolute majority of the Deputies comprising the Assembly, a condition which paralleled the procedure adopted for the appointment of the Prime Minister, since this could only be achieved by an absolute majority. However, these paper barricades proved ineffective: of twenty-one Governments, only six[9] were defeated according to constitutional procedure; the others resigned after being defeated by a relative minority, considering that they were thus deprived of the necessary authority (a further six cases); or even without facing a vote the outcome of which was likely to be

9. From January 1947 on. Before then there had been the provisional Government, led at first by General de Gaulle, then by Gouin and Bidault in 1945–6, and the short-lived Blum Cabinet in December 1946.

adverse (five cases). Two others were overthrown as soon as they were presented to the Chamber, and the last two were exceptional cases (Henri Queuille's resignation after the 1951 general elections, and the change of regime that ended in de Gaulle's government of 1958).

While votes of no-confidence passed according to constitutional procedure swiftly lost their political significance, the Government came to make frequent use of the question of confidence, as this was the only instrument still available to the Prime Minister for imposing his authority on the Assembly. The question of confidence was raised forty-five times during the first legislature (1946–51), seventy-three times during the second (1951–5) and forty-six times during the third (1956–8). The highest frequency occurred under Edgar Faure's first Cabinet, which raised twenty-three questions of confidence in forty days, while the absolute record is held by Guy Mollet (thirty-four times). The technique of the confidence question would be used to force the Assembly to agree to put a matter on its agenda, to squeeze out private Members' amendments or to force through the adoption of controversial measures: in short, it was the one all-purpose measure the Government leaders could apply.

The experience of the Fourth Republic had stimulated various projects for reform, some of which reappeared in 1958 in the new Constitution. The general philosophy of the new system tends to strengthen governmental leadership while stressing the distinction between the leadership and its political responsibility. The first aim leads to the arrangements already described concerning legislative procedure (committees, agendas, rejection processes etc.) and the Government's recognized power to ask the Assembly to decide by a single vote on all or part of a text under debate: this is the 'block vote' which thus makes it possible to link the adoption of a project as a whole and the approval of one of its disputed parts, while rejecting the amendments that otherwise would be attached to that section.[10] Until then this result could be obtained only by asking for a vote.

10. The block vote was used twenty-three times during the first legislature (1958–62) and sixty-six times under the second (1962–6).

The 1958 reformers had the second objective in mind when they limited the opportunities for politically significant votes and placed draconian conditions on the procedure for defeating a Government. Deputies were forbidden any indirect tactics intended to sabotage the government; the one remaining opening was the overt motion of censure. The censure motion must be signed by one tenth of the deputies, and the same signatories may submit only one such motion per parliamentary session. Finally, the Cabinet is overthrown only if the censure motion is carried by an absolute majority in the Assembly. From 1959 to autumn 1967, seven censure motions meeting these conditions were tabled (four during the first legislature, two under the second, and one in October 1967); of these only one was carried, in October 1962, leading to the dissolution of the Assembly.

To avoid the Government being paralysed by the rejection of its programme, the Constitution states that it could stake its responsibility on a Bill which would automatically be 'deemed to be carried' if no censure motion was forthcoming. From 1959 to summer 1967, there were eight censure motions tabled to handle this new type of issue of confidence; all were defeated. Four concerned the nuclear armaments budget, and three others the request for 'special powers' submitted in May–June 1967.

The Fifth Republic: Imbalance Reversed

The authors of the 1958 Constitution hoped to recreate, through procedural means, the behavioural patterns of the House of Commons, real or imagined. Some aspects of their undertaking were technically justified, but the plan was no less artificial for that, since it overlooked the key element of Cabinet government: the British Prime Minister does not rely purely on legal procedures for his authority, but is backed by a political reality, in that he acts as the leader of a disciplined majority invested with the confidence of the electorate.

The basic premiss of the Fifth Republic was that France lacked a parliamentary majority because of the multiplicity of parties and the fragmentation of public opinion. This assumption corresponded to observation of contemporary history, but the usual irony of fate saw to it that this hypothesis duly became invalid as soon as its extreme consequences were drawn. However, the unexpected appearance of a docile majority was brought about by a factor that had nothing to do with Parliament – this was, in short, the influence of General de Gaulle himself – while the pressure brought to bear by the presidential elections forced the Opposition to regroup itself. While at the end of the Fourth Republic in 1958 there had been a dozen or so groups, during the first two legislatures this number dropped to six,[11] and, during the third, to five (Table 2). The coalition between orthodox

TABLE 2. Groups in the National Assembly

Group	Second Parliament December 1966	Third Parliament April 1967
Communist Party	41	73
Socialist Party	66	
Rassemblement démocratique (Democrats)	38	
Federated Left (FGDS)*		121
Democratic Centre	54	
Progrès et Démocratie Moderne*		41
Independent Republicans	34	42
UNR–UDT–Union des Démocrates pour la Cinquième République (Gaullist)	230	200
Non-aligned	19	9
Total	482	486

* From 1967 on.

Gaullists and Independent Republicans gave the Government an absolute majority in 1962 and for the first time in French parliamentary history the legislature ran its course without a single Cabinet crisis.

As a result of this the Assembly's functioning has been affected in two ways: firstly, by the new constitutional measures, and

11. The minimum membership had, it is true, been raised from fourteen to thirty members; see Appendix 2 to this chapter.

secondly, by their application in the context of a majority system. But here we can see once more the principle of alternation, for the new system has simply led to a reversal of the former imbalance. The lop-sidedness survives, as the 'Presidential' and 'Parliamentary' forces still come into play, but now exclusively to the benefit of the Government.

In the first place, the distinction between Parliament and Government is still the cornerstone of the regime, but executive power is now stronger and more independent. Secondly, the split between a disciplined majority and a true Opposition now comes into operation, but to support the Government, not to regulate the functioning of the Assembly, which has been manoeuvred into a position of absolute Gaullist control. Two examples should illustrate this superimposition: the post of President of the Assembly, and oral questions.

According to the French tradition, the post of President of the Assembly is a political appointment; the titular office-holder acts to a certain extent as arbiter between the Government and the Deputies. With the advent of a cohesive government majority, the political character was strengthened and its submission to Government orders became total: M. Chaban-Delmas, Speaker of the Assembly since 1958, is a dedicated Gaullist who is keenly attentive to the desires of the President of the Republic. In no sense does he arbitrate between Majority and Opposition; he merely acts as the representative of the Majority.

Eliminated from presiding over commissions and from functioning as *rapporteurs*, the Opposition is unable to exercise any control in the old sense; it can only initiate debates. The Constitution allows for a weekly sitting devoted to questions, but as the agenda is arranged by the 'Presidents' Conference' in which Government supporters are in the majority, only questions approved by the Government are allowed. In other words, the only 'free' question time escaping from the rule of Government priority is virtually controlled by the majority, who strike out questions that might embarrass the Prime Minister.[12]

12. In his book '*Un Parlement pour quoi faire?*' André Chandernagor quotes telling examples of this censorship procedure.

Appendix 1 The Controlled Parliamentary System of the Fifth Republic

We have already mentioned the main changes of the 1958 Constitution: the new system of governmental responsibility and the censure procedure (Article 49), the distinction between regulations and legislation (Articles 34 and 37), the attribution of legislative power (Article 38), the block vote (Article 44) and parliamentary priority (Article 48).

Parliament meets in two plenary sessions of eighty and ninety days respectively, beginning on 2 October and 2 April. Extraordinary sessions may be summoned by the President of the Republic at the request of the Prime Minister or of the majority of Deputies, but the latter is possible only in theory: in March 1960 General de Gaulle refused, despite the provisions of Article 29, to summon an extraordinary session as in his opinion the moment was not opportune.

We noted elsewhere the general arrangements relating to the six standing committees: in addition, Article 43 of the Constitution allows for the creation, at the request of the Government, of a parliamentary group or standing committee or of special committees for special matters, but this procedure has scarcely ever been used: only seventeen special committees were created between 1959 and 1967.

Another interesting innovation of the 1958 Constitution was the creation of joint committees of the Assembly and the Senate, aiming at working out compromises between the two chambers in cases of complaint. But these committees are set up at the request of the Government, with the result that the Senate may bury a proposal carried by the Assembly if the Prime Minister so wishes, while on the other hand, if the Senate persists in its opposition to a Bill already passed by the Lower Chamber, the Government may ask the Assembly to decide by a final vote. The Government can thus use the two Chambers to suit its own ends.

Two other changes deserve to be mentioned:

(i) *The Constitutional Council:*

The existence and powers of the Constitutional Council are proof that the Constitution aims at limiting parliamentary sovereignty. The Council is composed of nine members, appointed for nine years; three are chosen by the President of the Republic, who also appoints the Council's chairman, three by the Speaker of the National Assembly, and the remaining three by the Speaker of the Senate. As the Speaker of the Assembly has been, since 1958, an orthodox Gaullist, M. Chaban-Delmas, the majority on the Council has always tended to support the head of State; several of his most loyal supporters have been appointed to it, including M. Pompidou, Gaston Palewski (the present Chairman), MM. Michelet and Chenot (who both belonged to the Government either before or after their appointment to the Council).

The Constitutional Council supervises the regularity of Presidential elections and referendums. If results are challenged, it decides on the validity or otherwise of the election of Deputies or Senators – control of such matters is in this way removed from the Assemblies, which formerly had final control in this field, although it must in fairness be noted that their decisions often gave rise to bitterly criticized abuses.

The standing orders of the Assemblies are submitted to the Constitutional Council; once, interpreting the Constitution in the narrow sense that anything not expressly authorized by the text was deemed to be forbidden, the Council prohibited the voting of resolutions, i.e. motions through which the Assemblies express political intentions.

Finally, at the request of the President of the Republic or the Prime Minister, or the Speakers of the Assemblies, it pronounces on the constitutional correctness of laws before they come into force.

In practice, the Council acts as a watchdog over the boundaries set to parliamentary action. This it does, firstly, by defining the limits of the legislative field, which are laid down in Article 34 of the Constitution: anything not figuring on this list is taken as belonging to the province of regulations (here the Council's interpretations have been balanced and, on the whole, liberal). Secondly, the Council forbids Members of Parliament to propose new expenditure or the reduction of State revenue (Article 40).

Thus the Constitutional Council emerges as an auxiliary of the executive, making sure its prerogatives are respected.

(ii) *Members of Parliament are expected to give up their seat on entering the Cabinet:*

Finally, it must be noted that membership of the Government is now incompatible with membership of Parliament. Deputies or Senators must resign their seats when appointed to ministerial posts. This measure was introduced with the open intention of putting a brake on personal ambition among Members of Parliament, who were tempted to overthrow Cabinets in the hope of belonging to the succeeding team. But it also indicates the regime's general desire to separate Government and Parliament.

In order to avoid constant by-elections, every candidate for the Assembly or the Senate must select a substitute who will replace him if, after return to Parliament, he is promoted to ministerial office.

This system has shown itself to be a complex, embarrassing fabrication, as former Deputies who have become ministers have continued to nurse their constituencies. In March 1967, all except two Ministers stood for election. Of the twenty-nine members of the new Cabinet, twenty-six had been candidates and twenty-four had been elected. Several Ministers stood for the first time with as their substitute the outgoing Deputy for the constituency.

Appendix 2 Parliamentary Groups

The concept of organized groups was long considered to be in contradiction with the idea of a representative system in which each elected Member was thought of as representing the entire nation and acting according to his own conscience. Until 1910 groups were unofficial and 'open' (i.e. a Deputy could belong to more than one group). Official recognition was then, after fierce argument, granted to groups, but their organization remained loose. The Fourth Republic tried to turn them into the normal mechanism through which Parliament could function: groups enjoyed prerogatives such as committee membership and parliamentary time, and material advantages such as secretarial help, as well as representation in the 'Conference of Presidents' which drew up the agenda. The minimum membership for a group was fixed at fourteen in 1946, but in 1958 it was decided to raise this to twenty-eight. Before this could be done, the Fourth Republic had disappeared and the Fifth took over the idea, fixing minimum membership at thirty.

The following table gives, as an example, figures showing the development of groups under the last legislature of the Fourth Republic.

TABLE 3. National Assembly 1956–8

Groups	February 1956	April 1958
Communist Party	144	142
Extreme Left	6	6
Socialists	96	96
'Radicals' and 'Radical Socialists'	58	43
UDSR and African Democratic Assembly (RDA)	19	22
Republican 'Left' and Republican Centre	14	14
'Democratic Left'	–	14
MRP (Christian Democrats)	73	75
Overseas Independents	10	–
African Socialist Movement	–	4
African Convention	–	7
Social Republicans (Gaullist)	22	20
Social Action Independents and Peasants	83	91
Social Action Peasants	–	9
Peasants	12	11
Poujadistes	52	31
Non-aligned	6	11
Total	595	596

Appendix 3 The Turnover of Political Personnel

In the 1958 election, 344 of the 475 outgoing Deputies who stood again were defeated; this represented a turnover rate of over 63% (as against 49% in 1885 and 59% in 1919). In the second Parliament, elected in 1962, there were only 90 Deputies who had held office in the last Assembly of the Fourth Republic. The Assembly elected on 5 and 12 March 1967 took the following form:

TABLE 4.

Group	Former Deputies	Senators	Former Senators	New Deputies
UDV^eR (Gaullist) 201 (*150*)*	7	2	1	41
Independent Republicans 42 (*27*)	–	–	–	15
Progressive Mod. Dem. 41 (*30*)	4	2	–	5
Federated Left 121 (*71*)	5	7	–	38
Communist Party 73 (*35*)	6	–	–	32
Non-aligned 9 (*7*)	1	–	–	1
All groups 487 (*320*)	23	11	1	132

* Figures in italic indicate 1962 seats.

Appendix 4 French Electoral Systems

Proportional representation, which was applied throughout the Fourth Republic, was based on lists for each *département* (an administrative division: France is divided into ninety-five *départements*). Each list included as many candidates as there were seats to be filled, the number varying with the population of the *département*. The distribution of seats was carried out by dividing the total votes cast by the number of seats to be filled, so as to obtain a *quotient*. Each list was allowed one elected member for each time it polled a multiple of the quotient. As this system seldom produced whole numbers, the distribution of seats entailed fairly complex calculations, either using the system of the 'highest average' or, as in the Paris area, the system of the 'highest remainder'. From 1951 on, the majority element was re-introduced by the organization of a network of relationships allowing lists to be grouped and their votes pooled, with a view to the joint allocation of seats (*apparentements*). This grouping procedure was designed to limit the representation in Parliament of the Communists and Gaullists (who in any case received over forty-eight per cent of votes), and indicated a defensive spirit among other parties rather than an agreement aiming at joint government.

Proportional representation strengthened the influence of parties and diminished the importance of the electorate in so far as: firstly, the main parties each won sufficient votes to reach the quotient; they were therefore fairly well assured of having their top candidates elected; and secondly, electors could not decisively change the composition of the Assembly, but merely modify the relative strength of each party.

There was consequently no collective choice corresponding to a national mandate; rather, a certain proportion of influence was handed over to party officials for them to use as they saw fit.

Since 1958 the country has returned to the system which applied throughout the greater part of the Third Republic: the *scrutin d'arrondissement*, i.e. a system of two-ballot, single-member constituencies. Each constituency (470 for metropolitan France in 1967, plus seventeen for overseas territories) elects one Deputy; to be elected it is necessary to obtain an absolute majority of votes cast (half the total plus one) at the first ballot. At the second (known as *ballottage*) it is enough to finish up ahead of the other candidates.

This system is known as *scrutin d'arrondissement*, since the electoral areas corresponded originally to administrative zones, but numerous modifications have been made so as to limit the excessive disproportion between the populations of different arrondissements. Since 1958 legislative areas have been defined independently of administrative divisions.

3 The Party System

Although the French Parliament tried carefully to carry out its duties in defending the interests and expressing the views of the different sectors of public opinion, it still could not fully play its part as a channel between voters and Government. The fragmentary, sectional nature of Parliament is closely related to the party system, which shows similar traits, though it cannot be stated which is the cause of the other. French politics has never been based on a system of organized parties, although the parties regularly took care of various specific functions: the selection of candidates, the discussion of governmental policies and the defence of social groups. Generally speaking, the main aim of the parties was to increase their influence, not to gain power; this is why they fitted well into the framework of the Deputy-centred Republic, in which their role was essentially marginal. Even the Gaullist UNR (Union pour la Nouvelle République) party, founded in 1958, has never attempted to play a part commensurate to its size and importance. The large number of parties and their consequent weakness cannot be interpreted in purely physical terms: rather, they reveal the almost insurmountable nature of the obstacles that hinder the installation in France of the type of party structure which, although inseparable from the idea of democracy, is still at the blueprint stage in that country. This phenomenon is not limited to the parties, but affects all associations: we could make similar observations about trade unions, which are broken up into three, if not four national organizations and have a relatively small membership.

Hence the emergence, sometimes fleeting (as in the case of the subversive 'leagues' in 1934, the Rally of the French People or RPF founded by General de Gaulle in 1947, or the Union for the

The Political Model

Defence of Shopkeepers and Artisans, founded by Poujade in 1955), sometimes lasting (e.g. the Communist Party), of movements which cannot be integrated into the normal democratic framework and from time to time exploit their position to express uninhibited discontent. This is due to the fact that traditional parties were unable to set genuine alternatives before public opinion, which was then manifesting its impatience, usually in a sporadic and negative fashion. The Communist Party, on the other hand, won itself the lasting support of millions of voters. However, it should be specified that this was largely due to the penetration of party politics into local government: out of 639 communes of over 9,000 inhabitants, 103 (including twenty-one towns of over 30,000 inhabitants out of the thirty-nine that constitute the Paris suburban belt) were run by Communists in the 1965 elections. Stripped of positive influence on Government policy, the Communist Party has gained numerous footholds in the day-to-day running of local government, and thus becomes integrated into the very society it is combating.

If we set aside such aspects of international Communism as the Cold War and Stalinism, and consider only the *French* Communist Party, we can see that in its own way it expresses the left-wing electorate's essentially protest-oriented attitude; it can thus be related to one of the two models provided by the French party system: Government parties or Opposition parties. At a time when this situation seems to be on the point of changing, a historical survey should help us to understand the contemporary situation.

The Formation of a Political Class: French 'Radicalism'

To what needs did the emergence of political parties in France correspond? They were needed to organize electoral campaigns and create a body of men capable of leading others and ensuring the functioning of the regime – in short, to train a political class.

At the beginning of the Third Republic, it seems that Freemasonry made a major contribution to the rapid, effective replacement of the Empire's political figures and thus avoided the

74

return of Royalist officials, which would have meant a Royalist restoration before long. Only the intervention of Freemasons can explain the astonishing caution shown by the Left when constitutional laws were passed in 1875, and the even more surprising discipline with which it respected the compromise that allowed the new regime to be established. Freemasonry, which had been the intellectual and moral stimulus of the Republican middle classes and claimed to be the heir of the 1789 Revolution, also provided the men who defeated Marshal MacMahon with the liaison they needed in order to take over a society in which the social and spiritual authorities, particularly the Catholic Church, as well as a good proportion of the administrative and military hierarchy, were hostile to them. It is also probable that it helped give French political life its oligarchic style, in so far as the egalitarian and collegial principles of Freemasonry were incompatible with any pronounced form of personal leadership.

After the failure of the attempts at party unification between 1876 and 1879 by the main Republican leader, Gambetta, a fragmented society composed of electoral committees, philosophical societies and newspapers fulfilled the functions of parties. The informal 'party' gathered together active citizens who probably represented a group roughly as large as the property-qualified electorate in 1830, i.e. approximately 200,000, according to Albert Thibaudet.[1] These were men who were interested in politics, and in a way, lived on politics, or at least depended on political activity for their place in society. Thus, from the very beginning, we can see the emergence of a clientele relationship with the Government party. Through the provincial networks set up by prominent Republican citizens (lawyers, public servants and doctors), the first French political party began to take shape; and one of its features was that the influence of political élites on the electorate increased in direct proportion to their own influence on the State, since the greater their influence, the more services they could do their friends and neighbours by interceding with Members of Parliament or people in authority.

1. Until 1848 the right to vote was reserved for citizens who paid a minimum amount of direct income tax (200 francs).

The Political Model

Whether they concerned licences to sell tobacco, which were granted by the Government, or scholarships for talented children (including the one given to the philosopher Alain, thanks to the efforts of a Deputy) or loans for road-building, these services created a bond between the man in the street and the party whose success in the elections was the guarantee that the system would continue to function. The threats that could be brought to bear on ordinary citizens by the 'forces of reaction' – right-wing notables, the aristocracy and the Church – stimulated this network of customer relationships and ensured that the Republic sent down deep roots. At the beginning of the century, Briand's reply to Maurice Barrès, a right-wing nationalist writer and Deputy, was: 'We've got the men for the job!'

The Republican Party, a decentralized, informal structure, developed into a system of communication between State and public. But it had no formal existence as an organization until the preparatory phases of the 1902 elections showed the need for more carefully planned coordination than had up till then been thought necessary. Consequently, the first French political party was founded at a congress which met on 21 June 1901; its organizers had obtained the support of 78 Senators, 201 Deputies, 476 committees, 155 Masonic lodges, 849 members of General Councils, local councillors, mayors and town councillors, and 215 newspapers. This party was named 'Republican Radical and Radical-Socialist Party', a complex title which indicates that it represented an *ad hoc* federation of men and organizations whose opinions ranged from just left of Centre to the fringes of the Socialist extreme Left. Such a body was made necessary by the fact that political activity now took place on a national scale, so that a permanent central organization was needed; the resultant many-sided organization seemed to have no clearly defined boundaries or rigid hierarchies. The Radical Party, chronologically the first French political party and the only one that was an original creation rather than the adaptation of an imported model, was reluctant to be considered a party in the strict sense of the term: in manifestos and speeches, spokesmen preferred to talk of 'French democracy becoming organized in an atmosphere of freedom and justice', to quote one of its leaders, Léon Bourgeois.

The Radical Party is in a way a condensed form of the traditional French political model, which it reflects in its performance and in its decline, and also in a certain lasting quality; it is curious to read, as one does quite frequently, that Gaullism (which took over several Radical dignitaries, including Michel Debré and Jacques Chaban-Delmas) is attempting to take its place, as if this new, ambiguous party embodied certain permanent features of French democracy, which can be summed up as a recognition of the personality of the State, tempered by an awareness of the electorate's demands; or, if one prefers, the Jacobin declaration of public interest humanized by the services rendered to the electorate.[2] The type of organization the Radical Party represents can be justified only by reference to the existing State – which it inevitably presupposes, for in itself it cannot (as do the Socialist Party and, even more, the Communist Party) embody its own aims. Deprived of contact with the seat of power, Radicalism is shrinking and withering, as we can see at present, but until this decline, its strength had stemmed from the irreplaceable role it had secured for itself, existing as a true party, not simply as a machine for winning elections, while keeping itself constantly poised for action over governmental issues. This type of balance was not preserved by other later parties; neither the Socialist Party organization, which was aimed principally at self-perpetuation, nor groups of the Right, which were no longer true parties but rather parliamentary machines, ever approached the balance achieved by the Republicans.

It seems that the Radical Party was practically the only one in which political debate remained open and through which public opinion could still influence the Government. Its tiny body of

2. This argument has often been used unscrupulously by Gaullist candidates. Robert Boulin, Secretary of State for the Budget, declared to his constituents at Libourne (Gironde) on 8 March 1967: 'If you give me a triumphal – and I *mean* triumphal – majority at the second ballot, the success will make me eligible for ministerial rank, so that I shall be in a position to be useful to this region and to each and every one of you: it stands to reason!'

supporters made it numerically unrepresentative but the flexible nature of its structure enabled it to follow trends in opinion with reasonable faithfulness.

Within the Radical Party we can discern a reduced-scale model of the parliamentary Agora, particularly when we look at an institution which it alone possessed: the General Purposes Committee. This was the equivalent of a café back-room group, except that its speakers often included Ministers, who had no formal authority in these meetings but yet wielded some influence; in this way the Committee formed a link between the top grades and the party militants. The party's Committee and its annual congress in fact provided two forums in which the most important problems in French politics over the last few decades were freely debated at the level of those responsible.

To Right and Left of Radicalism

Radicalism can be considered as the theoretical axis on which French public life centred from the beginning of the century onwards. It constituted a reference point in terms of which other parties grew up and developed their relationships with power. As it gradually tended to identify itself with the Government, it also produced its own Opposition-type reactions which initially served to balance its aspirations to govern.

At the beginning, the party had a single purpose: its late-nineteenth-century political committees constituted the original form of political organization. However, they developed in two diametrically opposed directions, on the one hand towards ensuring its voters' loyalty to the established power and, on the other, towards attacking this power. While one wing became increasingly involved in preparing for elections and maintaining the sympathy of its supporters in the periods between elections – by means of favours that required access to Ministers – the other was occupied in keeping watch over the elected Members, who were always treated as suspect, and criticized such Government actions as seemed unduly cautious. Here we can see the first signs of a shift towards the Left, which was later accelerated by social factors but still remains essentially political in character. Disconcerted by the compromises accepted by their Deputies, the electorate became inclined to vote for 'purer', i.e. more advanced, candidates. The disappointments of the first decades of the Third Republic led to a state of drifting which ruled out all possibility of stabilizing the party system, aggravating the rupture between Government parties, which became increasingly governmental, and Opposition parties which became more and more irresponsible. The Communist leader Jacques Duclos illustrated this phenomenon by declaring one day in the Assembly: 'My grandfather was a Radical Socialist; my father was a Socialist and I am Communist.'

In 1905 the Parti Socialiste Unifié was formed by the amalgamation of the two main movements in French Socialism: the parliamentary, reformist Socialism of Jaurès,[3] and the Marxist Socialism of Jules Guesde; the latter won the day, thus imposing on the party, which from 1920 on was to be called the SFIO (Section Française de l'Internationale Ouvrière), a revolutionary turn of phrase and mind that contrasted strikingly with the moderate positions actually held by most of its members in Parliament. It should be noted at this juncture that the Socialist movement in France has never been linked to a trade-union system; in 1906 the famous 'Amiens Charter' proclaimed the major trade union's independence from parties, and its refusal to take part in election politics. At that time Anarcho-syndicalism reigned supreme in the CGT, a fact which explains why parties claiming working-class adherents could not benefit from the union's support. The new Socialist party thus oscillated between rather gratuitous verbal extremism and, in actual practice, fairly pronounced political opportunism; because of its lack of direct links with working-class organizations it was never to break free from this situation.

3. An incomer from the Centre-Left, Jean Jaurès was the leader of French Socialism until 1914. He was assassinated just before the declaration of war. He was personally in favour of an alliance with Caillaux, the President of the Radical Party, to halt the drift towards war, but respected his own party discipline and held back from this action.

The Political Model

Even before it was officially constituted, French Socialism had broken with the middle-class Left by applying the decisions of the Amsterdam International Congress held in April 1904, so that the parliamentary Left could not unite its forces with a view to forming a Government. Instead of attracting large numbers of Radicals, as Labour attracted Liberals in Britain, the Socialist Party at first appeared bent on emphasizing its identity and keeping its distance from its Radical neighbours. It had to wait until 1936 before it faced, unwillingly, the problems posed by the exercise of power. But already, for the preceding sixteen years, it had been hard pressed from the Left by a competitor attacking it with criticisms similar to those it had itself levelled at the Radicals: the Communist Party, founded after the schism that took place inside the Socialist movement in 1920 after the Bolsheviks had taken power in Russia.

We have already said that the parties to the right of Socialism were above all parliamentary machines. This is not wholly true of the MRP (Mouvement Républicain Populaire) which could have led to the creation of a major conservative party if it had not immured itself in a contradiction itself illustrative of the complexity of French public life.

Succeeding the Christian Democrats of the Third Republic, the MRP hoped to concern itself with social questions, but its Catholic character placed it firmly on the Right. The contradiction between the opposing trends favoured by the party militants, who included a sizeable body of trade-unionists, and its mainly conservative electorate, was resolved only by the departure of the left-wing Christian element and the disaffection of the greater part of the conservative supporters, who had in any case been reassured only by the 'Christian' part of the party's title. Georges Bidault, who was its President after directing the CNR (Conseil National de la Résistance), realized that the small nucleus of Christian Democrats that had survived from before the Second World War could only hope to impose itself if it were sure of a foundation in society similar to the one enjoyed by the Republicans at the beginning of the century. According to Bidault, it was necessary to build a party including 'women and priests' (women were given the vote in 1945). The creation of a major Christian Democrat party on Italian or German lines would still have meant the absorption of the conservative wing of the Radicals and would have avoided the renaissance of a moderate Right. On both these counts the party failed.

Although the MRP's militants and a good proportion of its Deputies considered Radicals as a whole as conservatives, the old splits were still deep enough to cause the MRP to be rejected as a right-wing party, so that it could not win the support of the traditional Republican Centre. This combination, logical enough in the abstract, in practice came up against insuperable psychological difficulties, as it had to deal with two modes of thought which, though probably close enough in their ways of approaching problems, were descended from two hostile traditions. Throughout the Third Republic, attempts at uniting the various Centre movements had come to nothing because of reflexes of this type, which prevented the MRP from expanding into the old secularist Centre.

Neither could it prevent the reconstruction of a moderate Right, since, given its attitude to social matters, it refused to play the trump-card of economic liberalism, but pronounced itself in favour of State intervention. Many others played this very card to attract the conservatives, who had become dispersed and discredited after their compromises with the Vichy regime. In 1949 a former Radical Deputy who had become a Senator, Roger Duchet, joined with two other Senators (one of whom, René Coty, was to be elected President of the Republic in 1953) to found the CNIP (Centre National des Indépendants et Paysans).

Like the Radical Party in 1901, the CNIP comprised a variety of elected representatives, such as mayors, Senators and members of the General Councils as well as Deputies to whom it offered a national party label. It also grouped together various small parties (e.g. the Peasant Party and the Republican Liberty Party), and attracted a not inconsiderable fraction of Gaullists after the failure of the RPF. In 1952, after the rise to power of Antoine Pinay, who was their star member, the Independents seemed on the point of becoming the major conservative party that until then had been lacking in France. But it fell victim to the Algerian war, which led to its disintegration. Moreover, unlike the Radicals, the CNIP structure was a purely electoral machine; it had no militant infrastructure, but only a network of clients who were liable to transfer their loyalties as soon as other, more efficient or glamorous 'bosses' came their way, as indeed happened after General de Gaulle's return to power.

Parties and Governments

After the Second World War there was much talk of 'spiritual families' corresponding to the various political alignments. These were thought of as the natural expression of an underlying diversity that it seemed should be recognized officially, through proportional representation in particular, so that this pluralism could be reflected in the regime. The idea of coalition, which under the Fourth Republic had been imposed by force of circumstances, was thus granted some measure of official blessing, while attempts were made to bring it in line with the current situation. But the effect of juxtaposing divergent trends was to accentuate former rivalries, in terms of which each party fought to gain ground at the others' expense. This built-in mechanism of dispersion had proved its worth throughout the Third Republic; it gained systematic form between 1946 and 1958 and continued to give party structures a rather artificial cast.

It is perhaps useful to compare the relationship between Governments and parties. From 1920 to 1940, there were 47 Cabinets, 15 of which were run by Radicals, 2 by Socialists (the 1936 and 1938 Léon Blum Cabinets) and the rest by individuals from various parliamentary groups that did not correspond to nationally organized parties.

After 1946, attempts were made to introduce a party system, but the main result of this was to deepen the split between the various groups aspiring to power (they soon shrank to politically insignificant mechanisms) and the Opposition parties, which stuck to negative, essentially parasitic positions, despite their increasing representation.

This split shows clearly in the leadership of the twenty-one Governments of the Fourth Republic, which break down as follows:

10 Radical Cabinets (almost half the total) headed by André Marie, Henri Queuille three times, Edgar Faure twice, René Mayer, Pierre Mendès-France, Maurice Bourgès-Maunoury and Félix Gaillard;

4 MRP Cabinets (Robert Schuman twice, Georges Bidault and Pierre Pflimlin);

2 Socialist Cabinets (Paul Ramadier in 1947 and Guy Mollet in 1956–7);

2 Centre-Left Cabinets headed by René Pleven, leader of the key UDSR (*Union Démocratique et Socialiste de la Résistance*);

2 Cabinets headed by members of the CNIP (A. Pinay and J. Laniel);

1 Cabinet headed by General de Gaulle on his return to power, from June 1958 to January 1959, when he took office as President of the Republic.

These figures confirm that the Fourth Republic led to an extreme, rigid division between those parties aspiring to Government power and the others, which settled for positions of irresponsible criticism. It should be added that the coalition attempted in 1946 between the three main parties – MRP, Socialist and Communist – came to an end in 1947 with the dismissal of the Communist Ministers; from then on the Communists played no part in any Government. The Radicals then reappeared and figured in every Cabinet, as did the MRP. The Socialists were left out of Governments from June 1951 to February 1956, the life-span of one Parliament.

During this period the function of the Government can be looked on as primarily administrative; there had to be a Cabinet of some sort, an imperative requirement that was imposed, almost as a technicality, on all parties not rigorously controlled by bureaucracies outside the Assembly. The Socialists themselves often gave their support, at least in the early stages of Cabinets, but retained the right to withdraw their goodwill should any action taken by the Prime Minister displease them. This leads us to another side of the divorce between Government and Opposition, which manifests itself as a divergence in behaviour between militants and elected members inside the same party.

From 1924 on, Socialist Deputies had been willing to take part in left-wing Governments, but their party leadership constantly forbade this – even, as in 1929, after the group had voted for a favourable reply to the offer made by Édouard Daladier, the Radical Prime Minister, who thereupon gave up trying to form a Government. In 1954 Pierre Mendès-France offered five Ministerial portfolios to Socialist Deputies, but Guy Mollet, Secretary General of the SFIO since 1946, opposed this, according to the decisions of a party congress at which Members of Parliament had, inevitably, been in the minority. Constant disputes over this question set the parliamentary party against the Executive, and in 1948 a joint committee had been set up to deal with them. But behind the sporadic disagreements there lay a more fundamental enmity between elected Members, who felt they held direct mandates from their constituents, and the line taken by Guy Mollet, that a Deputy's status was subordinate to that of a member of the party's executive.

One of the traits that distinguishes Opposition and Government parties is that in the former decisions belong to party authorities, as elected members are committed to reform, which alone justifies their participation in the challenged regime. So that considerations concerning the functioning of the regime should not take precedence in the eyes of Deputies over their own commitment to reform, directives are issued by the reformist party bureaucracies to indicate the line to be followed; but for the system to be viable, further mechanisms must be created to resolve conflicts between militants and electors. These mechanisms were in fact lacking, and existing procedures functioned precisely in such a way as to hinder this type of adjustment; the electoral weakness of the SFIO made it impossible for it to exercise power alone, since this party could not reasonably hope that universal suffrage would give it a mandate to act entirely according to its own convictions. It therefore had to enter into compromises with others, but in arbitrarily chosen circumstances, since its decision was by then not dictated by its electors but depended on the judgement of the party chiefs. There was some excuse for adopting this type of attitude, particularly in view of the Communist Party's constant outbidding tactics; however, the position of immobility that was chosen made any democratic outcome impossible.

The Socialists' refusal to share the responsibilities of power save in exceptional circumstances accentuated the opportunism of the Radicals, who gradually gave up their reforming ambitions and acted merely as a cog in the governmental machine. This functional behaviour manifested itself in the picturesque section of the party rules laying down policy during Cabinet crises. In such cases, the party bureau would meet with Members of Parliament to form what was familiarly known as the 'Cadillac Committee'[4] to decide the position to be adopted by the Deputies; unlike the Socialists, Radical Deputies were not subordinated to the party bureaucracy, but the consultations which took place on such occasions none the less made for a modicum of compromise between party feelings and the behaviour of Deputies. Party congresses played a similar part, and while they took care to avoid issuing directives, the positions they took up were not without influence, as they arbitrated between various factions, all led by Deputies, the winners being entitled to speak in the name of the Radical Party: the rivalry between the 'two Édouards' (Herriot and Daladier), who followed one another as party chairman, enlivened the inter-war political scene. The decline of the influence of the external party over parliamentarians, who came to behave increasingly like a Friendly Society of Deputies, heralded the decrepitude of Radicalism – which still had some spasms of life left in it, particularly when Pierre Mendès-France took over as party chairman; but in due course he too gave up after a skirmish with the parliamentary group in 1957, without

4. The 'Cadillac Committee' gained its name from the fact that it was founded at the suggestion of the Radical Party of the town of Cadillac, near Bordeaux.

forcing his opponents to defend their points of view before a party congress that might well have disowned them.

Parties under the Fifth Republic

The Fifth Republic seemed at first to perpetuate the system we have just described. Once cut off from the governmental power its life depended on, Radicalism withered away, but the other parties happily vegetated on. A minority of Socialist and Radical activists banded together with other left-wing groups to form the PSU (United Socialist Party), held together by their opposition to de Gaulle, who had rallied together the leaders of the traditional groups in 1958. But this apparent standstill lasted only until the end of the Algerian war; since 1963 the situation has been changing fast, tending towards an overall simplification of the system and a revision of existing rules.

In purely numerical terms the simplification has been spectacular. At the 1956 elections there were eighteen 'national' (i.e. officially recognized) parties, the qualifying condition for this title being to present candidates under the same party label in at least thirty *départements*. But many of these eighteen parties were merely election-oriented devices, serving to provide candidates with a common label, and did not correspond to organized groupings. After 1958, proportional representation was replaced by a single-member, two-ballot system, and the title of 'national' was given only to parties presenting a minimum of seventy-five candidates; in 1958 there were still twelve national parties, but the number fell to seven in 1962 and five in 1967. These five were:

(i) The 'Fifth Republic Action Committee' (Comité d'Action pour la Cinquième République) composed of the UNR–UDT (Gaullists), Giscard d'Estaing's Independent Republicans (former members of the CNIP who had opted for Gaullism), several tiny groups of more left-wing persuasions, and individuals without formal affiliations.

(ii) The 'Federation of the Left' (Fédération de la Gauche Démocrate et Socialiste), which included the Socialist and

Radical parties and the 'Convention of Republican Institutions', a group of political clubs led by François Mitterrand.

(iii) The 'Democratic Centre', comprising the MRP and the non-Gaullist members of the CNIP.

(iv) The Communist Party.

(v) The PSU, whose key figure was Pierre Mendès-France, although he stayed somewhat aloof from the party organization.

But the change is not merely arithmetical, if we compare this situation with the past. It indicates the emergence of a type of majority system in which the electorate is now able to take a stand for or against the sitting Government.

As Philip Williams has pointed out:

The French electorate seemed ready, like the British, to vote for or against a Cabinet and to expect their representatives to keep it in power rather than turn it out whenever some unexpected crisis or an unpopular reform offended an interest in the country and a marginal group in the Assembly.

With de Gaulle in power, the parties were obliged to adapt themselves to a system in which the hierarchy was no longer the same as before. There was no longer any question of ensuring the exact representation of varying opinions and interests, which had instead to be conflated into a single national response. The law of dispersion which had hitherto prevailed gave way to the opposite tendency, which spurred neighbouring groups to come together and played down minor rivalries. The new system took shape in two stages, firstly to the advantage of the Gaullist majority, then in favour of the left-wing Opposition.

The first step was taken in November 1962 after the dissolution of the National Assembly. General de Gaulle intervened personally on the eve of the polls to point out that the issue at stake was his remaining in power; a massive proportion of MRP and right-wing voters promptly abandoned their old parties and flocked to rally round the Gaullist cause, which emerged from the polls with 230 UNR (orthodox Gaullist) seats and about thirty Independent Republicans (Conservatives allied to Gaullism). For the first time there was a homogeneous disciplined majority in Parliament. This was to bring about profound changes in the public's attitude to political life and, consequently, lead the other parties to speculate on their own future.

This change in the framework did not, however, correspond to a comparable change in content. 'UNR' had served only as a flag of convenience for the elections, and despite the efforts of some of the party leaders, the UNR does not possess an organization adequate for the size of its representation in Parliament. It is, in fact, scarcely more than a tool in the hands of the General, possessing little life of its own and controlled from above by a small group of men. Its existence seems to be linked to the presence in power of a personality capable of welding together a rather ill-assorted body of men who are united only by an awareness of what their fate would be otherwise. And, indeed, politicians who have left the UNR have been ruthlessly eliminated by their electors, who have given the party's candidate a simple but imperative mandate: observe discipline and support the General.

The situation of M. Giscard d'Estaing's Independent Republicans is somewhat different, as their decision to join the majority results from calculations based on the attitude of the conservative electorate, which has been won over to Gaullism, as well as from a realization of the implications of the new majority regime, in which there is no longer any place for outsiders, but only for one Majority and one Opposition.

The December 1965 Presidential elections provided the left-wing Opposition with an opportunity to overcome its internal rivalries and divisions. We have already seen that the grouping together of the non-Communist Left could have taken place at constituency level as well as in Parliament, but that the attitude of the Socialist leaders was as much of an obstacle as was the desire of the Radicals to belong to all successive Governments. Circumstances took care of the latter problem, and the other difficulty was to be overcome as a result of the election of the President of the Republic by universal suffrage. It was in fact against the advice of Guy Mollet that a leading Socialist, Gaston

Defferre, decided at the end of 1964 to stand as a candidate for the Presidency, and set off an inexorable chain of events. Left-wing opinion, both inside and outside the parties, then began to look at politics in terms of government power that might, after all, be won directly and collectively, instead of worrying about maintaining a few electoral positions in order to obtain representation in Parliament. M. Defferre was unable to carry his plan through to its conclusion, for he made the mistake of getting caught up in negotiations with the MRP, on whose support he was counting. He was followed in autumn 1965 by François Mitterrand, a Centre-Left politician who had become the spokes-man for the political clubs that grouped together former supporters of Mendès-France and newcomers to politics.

The emotions touched off when M. Defferre stood down had in any case convinced the Socialist and Radical leaders that something had to be done, and they resigned themselves to giving up some of their independence by creating a Federation of the Left, of which M. Mitterrand became president. The Communist Party, faithful to its position as a party of challenge, did not aspire to presenting a candidate in the forthcoming presidential elections, particularly as it suspected that the protest-oriented nature of its traditional vote might be put off balance in a com-petition in which power, not opposition, was the prize. Communist electors may want to be represented by the most extreme left-wing Deputies they can find but they do not necessarily dream of being *governed* by the Communist Party. . . . The party therefore promised to support M. Mitterrand's candidature; in this way he obtained 34% of votes at the first ballot and 44·8% at the second. His position as leader of the Federation of the Left was thus con-firmed and from then on its members knew that they could not break apart, as their fortunes were bound up together. At the March 1967 legislative elections, the Federation managed to im-pose nationally planned discipline on its candidates, 116 of whom were elected (it had 90 outgoing Deputies) and formed a single bloc in the National Assembly.

A very different demonstration of this change in the rules of the parliamentary game is provided by the failure of the 'Demo-

Appendix 1 General Elections (1958–67)

The results of the three general elections of 1958, 1962 and 1967 given below are those obtained at the first ballot. At the second, voting takes place only in those constituencies in which the seat is not filled at the first ballot. Many of the first-ballot candidates stand down at the second, either because they realize they have no hope of winning the seat, or because they hope to favour the election of some other candidate with views similar to their own, or in order to prevent the election of an opponent.

The three tables below give the official results for metropolitan France, published by the Ministry of the Interior. For several reasons, the figures are not exactly comparable. Firstly, the various parties are not all represented in all constituencies; only the Communists (and in 1967 the Gaullists) had candidates everywhere. Furthermore, the Ministry of the Interior's classification system tends to vary, and political labels are not consistent from one election to the next. Lastly, candidates' labels do not always correspond to a precise parliamentary party; for instance, Deputies elected on a 'Centre-Left' label in 1962 could be supporters of either the Rassemblement Démocratique or the Centre Démocratique.

TABLE 5. Parliamentary Elections, 23 November 1958

Electors	27,236,491
Abstentions	6,236,694
Votes cast	20,484,709

Party	Number of votes	Percentage of votes
Communist	3,882,204	18·90
Other left-wing	347,298	1·04
Socialist (SFIO)	3,167,354	15·50
Radicals	983,201	4·80
Centre-Left	716,869	3·50
UNR	3,603,958	17·60
MRP	1,858,380	9·10
Christian Democrats	520,408	2·05
Centre Republican	647,919	3·02
CNIP	2,815,176	13·70
Moderates	1,277,424	6·20
Extreme Right	669,518	3·03

The 'Christian Democrats' were in reality a variant of the MRP, which looked to Georges Bidault as its leader. The 'Centre Republican' party was a dissident Radical group.

TABLE 6. Parliamentary Elections, 18 November 1962

Electors	27,526,358
Abstentions	8,608,199
Votes cast	18,333,791

Party	Number of votes	Percentage of votes
Communist	4,003,553	21·84
Extreme Left	427,467	2·33
Socialist (SFIO)	2,298,729	12·54
Radical and Centre-Left	1,429,649	7·79
UNR and UDT	5,855,744	31·94
MRP	1,665,695	9·08
Independents	1,089,348	5·94
CNIP	1,404,177	7·66
Extreme Right	159,429	0·87

TABLE 7. Parliamentary Elections, 5 March 1967

Electors	28,291,838
Abstentions	5,404,687
Votes cast	22,392,317

Party	Number of votes	Percentage of votes
Communist	5,029,808	22·46
Extreme Left (including PSU)	506,592	2·26
Federation of the Left	4,207,166	18·79
'Fifth Republic' (Comité pour la Cinquième République)	8,453,512	37·75
Centre Democrats	2,864,272	12·79
Others	1,136,191	7·66
Extreme Right	194,776	0·87

The Communist Party

The French Communist Party was founded as a breakaway from the Socialist Party in 1920. From 1930 to 1964 it was led by Maurice Thorez, who was succeeded after his death by Waldeck Rochet.

Approximately one million party cards were issued in 1946, but party strength then took a downward turn, particularly after 1958, and began to rise again only in 1961. At the 1967 party congress, it was stated that the French Communist Party had 50,000 members more than in 1961 and that 425,000 party cards had been issued (not all, however, were taken up). About a quarter of the members are women, and a third of the membership belongs to the 26–40 age group.

TABLE 8.

Parliamentary elections	Votes	Percentage	Number of deputies	Number of Départements represented
10 11 46	5,489,000	28·6	159	79
17 6 51	4,910,547	25·67	97	41
2 1 56	5,454,589	25·38	139	69
23 11 58	3,882,204	18·9	10	5
18 11 62	4,003,553	21·84	41	18
5 3 67	5,029,808	22·46	72	29

The Socialist Party (SFIO)

Founded on 25 April 1905, the Socialist Party was officially named Section Française de l'Internationale Ouvrière (French Section of the Workers' International) after the schism at the 1920 Tours Congress that led to the foundation of the Communist Party. Under the leadership of Jean Jaurès until 1914, then of Léon Blum until 1946, the SFIO became the largest party of the Third Republic. Since 1946 its Secretary-General has been Guy Mollet, who heads both the political and administrative sides of his party.

Membership, around 335,000 in 1945, has since dropped to less than 100,000.

TABLE 9.

Parliamentary elections	Votes	Percentage	Number of Deputies	Number of Départements represented
10 11 46	3,432,000	17·9	90	64
17 6 51	2,744,842	14·35	95	58
2 1 56	3,180,656	14·8	89	54
23 11 58	3,167,354	15·5	39	21
18 11 62	2,298,729	12·54	64	30

In 1967, 76 Socialist Deputies, belonging to the Federation of the Left group, were elected, representing 38 *départements*.

The SFIO professes a doctrine inspired by Marxism; it has considerable representation in local councils: of 639 communes of over 9,000 inhabitants, 145 had Socialist mayors after the March 1965 elections (compared with 103 Communists and 81 Gaullists).

The Radical-Socialist Party

The Radical-Socialist Party was founded in 1901, and gained its largest number of parliamentary seats in 1913, with 172 members returned. Between the wars it was overtaken by the Socialist Party. Weakened by later events, it gradually regained importance; it had a membership of about 80,000 in 1955–6, when it was led by Pierre Mendès-France; since then its strength has dropped to a quarter of that figure.

TABLE 10.

Parliamentary elections	Votes	Percentage	Number of Deputies	Number of Départements represented
10 11 46	2,381,000	12·4	58	42
17 6 51	1,887,583	9·87	78	50
2 1 56	2,876,698	13·4	74	45
23 11 58	1,700,070	8·3	35	25
18 11 62	1,429,649	7·79	43	37

The number of votes indicated is approximate, as the classification system changed between elections. Of Radical Deputies proper, defined in terms of strict party membership, there were 17 in 1958, representing 14 *départements*, and 25 representing 23 *départements* in 1962 and 1967.

The MRP (Mouvement Républicain Populaire)

The MRP has steadily declined in strength ever since its foundation shortly after the Liberation. It was even due to be disbanded after the creation of the Democratic Centre party in 1965, but none the less it has survived. In 1946 it had 200,000 members; twenty years later it had slightly over a tenth of this figure.

TABLE 11.

Parliamentary elections	Votes	Percentage	Number of Deputies	Number of Départements represented
10 11 46	5,058,000	26·3	158	77
17 6 51	2,369,778	12·39	78	52
2 1 56	2,374,221	11·05	73	40
23 11 58	2,408,370	11·7	54	36
18 11 62	1,635,452	8·92	34	26

In the 1967 election only 15 MRP Deputies, representing 14 *départements*, were elected; they belonged to the centre groups known as 'Progress' and 'Modern Democracy'. However, 7 other Christian Democrats were also elected on a Fifth Republic ticket.

The CNIP (Centre National des Indépendants et Paysans)

Founded in 1949, the CNIP has gradually brought together various conservative groups, but it divided once again over General de Gaulle's Algerian policy; after 1962, it went into hibernation. Voting for the various conservative parties was as follows:

TABLE 12.

Parliamentary elections	Votes	Percentage	Number of Deputies	Number of Départements represented
10 11 46	2,466,000	12·9	71	43
17 6 51	2,433,000	12·3	85	50
2 1 56	3,086,000	14·3	94	58
23 11 58	4,112,191	20·1	111	56

In November 1962 the Ministry of the Interior assigned 1,404,177 votes (7.66% of total votes cast) to the CNIP candidates, who thus obtained 27 seats in Parliament. But 16 of these Deputies eventually rallied to Gaullism, under M. Giscard d'Estaing, while most of the others joined the MRP to form the Democratic Centre.

In 1967 M. Giscard d'Estaing's party, the Fédération Nationale des Républicains Indépendants, founded the preceding year, obtained about forty seats. The CNIP candidates within the Democratic Centre had only 9 seats in 8 *départements*. The CNIP has no militants but only local constituency committees.

The UNR (Union pour la Nouvelle République)

In April 1947 General de Gaulle launched the RPF (Rassemblement du Peuple Français) which rocketed into prominence only to plummet out as abruptly in 1952. After de Gaulle's return to power, in October 1958, the Gaullists founded the 'Union for the New Republic' (which became UNR–UDT in December 1962 after taking over a small left-wing Gaullist group, the Union Démocratique du Travail).

From 1958 to 1967, the UNR held only three national congresses. Its organization, which is alleged to have 80,000 active members, is run on rigidly hierarchical, centralized lines and hinges on the authority of a small circle of the General's more faithful supporters. Gaullist representation has fared as follows:

TABLE 13.

Parliamentary elections	Votes	Percentage	Number of Deputies	Number of Départements represented
17 6 51	4,134,885	21·7	104	52
2 1 56	948,854	4·42	16	15
23 11 58	3,603,958	17·6	195	69
18 11 62	5,855,744	31·94	229	68

In 1967, the overall votes cast for the majority were conflated without distinguishing between UNR and other members of the Government coalition. 192 Deputies, representing 67 metropolitan *départements*, are officially registered with the parliamentary party of the Union des Démocrates pour la Cinquième République (UDV^{e}R: Fifth Republic Party) which has replaced the UNR–UDT; but 18 of them are only 'attached' to the group.

4 The President of the Republic: Guardian or Leader?

The function of the Presidency must be understood within the general context we have just described; it reflects all the ambiguity and fluidity of the system in that the position of the head of State, placed slightly apart from the main conflicts, leads him to intervene only as far as the State needs his support. He can indeed provide the strength needed, for he possesses the key attributes the Government lacks: above all, stability and independence. Yet on the other hand, he used not to have the direct authority which comes from being elected directly by the people. It might therefore be said that the President of the Republic acts as a 'spare wheel' for use when the French parliamentary system is unable to function on its own. But over a period of eighty years, from Marshal MacMahon to General de Gaulle, this reserve role remained a subsidiary one to such an extent that we could almost, on the institutional plane at least, look on de Gaulle's return to power in 1958 as retaliation for the defeat of the earlier soldier.

The Two-headed Executive

One of the most peculiar and least well-known features of the French parliamentary system is the permanent dualism that characterizes the executive branch. The relationship between the President of the Republic and the head of the Government has always been ambiguous as their respective influences vary according to considerations of personality and situation and the problem in hand; however, we could say that the President's role goes beyond what is normally conceded to a parliamentary head of State. This aspect of the regime has generally been overlooked, since it did not contradict the rules of the Deputy-centred republic; while in retrospect it may appear abnormal, this is largely by comparison with a system based on the supremacy of universal suffrage. Here we see yet again the events that set the Third Republic on the lines that persisted until 1958, despite the fact that the circumstances surrounding the beginnings of the regime were similar to those surrounding other new regimes which none the less developed along different lines.

When, in 1873, even before a Constitution had been adopted, the leader of the parliamentary monarchists, the Duc de Broglie, carried through the law fixing the head of State's term in office at seven years, he intended to organize the provisional regime that had governed France since the fall of the Empire without prejudicing the possibility of a royalist restoration. The plan was that Marshal MacMahon was to occupy this seat for seven years, in order to keep it warm for the pretender to the throne. The powers of the President of the Republic were truly defined in 1875, with a view to their possibly being wielded by a monarch. The President, elected by Parliament, is the embodiment of the State authority, which is translated into action through Ministers appointed by the President and answerable to the Chambers.

The basic principles of the parliamentary regime were thus laid down in a wholly pragmatic fashion, since the Royalists wanted only to safeguard the future, and the Republicans asked only to have the title of President of the Republic recognized. Neither side seems to have given any thought to the Prime Minister, who was not even mentioned in the constitutional laws.

The second step was every bit as pragmatic. Marshal MacMahon hoped to exercise direct influence over Cabinet policy, and consequently came into conflict with the Deputies (the majority of whom had been, since the 1876 elections, Republican). After the dissolution of the Chamber on 16 May 1877 and the return of another Republican majority, the supremacy of universal suffrage came to be imposed, and with it the fundamental principle of ministerial responsibility, which implied diminished responsibility and, therefore, status for the head of State.

All was set, or so it seemed, for an uneventful evolution towards Cabinet government, but this was not to be the case. In Chapter 2 we mentioned the importance of the action of Jules Grévy, MacMahon's successor, when he refused to call on the main Republican leader to lead the Government, and appointed instead Senator Waddington. The head of the Cabinet was therefore merely a coordinating Minister, a *primus inter pares*, lacking the type of authority that comes from being at the head of a majority. The President of the Republic continued to preside over the Council of Ministers, although the parliamentary head of the Government acquired the rather paradoxical title of 'President of the Council'. After keeping Gambetta out of office in 1879, Jules Grévy who, despite his retiring appearance, was extremely jealous of his personal authority, carried on with the same tactics: when Waddington resigned at the end of the year, he appointed Freycinet ('the white mouse') to succeed him.

The arbitrary character of presidential appointments was made possible only by the absence of political parties as such, i.e. instruments enabling the electorate as a whole to participate in the choice of the head of the Government. The practice introduced by Jules Grévy did much to stir up rivalry between the main majority leaders, who could all lay claim to the Cabinet leadership, and consequently fostered the tendency for Deputies to divide up into competing groups. Free to choose the Prime Minister out of the loose parliamentary majority, Grévy carried on with his own personal game by keeping out men whose personal authority risked encroaching on his own, or calling on them only when they were worn out by too much waiting and their colleagues' jealousy. For instance, he twice passed over Georges Clemenceau, who had defeated the Ferry cabinet in 1885 and the Freycinet cabinet in 1886, although Waldeck-Rousseau in 1885 and Freycinet himself in 1886 had advised him to call on the man who had caused the crisis in the first place.

After playing an instrumental role in forming the basic characteristics of the French parliamentary system, the President of the Republic duly reaped the benefits of the situation he had created; as a result it became necessary for him to intervene personally. It had indeed become indispensable to have an independent 'referee' to choose the Deputy best fitted to gain the support of a majority and lead the Government. This role came to develop as a corollary of the regime without an elected majority which we described in Chapter 2, and if it happened that an election produced a new leader, as in the cases of Herriot in 1924, Poincaré in 1928 and Léon Blum in 1936, it was still necessary to call on the President of the Republic when that particular majority broke up and a new one had to be formed.

Under the Fourth Republic, the lack of political cohesion, aggravated by the new electoral system of proportional representation, led the first President, Vincent Auriol, into almost immediate conflict with his own Socialist Party whose demands were preventing him from building a Government.

Although the Constitution of 1946, which proclaimed the Fourth Republic, had aimed at limiting presidential powers and only allowed the head of State to suggest a candidate for Assembly investiture, the first President of the new regime, Vincent Auriol, found himself led by circumstances to take personal steps in order to solve, from week to week or month to month, the difficult problems raised by parliamentary arithmetic. When considering the demands of the various groups, he had also to take into account their respective numerical importance and work out the combination likely to produce even a short-lived majority. By force of circumstances (and in accordance with his own temperament) Vincent Auriol interpreted his functions in dynamic terms: he stage-managed crises, brushed aside solutions he considered dangerous, impracticable or simply premature, eliminated men whose time he felt had not yet come, and catapulted others into power. He played on suspense and anxiety, waiting for the moment he judged propitious for the success of the solution he wanted to put through. The 'spare wheel' was now in almost constant use, a key component of the new parliamentary machinery. If a less prosaic comparison is preferred, we might say that by virtue of his flair for choosing unexpected men for elevation to the front ranks (as with Antoine Pinay in 1952), by the practice of consultation and exploratory missions (at which René Pleven excelled), and by the solemn warnings he issued at psychologically strategic moments, this theoretically retiring arbiter became the veritable *deus ex machina* of the regime. But this quasi-supernatural aid was made necessary only by the fact that the machine failed to run smoothly when left to its own devices.

The resolution of crises could not, obviously, be reduced to a simple technical operation, for the choice of a viable parliamentary formula was in practice inseparable from the President of the Republic's own conception of the national interest. Vincent Auriol's successor, René Coty, was elected at the end of 1953, and seemed inclined to play a less active part in the conduct of State business; he carried discretion to the point of vanishing of his own accord on the arrival of General de Gaulle in 1958. Yet previously, in 1956, he had taken what turned out to be a momentous step in appointing Guy Mollet rather than Pierre Mendès-France as head of the Government. Behind the pretexts issued (Mollet was the head of the Socialist Party, which was larger than the Radical Party), there was a characteristic refusal to pay attention to public opinion, which had looked on Mendès-France as the uncontested leader in the election campaign; there was also an element of political preference: René Coty considered Guy Mollet more of a 'European', who thus would be more acceptable to the MRP than Mendès-France, and further, this more traditional line of policy was more in tune with the President's personal views. Therefore, by occasionally conjuring up new figures, the President of the Republic could exercise a determining influence through his choice of men, by setting national policies on one particular course which he, rightly or wrongly, judged preferable to others.

The Participation of the President of the Republic in Governmental Activity

Apart from his right to choose the Prime Minister – a prerogative which, as we have seen, only gained its later importance because it fell within one man's discretion – the President of the Republic was granted certain other powers by the Constitution. In Cabinet-governed regimes, the exercise of these was transferred to the responsible Ministers, while the head of State remained only symbolically as titular holder. In France for these very reasons and in spite of his non-accountable position, the President of the Republic has retained a by no means negligible degree of participation in Government affairs.

Firstly, he is closely associated with the work of the Cabinet, since he presides over the Council of Ministers during whose meetings the most important decisions are taken. In contrast to the common law of parliamentary regimes in which 'the King reigns but does not govern' the President of the Republic not only holds office for seven years but also influences the Government, sometimes discreetly, sometimes more overtly. The full scope of his role will be appreciated if we remember that Cabinets survived for only a few months and the President of the Republic naturally became the one lasting element in the endless to-and-fro between the seats of power. He was no longer a merely symbolic head of State, but also the regime's memory (before 1946 minutes were not kept at meetings of the Council of Ministers, and since then they have been filed in the Élysée). The President's position as effective chairman of Government meetings in which he represented the element of continuity gave him a twofold advantage which was exploited by the various office-holders to a degree that varied with the strength of their personalities and the character of the head of the Government; however, the situation clearly provided openings for influence for those who saw fit to use them. The one limitation they had to accept stemmed from the existence of ministerial responsibility, which they were obliged to accept. When open disagreement emerged between the President and a Minister, the Minister usually seems to have won (at least in our own times), but often the President had only to wait for the next crisis to acquire more understanding colleagues. Furthermore, the occurrence of this type of political argument depended on the nature of the questions under debate; the President was powerless when a question caught the interest of the Chambers, as it was on those very questions that Governments were most often called on to answer for themselves; questions that did not interest Parliament were in general willingly left to the President.

In this way the logic of the Parliamentary regime exercised a general influence over domestic politics, but was easily set aside when foreign affairs or defence came under scrutiny. Since the 1875 constitutional laws the President of the Republic has been empowered to negotiate and ratify international treaties (subject to informing the Chambers as soon as is compatible with national security and the national interest) and to control the armed forces. It was therefore accepted that these fields constituted a sort of special prerogative, since it was essential to keep them above the everyday bickerings of domestic politics. Presidential power was certainly interpreted in this way by Jules Grévy; he confidentially told a Deputy: 'There are two things I will allow nobody else to touch: foreign affairs and war. As far as the rest is concerned I'm very easy-going.' It was only when external crises and domestic conflicts coincided, or could serve as pretexts for them, that Parliament attacked diplomatic problems; in this way Jules Ferry[1] was unseated in 1885 over the Tonkin expedition and Caillaux lost his position in 1912 because of an incident in Africa. This led to a gradual division of responsibility between the President of the Council, who handled domestic affairs and relations with Parliament, and the President of the Republic, who watched over diplomacy and the Army. We have an unvarnished account of this division of power from one Prime Minister: Émile Combes, who engineered the separation of Church and State between 1902 and 1905. The President of the Republic, Émile Loubet, who had called on Combes, gave his agreement to these anti-clerical measures – more because he was resigned to the overwhelming feeling among the Deputies than through genuine approval; in return for this, the President of the Republic told Combes that he hoped that the Ministry of Foreign Affairs

1. Jules Ferry (1832–1893) headed two Governments, in 1880–81 and 1883–5. He organized the primary education system, encouraged colonial expansion and extended French influence through Tunisia, the Congo and Tonkin, where a military defeat led to the downfall of his Government.

would be left in the hands of Delcassé[2] with whom, as he explained, he was used to working. ... A little later, Poincaré played what some historians have interpreted as a determining role in shaping the policies that led to the First World War. After the Armistice, Millerand lost patience with the way the Prime Minister, Aristide Briand, was taking over the running of French diplomacy, and played a major part in bringing about Briand's defeat as a result of the 1922 Cannes Conference. However, soon after this Millerand made the mistake of intervening in the electoral campaign – i.e. in domestic politics – and was forced to resign in 1924 after the victory of the left-wing 'cartel'. His successors learned from this experience and behaved in a more circumspect way.

In 1946 the powers of the head of State were reduced, at least in theory: in practice Vincent Auriol turned out to be far more active than Presidents of the end of the Third Republic. He received diplomatic reports and despatches twice daily, conferred with ambassadors and military chiefs, and when the occasion demanded, he could take up spectacular stands, in particular when he was opposing German rearmament. According to the French political scientist Alfred Grosser,[3] he also played a far from negligible role in stifling the plan for a European army. However, the MRP's interest in these questions and the almost constant presence of its representatives in the Ministry of Foreign Affairs acted as a brake on the influence of the President of the Republic. After Auriol, René Coty followed a more self-effacing line, which he departed from only to support the French presence in Algeria.

The respective weight of the President of the Republic and the Prime Minister depended mainly on personalities and circum-

2. Born in 1852, Delcassé was Minister of Foreign Affairs for seven years (1898–1905). He followed a policy of *rapprochement* with Great Britain, leading to the Entente Cordiale in 1904, but he also strengthened the alliance with Russia and obtained a promise of neutrality from Italy. Germany considered itself hemmed in by these measures, and used Morocco as the pretext for a military incident, after which Delcassé was forced to resign in 1905.

3. Alfred Grosser, *La IVe République et sa politique extérieure*, Paris, 1961.

stances. But the same man could move from one post to the other, and it is clear that he did not change character when he changed title; at least, when he *had* a character of his own, which in fact was the case with some of the politicians who filled both posts. Poincaré, for example, had been a very popular Prime Minister before he became President of the Republic in 1913, and later on he returned as Prime Minister in 1922–4 and 1926–9. During the war his influence had been eclipsed after 1917 by the head of the Government, Georges Clemenceau, who played a Churchillian role. Clemenceau made a bid for the presidency of the Republic in 1920, but Deputies feared his popularity and authority and withheld their support. Millerand, whose misadventure in 1924 has just been mentioned, had been Prime Minister in 1920 before he moved to the Élysée. Lastly, Gaston Doumergue, President of the Republic from 1924 to 1931, was called back to head the Government after the Paris riots of 6 February 1931.

At this time the increasingly defective functioning of the parliamentary system had sparked off a movement for revising the Constitution with a view to strengthening Presidential authority. The main aim was to limit the powers of Parliament, but this view unfortunately overlooked the fact that a strong executive could be based only on universal suffrage, so that the reforms envisaged by Doumergue met with the hostility of the entire left wing. Indeed, the whole project aimed at establishing a sort of tutelage over national representation, a tutelage 'above parties'; the idea was abandoned for some years but it was to come into its own in 1958.

The Gaullist 'Principate'

The text of the 1946 Constitution began with Parliament: that of the 1958 Constitution begins with the President of the Republic. The order in which the document is drafted reflects the underlying conception of the hierarchical arrangement of the State, and shows that the new regime was not limiting itself to correcting certain flaws of the Fourth Republic: it was attempting to go back to the initial stage in the development of Republican institutions, to orient them in another direction. M. Michel Debré, who played an essential part in working out this Constitution, once said that the French Parliamentary system had begun to go off the rails in 1872. The ideal model Michel Debré used for reference was not unlike that imagined by the conservatives at the beginning of the Third Republic. The State had to have a monarch or a quasi-monarch (in 1943 Debré expressed his hope for a 'republican monarch') but it was also inevitable that universal suffrage should have its role to play as well. This was to lead to a system in which a controlled, limited parliamentary regime would exist side by side with arbitrary power which would intervene when needed, to 'ensure the regular functioning of public power'. In the absence of a dynasty, the head of State was to be designated by a college of notables identical to the electoral college that chooses Senators. These notables, about 70,000 in all, are the delegates of municipal councils and members of the General Councils. The President of the Republic was thus no longer chosen only by Members of Parliament, but by a much larger, though still restricted, electorate, largely rural in its origins and conservative in its beliefs. In terms of this type of system, the upper Chamber, the Senate, emerges as an auxiliary of the executive power, which it assists in controlling the National Assembly, the one government organ elected by direct universal suffrage.

The President of the Republic disposes of two types of power. The most typically 'Gaullian' powers are designed to cope with crisis situations: the famous Article 16, which institutes a sort of temporary presidential dictatorship when:

the institutions of the Republic, the independence of the nation, the integrity of its territory . . . are seriously and immediately threatened, and the regular functioning of constitutional public power is disrupted.

The others apparently reproduce the powers of Presidents of the Third Republic, but whereas the latter had become largely symbolic, General de Gaulle showed that he intended to interpret them literally, if not actually to go further.

108

Starting from the idea of the head of State as 'guarantor of the independence and integrity of the nation', with the right and duty 'to ensure the continuity of the State and the functioning of power', the General considers that his various prerogatives correspond to powers that he can genuinely exercise in person.

The choice of Ministers, and in particular of the Prime Minister (the new title given to the post of President of the Council), comes entirely within the President's province. The Cabinet no longer receives its mandate from the Deputies: a Government exists once it has been appointed by the President. He may ask for a vote of confidence from the Assembly, but according to the interpretation of the Constitution which prevailed, he is not obliged to ask for a vote of confidence. M. Debré sought confirmation in this way in 1959, as did M. Pompidou in April and December 1962: however, at the formation of the third Pompidou Cabinet in January 1966, after the Presidential election, and again in April 1967, after the legislative elections, the Prime Minister did not see fit to ask for a vote. It is clear that the making of the Government rests entirely with the head of State, and now the Assembly's only means of action against a Government is to unseat it, assuming the Deputies can muster the necessary strength. The Government must still answer to Parliament for its actions, but in practice things are run as if the Cabinet was responsible primarily to the President who appoints and dissolves Governments. The demands of political reality have proved too great for constitutional measures, which did not allow for this second type of responsibility.

Moreover, the fact that the President chairs the Council of Ministers, which is now expanded to include not only all Members of the Government, but also the Secretaries of State, who previously were not entitled to membership, implies for all practical purposes presidential direction of Government action. The decisions published by the Council of Ministers are taken by the head of State, whose signature is no longer a mere formality, but a positive act. Furthermore, contrary to the common law of parliamentary regimes, a certain number of presidential decisions (dissolutions and referenda) no longer have to be countersigned by a responsible Minister. The right to make civil and military appointments is a genuine power and not, as formerly, the ceremonial confirmation of decisions made by others.

In the fields of foreign policy and defence, the President intervenes directly and his authority is total. We have seen how the first Presidents of the Third Republic kept a measure of personal influence in these matters, in spite of the fact that Ministers were answerable to Parliament. At present, diplomacy and the army are the private preserve of the head of State.[4] This does not represent a revolution as complete as is claimed by opponents of the regime; it is, however, a major reorganization.

In terms of the initial plan for the Fifth Republic, a parliamentary regime was to function on probation under the active tutelage of the President of the Republic. The latter was, like his predecessor, associated with Government life, but more closely than before, and he possessed far greater influence; he was still not a leader, but an arbitrator, in as much as his interventions aimed, theoretically, at maintaining the regular, stable functioning of power. He did not take sides in debates, but 'observed' the national interest without committing himself personally.

This system as it stood was basically unrealistic and functioned only for a few months, from January to September 1959. Its one effect was to consummate the eclipse of Parliament, which was subjected to the severe discipline of M. Michel Debré and stripped of all ability to act, except through censure motions. To understand this situation we must remember that General de Gaulle was called on after the Algiers riots of 13 May 1958, and that he had received a personal mandate, whatever the legal position may have been; by giving their support to the new Constitution in September 1958, by 17,668,790 assenting votes of *oui* to 4,624,511 votes of *non*, the French electorate had in reality, as the French Socialist politician André Philip noted at the time, 'elected General

4. This was first stated publicly (using the expression '*domaine réservé*') by M. Chaban-Delmas, President of the National Assembly, on 15 November 1959 at the UNR Congress in Bordeaux, in an attempt to dissuade the Gaullists, who then supported the French presence in Algeria, from taking up a stand on this issue.

de Gaulle President of the French Republic'. Moreover, they had voted him this power in order to resolve the Algerian problem. Consequently, for public opinion as for most Members of Parliament, he was the true leader of the country. The contradiction between this political situation and the President's role as arbitrator, as defined in the Constitution, was bound to come to a head as soon as an important decision had to be made. And indeed, on 16 September 1959, General de Gaulle intervened to propose self-determination to the Algerians: he stepped in again, more directly, after a new series of riots in Algiers in January 1960. The Government led by M. Michel Debré was there only to carry out presidential policy, and its increasingly factitious responsibility to the National Assembly served exclusively to allow the head of State to stay aloof, preserving his freedom to act and maintaining uncertainty as to his real intentions.

The illusory accountability of the Debré Cabinet enjoyed the complicity of the greater number of Deputies, who had in a way surrendered all their power to General de Gaulle. They would have preferred to keep some of their functions as representatives of interest groups (particularly in the field of agriculture), or as ideological spokesmen (e.g. over the plan to extend state subsidies to religious education), but the President of the Republic made it brutally clear that they would be ill advised to count on this. They protested a little, then resigned themselves to the new situation and waited for the Algerian war to come to an end.

The gradual atrophying of parliamentary representation made General de Gaulle feel the need to have his Algerian actions ratified by public opinion. He proceeded to do this by means of two referenda, in January 1961 and April 1962, which bypassed the Deputies. It was becoming clear that, however great the prestige and personality of the head of State, central power could not dispense with the support of the electorate at large; since it no longer used the intermediary of the National Assembly, another way had to be found, and the referendum seemed, albeit in a rather unorthodox way, to provide the solution; the logical outcome of this trend was the direct election of the President of the Republic by universal suffrage.

The Political Model

In order to put an end to Parliament's hankering after a return to a Deputy-based Republic, General de Gaulle was thus led to propose a modification of the Constitution which had been ruled out in 1958 as incompatible with the idea of a parliamentary regime and the neutral role of the head of State. This reform appears to have been a pragmatic compromise with the facts of mid-twentieth-century life, which laid down that monarchical tutelage is unacceptable and that the only possible type of authority must depend on universal suffrage.

Once peace in Algeria had become a reality, the position of General de Gaulle was in many ways comparable to the situation of 'Monsieur Thiers' in 1873, after the Communard insurrection had been repressed and the Prussian occupying forces evacuated. He had carried out the mission entrusted to him, and he must have been aware of the impatience with which Parliament was still knuckling under to his authority: so he decided to challenge Parliament on the issue of constitutional reform, which he put to the national vote in the referendum of 28 October 1962. It is strange to recall that Thiers himself had not been in favour of the parliamentary regime and, conscious of his own influence over public opinion, he had proposed the election of the President by direct suffrage. But he was not given the opportunity to push this scheme through – a scheme that had also attracted Napoleon III, who had been elected President by universal suffrage before organizing the *coup d'état* of 2 December 1851 which enabled him to scatter the Deputies. The Gaullist reform therefore represented a genuine return to the origins of the Third Republic and not, as M. Debré claimed, to its parliamentary, conservative sources; the problem of governing France was tackled once more, but this time on the basis of a link with an even more distant past.

From Arbitration to Leadership

General de Gaulle was re-elected President of the Republic on 9 December 1965, at the second ballot. The 1962 reforms envisaged a presidential election based on two ballots; in the first round any citizen could stand as candidate providing he received at least one hundred nominations signed by Members of Parliament, members of General Councils, or mayors in at least ten different *départements* – the qualifications were intended to ensure that only serious candidates stood, but practice showed them to be insufficiently strict. The second ballot concerned only the top two candidates (allowing for the possible withdrawal of others): thus the President of the Republic is necessarily elected by an absolute majority, since only two candidates are left at the second ballot.

TABLE 14. Results of the 1966 Presidential Elections

	5 December		19 December	
Electorate	28,913,422		28,902,704	
Votes cast	24,502,957		24,371,647	
Valid votes	24,254,554		23,703,434	
	Total votes	Percentage	Total votes	Percentage
Barbu	279,683	1·1		
de Gaulle	10,828,523	44·6	13,083,699	55·1
Lecanuet	3,777,119	15·5		
Marcilhacy	415,018	1·7		
Mitterrand	7,694,003	34·7	10,619,735	44·8
Tixier-Vignancour	1,260,208	5·1		

These results cover the entire electorate and therefore include the 500,000 votes cast in overseas territories and *départements*.

While the elections of 19 December 1965 did not lead to any legal transformation of the preceding system, they did lead to a political modification. The President of the Republic was led to abandon, at least during the period of his electoral campaign, his privileged position of irresponsibility and submit to the discipline of the competition. One of the most remarkable features of the campaign was that, after qualifying for the second ballot, the President found himself in a situation in which he had to justify his policies. On this occasion he left off his role of arbitrator above party politics, and became a leader bidding for the support of the electorate. At the same time it became evident that he was the real head of the executive, and that the Government was consequently no more than a set of presidential advisers.

The logical consequences of this were drawn almost immediately since, as we have seen, the new Pompidou Cabinet appointed on 8 January 1966 did not bother to ask Parliament to consider the Government's programme and give a vote of confidence. On 8 April 1967, after the legislative elections, the Prime Minister, who once more found himself heading a new Cabinet, again dispensed with the step of asking the Assembly to approve his plans: he contented himself with making a general policy declaration without a vote.

But the first signs of the changed state of affairs could be seen as early as the end of the Algerian war. In April 1962 General de Gaulle had removed Michel Debré (without there having been any indication of parliamentary hostility towards him), replacing him with a former Cabinet leader, M. Georges Pompidou, who at that time was not even a Member of Parliament.

With this new appointment, the old system of sharing work between the President and the Prime Minister was discarded, to be replaced by a hierarchical organization of Government work in which preparation fell to the Prime Minister and final decisions were made by the President. To arrive at his decisions, General de Gaulle gathered together the main figures concerned with the problem, Ministers and high-ranking officials: these men form the Councils which the President holds at the Élysée, which study all the important business that cannot be dealt with at lower levels (i.e. at Prime Ministerial level). Consequently, there is no longer a 'private preserve', as the expression would imply that the President left other matters to the Government: he now takes it upon himself to handle everything, from the reorganization of the Paris area to colour television or Common Market agricultural policy. The result is a presidential Cabinet in which the Prime Minister, to quote a prominent Gaullist, the jurist René Capitant, serves only as a sort of 'civilian staff officer' for the President.

However, the regime is still trying to reach a state of balance, and it pursues this aim in several ways. The implications of having a set of presidential advisers (known as the *cabinet présidentiel*) would lead us to expect Ministers to be recruited mainly among civil servants or non-political figures. The contrary has been the case: it was while the parliamentary fiction of the Debré Cabinet lasted that the number of Ministers drawn from Parliament continually shrank in favour of higher civil servants – *les grands commis*. The reversal of this tendency dates from the end of 1962, when 15 members of the second Pompidou Cabinet stood at the elections. Since then, new Ministers have almost always been chosen from among the Deputies. At the 1967 elections, 25 of the 27 members of the third Pompidou Cabinet stood as candidates, and of the 28 members of the fourth Pompidou Cabinet, constituted on 8 April 1967, there were only five non-parliamentary Ministers (including two defeated candidates: MM. Couve de Murville, Minister of Foreign Affairs, and Messmer, Minister of Defence: MM. Malraux and Jeanneney had not stood and M. Ortoli, a former commissioner to the Economic Plan, was a new Minister.)

Ultimately it is not enough that the President of the Republic be elected by universal suffrage; he must also have a parliamentary majority and this requirement could explain why General de Gaulle sent his Ministers out to fight electoral campaigns. In the 1962 and 1967 elections the voters decided in terms of the General's power, so that the existence of a majority in the Assembly does not really mean that new parliamentary codes of behaviour have emerged, but rather gives the measure of the influence the President of the Republic wields over the Deputies. The head of State, and not the Prime Minister, is the political leader who maintains a coalition – which, it seems legitimate to assume, would break up without him.

Consequently, the President still acts as a *deus ex machina*, but he has adapted his techniques of intervention to meet the demands of a political situation whose striking new characteristic is its dependence on majorities. But the majority is presidential first and foremost: only at a secondary level is it a parliamentary one.

because his son-in-law was found to be selling decorations of the Légion d'Honneur; Sadi Carnot was assassinated; Casimir-Périer aspired to direct influence, and as he was unable to achieve this as he wished, he decided to resign; Félix Faure died suddenly; Émile Loubet's term in office ran its normal course, as did those of Fallières and Poincaré; Deschanel had a nervous breakdown; Millerand was forced to resign after the victory of the left-wing cartel; Doumergue served his full seven years; Paul Doumer was assassinated; Albert Lebrun stood down in favour of Marshal Pétain during his second term in office; Vincent Auriol served his full term; and René Coty stood down in favour of General de Gaulle.

Appendix 2 The Organization of the Executive

In the organization of the executive in France, the highest authority is the Council of Ministers. This Council adopts Government Bills before they are submitted to the Assemblies; it also issues the most important decrees and decides on appointments to the highest posts in the civil service and the armed forces.

The Council of Ministers is always chaired by the President of the Republic; however, its composition has changed. Before 1959 membership was restricted exclusively to ministers; Secretaries of State were admitted only for business directly concerning their work (Secretaries of State are members of a Government in charge of sections of departments under a Minister whom they assist); on the other hand, the entire Government used often to meet in what was known as 'Cabinet Council' under the chairmanship of the Prime Minister, without the President of the Republic. Cabinet Councils were frequently the scene of political arguments between members of different parties forming the coalition; the main arbitration was carried out at this level, then officially confirmed by the Council of Ministers.

Things have changed since 1959. Cabinet Councils no longer exist, and the Council of Ministers includes every member of the Government, including Secretaries of State. Consequently it has become the one collective organ of Government action, not only in theory but also in practice. It is through the Council of Ministers that the Government carries out the task assigned it in Article 20 of the Constitution: 'to decide on and execute national policy'.

(i) The real power, however, is shared between the President of the Republic and the Prime Minister. *The Prime Minister*, a title which under the Fifth Republic has replaced that of 'President of the Council', is entrusted with 'directing Government action' (Article 21 of the Constitution). Accordingly he has under him a number of special agencies designed essentially to ensure coordination.

The most important of these is the General Secretariat of the Government, which includes a legislative office through which all Government Bills drawn up by the various Ministries must pass. The General Secretariat prepares meetings of the Council of Ministers, at which the Secretary-General is present and keeps the minutes. The General Secretariat also sees that once legal documents have been ratified they are sent to the *Journal Officiel* for publication. (Laws and decrees come into force only after they have been published in the *J.O.*, an official bulletin issued by the Government printing agency, which belongs to the Prime Minister's services.)

There are also other coordinating bodies, such as the National Defence General Council and the General Secretariat of the Interdepartmental Committee for European Economic Co-operation.

The General Planning Commissariat, a research and development organization, to which we shall return, also comes within the Prime Minister's purlieu, as do the Board for Town and Country Planning and the General Board for Scientific and Technical Research, which are the instruments through which overall policies involving several ministerial departments are developed.

The Prime Minister presides over a certain number of regular and *ad hoc* interdepartmental committees. He acts essentially as the agent in charge of executing the Government's general policy.

(ii) General policy is officially decided in the *Council of Ministers*, but the main guide-lines and the fundamental choices have been decided upon by the President of the Republic since General de Gaulle took over the post. To assist him the President has a General Secretariat of his own, which was headed first by M. Geoffroy de Courcel, who in 1962 became French Ambassador in London, then by M. Burin des Roziers, and from 1967 by M. Bernard Tricot. In 1967 the General Secretariat included four technical advisers who were each responsible for a major sector of government; responsibility for the economic field fell to M. Dromer, who at the same time looked after the functioning of the Interdepartmental Committee for European Economic Co-operation. It can be seen that this system facilitated close links between the two levels of executive power, especially as the four technical advisers were assisted by ten or a dozen *chargés de mission* and the members of the General Secretariat often took part in the interdepartmental committees called by the Prime Minister.

As a result, the structure of the President's General Secretariat parallels that of the administrative organization; though it is without hierarchical power over the services headed by the Prime Minister, it is closely associated with their functioning and enjoys considerable influence.

There is also a presidential 'Cabinet' composed of a small staff of advisers in close touch with the President, as well as a General Secretariat for African and Malagasy Affairs, and a personal Military Staff.

(iii) *The decision-making process* within this framework is dictated by the nature and importance of decisions. The Prime Minister supervises the normal workings of the State administration and deals with day-to-day business at this level; draft Government Bills, decrees or appointments are prepared by him and submitted to the Council of Ministers. In short, he prepares the business for the meetings of the Council of Ministers, which take place every Wednesday at the Élysée Palace.

Matters that cannot be dealt with at Prime Ministerial level, whether because of their importance or because they raise particular difficulties, are taken over by the President of the Republic, who calls *ad hoc* committees of Ministers and top officials in order to prepare the final decision to be confirmed officially by the Council of Ministers.

Such committees are statutory in some fields, as is the case for Defence. The National Defence General Secretariat plays a specialized role, similar to that of the Government General Secretariat in relation to the Council of Ministers, preparing the business to be dealt with by the Defence Council, which meets fortnightly under the chairmanship of the President of the Republic. The Secretariat then transmits the Council's decisions to the appropriate armed service departments and supervises their application. In this it assists the Prime Minister, who intervenes in his own right to ensure coordination between Ministries for the carrying out of projects.

In the field of foreign policy, the coordinating and executive roles of the Prime Minister are radically curtailed since, except in relation to European economic cooperation, the main agent of Presidential policy in this field is the Minister of Foreign Affairs, a post held by M. Couve de Murville since 1958.

In all cases, the structure is the same – one level for administrative preparation and a higher level for political decision-making. The Council of Ministers stands at the highest rung of this particular ladder whenever the steps to be taken have to be given a legal form. But in Gaullist practice, the Council of Ministers is only exceptionally a deliberating body: it solemnly records, after being duly informed, decisions prepared and taken elsewhere.

Part Two The Administrative Model

Part Two The Administrative Model

There is a striking contrast between the stability of French administrative structures and the instability that characterizes political life; these two qualities have been so pronounced for so long that it is a commonplace to compare the administration, which remains, with Governments, even with regimes, which duly come and go. The permanent nature of the State and the independence of its apparatus from political contingencies seem to compensate for the more inconvenient aspects of a turbulent political life, by ensuring the minimum of order and continuity necessary for the nation's survival. According to some authorities, it is because of this that France has managed to emerge relatively unscathed from the various revolutions and crises that punctuate the country's history; the administration acts as a tutelary element, watching over society and protecting it from the extravagances of politicians.

Without going all the way with this optimistic rationalization, we may still interpret the jealously guarded continuity of public service as an instinctive defence mechanism set up by the social body, which sensed itself exposed to two major risks: from within, due to society's own inherent tendencies, and from outside, because of the presence of constantly threatening neighbours. Foreign invasions and revolutions together make it essential for the basic minimum of organization and public order to be preserved – and in the name of continuity, this task must fall to the State.

It is, however, possible that the very existence of this type of guarantee may foster a state of mind prone to crises. Once the population had acquired the habit of falling back on the good offices of the centralized State and officialdom for the solution of everyday problems, it could cheerfully switch from one extreme to the other, from apathy to revolt. What we have already seen suggests that Parliament's reactions were nothing more than a faithful reflection of the attitudes of the electorate. As a result of this, the characteristic features of French public life led some sociologists to suggest that institutional and governmental instability was the consequence rather than the cause of the State's particular structure. For instance, according to Michel Crozier: 'the crisis mechanism is one of the essential components of the style of collective action that appeals to the French', because of the bureaucratic, centralized nature of the State. Given a situation in which it is impossible to find solutions for everyday problems through pragmatic adjustments, people are inclined to periodic reassessments of power at the level of Governments or even of regimes. Adaptation to changing circumstances, the main challenge of modern times, is achieved not by decentralized adjustments left to the initiative of the groups involved, but by sudden State action, which then reverberates through the hierarchy and duly penetrates the lower levels.

Michel Crozier's analysis is all the more interesting as it was worked out by a sociologist profoundly affected by Anglo-American thinking; at a distance of a century, it recalls the work of Tocqueville, who considered Britain and the United States as examples of free societies. It has, however, been challenged by other sociologists for whom the French model is neither particularly archaic nor strikingly modern, neither more cumbersome nor less rational than any other: it is simply different. If we were to admit the inferiority of this model, we should have to conclude that by comparison with others French society has failed, and there is no proof of failure of this order. France has gradually produced a model of collective action strongly influenced by 'an interventionist, organizational State' periodically shaken by major social movements,[1] and it is only by remaining

1. Alain Touraine. For a summary of Crozier's theses and Touraine's reply see Touraine, *Tendances et volontés de la société française*, Paris, 1966, esp. pp. 426, 475–89.

faithful to the national type – that is, by being oneself – that national problems can be solved.

Does the French political system appear defective by comparison with Anglo-Saxon standards? Perhaps it does, but it must be considered as a whole, bearing in mind the importance of State mediation as dictated by history. With this in mind, we propose to give a short outline of history before the 1789 Revolution as background to the development of the State as an autonomous political force during the formative period of the Third Republic. In our examination of this question, we shall concentrate on two typical instruments of power: Prefects and 'ministerial cabinets'. We shall then examine the modern transformations of the State, which have two main features: firstly, modernization is a recursive process, into which we can fit Gaullism in historical terms; and secondly, specific instruments of power have made their appearance, corresponding to the new economic, technical and social conditions of State action. As an example we shall take the École Nationale d'Administration (National School of Administration) which trains the upper ranks of civil servants – the *grands corps* of the State set up at the beginning of the nineteenth century.

The second chapter will be devoted to one of the main characteristics of the French State: its independence. Through two significant institutions (the Council of State and the General Planning Commissariat) we shall see how the State can achieve regulation of its own activity from within.

The centralization of power, another distinctive trait of the French system, will be the object of our third chapter. Naturally, we shall return to Prefects when we talk of geographical centralization, but we shall also mention the financial controlling bodies which operate as organs of centralization on the functional plane. The relationships between Paris and the provinces will also be dealt with in this chapter.

Finally, in the fourth chapter, we shall outline a description of the type of society corresponding to the traditional model and the internal tensions that are presently at work in it.

Following the procedure adopted throughout this book, we

shall begin our analysis at the top, in this case with centralized power, work our way down through intermediary systems and arrive finally at the actual society controlled by this power. Some institutions and officials will appear more than once, in so far as they function at different levels and illustrate the different facets of a complex system. As in the first part, the reader will find appendices of documentary material which should provide some essential information about these institutions and officials.

5 The State as a Political Force

The State is not a lifeless machine. While it may be thought of as an instrument designed to serve the community, it is also the guardian, sometimes the inspiration, of society. The development of democracy displaced rather than resolved the problem of the relationship between State and society; the Republican regime simply introduced a new type of compromise between authority and the people.

In the first part of this book, this particular compromise was studied at the level of national institutions; it should now be considered in another light, in terms of the relations between public power and the intermediary bodies. Dealings between them have often taken on overtones of rivalry, even of direct conflict, the reasons for which can be traced back to the Middle Ages when the monarchy's policies of unification first clashed with the claims of the military feudal aristocracy, which Richelieu[1] brought to heel in the seventeenth century. The resistance was then continued by other privileged classes (judges, churchmen, etc.) who none the less took care to avoid giving their position a political turn: as Herbert Lüthy pointed out, the constitution of the Old Regime was economic and social, not political.

In return for forfeiting all influence over royal decisions, these privileged groups received guarantees that their traditional rights would be preserved, and thereby thwarted in advance any attempts at reforming society. In these terms the 1789

1. Cardinal Richelieu (1585–1642) was Prime Minister under Louis XIII from 1624 until the King's death; he eliminated the Protestants from power and brought down the aristocracy. He is remembered as the architect of Royal absolutism and centralization (he instituted the office of Intendant, the predecessor of the Prefect).

Revolution was only the paradoxical outcome of a century-old course of action followed by the monarchy; indeed, one of the most perspicacious politicians of the time, Mirabeau,[2] wrote secretly to Louis XVI:

Part of the decisions of the National Assembly, indeed the most considerable part, is clearly favourable to monarchical government. Is it a question merely of dispensing with Parliaments, States General, clergy, nobility or privilege? The idea of creating a single class of citizens would have pleased Richelieu: so smooth a surface must ease the exercise of power.

The endless multiplication of privileges was a result of the lack of any representation of the people. To avoid the emergence of an authority which it would have been obliged to take into account, the French monarchy thought it wiser to maintain an archaic, uncoordinated system of judiciary bodies, known as the 'Parliaments', in which seats were inherited or bought. When the royal Ministers had their monarch's edicts recorded by 'Parliaments', as Prince de Montbarey remarked, they

believed that such a device could replace the assent of the Kingdom and that the King would be more sure of having his edicts recorded in eighteen separate bodies than if he were forced to call on a meeting of Deputies from all the corners of the Realm.[3]

This constant, deliberate policy had some immediate advantages, but it was not wholly free from drawbacks. It identified the demands made on central power with the defence of the privileges of the constituted bodies. The transfer of royal authority to the aristocracy, then from the aristocracy to the people, which is looked on as the greatest achievement of British democracy, contrasted with a rigid distribution of social influence in France which made peaceful development between the classes impossible.

2. Mirabeau (1749–91) favoured a constitutional monarchy, but met with the hostility of the absolutists and the animosity of his colleagues in the Assembly. He died prematurely.
3. Quoted by Edgar Faure, *La Disgrâce de Turgot*, Paris, 1961, p. 120.

It is not surprising that, given this barrage of acquired rights
solidly entrenched in ancestral privileges and bought offices, the
idea of an enlightened, egalitarian, reforming despotism took root
among advanced thinkers. The incompatibility between the
notion of progress and the principle of intermediary bodies was
first felt in the middle of the eighteenth century and the idea
spread rapidly, not only among public officials, long imbued
with a conception of their role as servants of the kingdom's
interest, but also among the rationalist philosophers whose
influence made a profound impression on the national psychology.
When Louis XV and his Minister Maupeou disbanded the
judicial 'Parliaments' in 1771, their members managed to stir
up strong public emotion by denouncing the abolition of these
institutions as the destruction of 'the last barrier against arbitrary
Royal power'; on the other hand, Voltaire[4] considered the royal
edict 'full of useful reforms. The destruction of paid offices, the
provision of justice gratis, and making the King bear the expense
of lordly justices must surely be great services to the nation.'
Attacking these 'insolent, thankless bourgeois', Voltaire added,
'In my opinion the King is right and, as we are bound to serve,
I consider it better to serve under a well-born lion, who is born
much stronger than I, than under two hundred rats of my own
kind.'

Voltaire's attitude will seem legitimate or irritating according
to one's personal point of view. For admirers of English institutions, among them Tocqueville, the French had, on the eve of the
Revolution, conceived notions of government which were

almost contrary to the existence of free institutions. They had admitted
as the ideal society a people without aristocrats other than public
officials, a single, all-powerful administration to direct the State and
control individuals. In their striving towards liberty, they never thought
of departing from this first notion; they simply tried to reconcile it with
the idea of liberty.

4. Voltaire (1694–1778) was the most famous writer of his time; he cham-
pioned freedom of thought against the church and justice against Parliaments.

If, on the other hand, we take the state of French society into account we are tempted to admit that in the middle of the eighteenth century, 'setting aside their doctrinal quarrels, all progressive thinkers place their hopes in enlightened despotism, the one revolutionary force they can conceive that can sweep away all private privilege.'[5] The twentieth-century political scientist Bertrand de Jouvenel considers that the main vice of the declining Old Regime was not so much the arbitrary nature of royal power, but rather its inability to promote the necessary changes. What led to the downfall of the monarchy, was, he wrote, 'the powerlessness of a body of officials steeped in New Deal idealism to get the necessary reforms through the "Parliament", the last guardian of vested interests'.[6]

We can thus discern, at the very foundations of modern French society, a conflict between the idea of progress and the existence of intermediary bodies, a conflict that was to survive long after these bodies had, with the introduction of electoral procedures, become representative. The mediation ensured by political suffrage was not to overcome this contradiction as it has done in other countries, but left intact a higher circle inaccessible to the influence of private citizens – a summit from which the general interest could be viewed. The conviction that reforms, even revolutions, are directed from above was naïvely expressed by a writer of the period:

> The situation of France is infinitely better than that of England; for here we can carry out reforms that change the face of the country in an instant, whereas in England such reforms can always be blocked by the parties.

This belief was to survive the collapse of the monarchy and also the reconciliation attempted by the Republic. But was the Republic itself not the legitimate, rational form of enlightened despotism, with the State as its indispensable agent?

5. Herbert Lüthy, *Le Passé présent*, Paris, 1965, p. 129.
6. Bertrand de Jouvenel, *L'Art de la conjecture*, Monaco, 1964, p. 309.

The Republican Synthesis[7] – 'The Administration as Manager for Democracy'

The expression 'republican synthesis' is taken as referring to the reconciliation between the State and democratic forces that took place at the end of the nineteenth century. It stemmed less from a systematization of the part representative organs played in the functioning of the regime, than from a transformation of public power itself, which became converted to republican practice as the result of assimilating republican principles. The Republic was in reality more than simply a form of government. It could not be reduced to a legal arrangement of power; in the eyes of its supporters, it was also, above all, a philosophy of society based on revolutionary principles, a radical secularization of the social order. Formulated for the first time in 1789, these principles went far beyond the devolution of power and kept, a century later, their subversive strength. A 'Radical' leader, Pelletan, once suspiciously asked a meeting of Republican Catholics, 'You accept the Republic, gentlemen, that much is clear, but do you accept the Revolution?' The great Catholic orator Albert de Mun had, in 1878, stood up in the Chamber precisely to denounce the Revolution as 'a doctrine that claims to base society on the will of man rather than on the will of God'. In reality, this was not so much a question of metaphysics as nostalgia for a traditional social order founded on the principles of authority and hierarchy, which the ideas of the 1789 Revolution had completely and utterly challenged. Throughout the nineteenth century, the Republic played the role of an anti-Establishment in the eyes of supporters of the old order, a challenge that was aimed less against religious beliefs as such than against the established order, the cornerstone of which was the temporal power of the Church. Free thought and its corollary, equality, seemed an intolerable challenge; the enormous importance of the Dreyfus Case at the end of the century stemmed from the fact that behind the moral problems involved, the general principles according

7. The expression is borrowed from Stanley Hoffmann, *In Search of France*, Harvard University Press, 1963, but with a slightly different meaning.

to which society was organized were under attack. For the Right, it was inconceivable that decisions taken by the authorities should be questioned and controlled by public opinion; by its passionate refusal to reopen the Dreyfus Case, political Catholicism manifested an all-embracing hostility towards individualism, or the primacy of justice and freedom over order and hierarchy.

For a whole sector of the French population the idea that the law of numbers might be taken as the sole basis for legitimacy produced a revulsion so intense that the formation of a true conservative party was held back for over half a century. But the administration as a body did not share such reactionary prejudices: undoubtedly a certain number of its members individually professed very un-republican beliefs, but their loyalty to the State took precedence over subjective preferences, especially as the new ideas were in harmony with permanent attitudes of the French administration.

This affinity showed through on the occasion of the separation of Church and State which was the long-term consequence of the Dreyfus Case, although its origins went back much further. The French monarchy had fought incessantly against encroachments by the Church: the last expulsion of the Jesuits was as recent as 1828, and Republican legalists saw no objections to quoting royal edicts against religious congregations. They considered they were defending the rights of the State by pursuing a policy of secularization which dated from the Old Regime, but which took on an explosive character as a result of the antagonism between the traditional order and the society that had developed out of the Revolution. It was no longer a question of rivalry between two competing types of authority, but of a direct confrontation between two systems, between two conceptions of society, the irreconcilable nature of which was brought out into the open by the Dreyfus Case.

The principal politicians of this period (Gambetta, Jules Ferry, Waldeck-Rousseau) were for the most part lawyers, steeped in a Roman conception of public power; they also showed complete confidence in the virtues of reason applied to the service of the general interest and this twofold influence gave added justification to the idea of autonomous action by the State. With the Republic, the State gave itself an objective about party politics (the general interest) which it pursued with the aid of a privileged instrument (public service) in terms of a set of values laid down by the Declaration of the Rights of Man. It thus possessed a body of principles enabling it to regulate itself, quite independently of any political pressures. The machine could function on its own and take the necessary initiatives.

The part played by political representation was itself defined in this same framework: the legislator, as interpreter of national sovereignty, laid down the rules governing the activity of the administration, but once the laws were passed, their application was handed over to the secular arm of the State.

In my opinion [said Waldeck-Rousseau], the fundamental rule of a democracy is that opinions must be expressed with the greatest possible degree of freedom. One must be able to write, speak and meet freely. . . . After such discussions, the whole nation is the judge; it decides, and its will must be obeyed by everyone. And this is where the role of authority begins: this is why we must have a system of government which is respected and which, through its agents throughout the land, ensures the execution of this sovereign will. If we look at it this way, what is authority, if not legal force given to the decisions of a free people?

It might be noted that this philosophy can be defined in terms of procedures: for the republic to function, it is essential – and it is enough – that the formal conditions for the free expression of the nation's 'decisions' be present. It is then the State's business to see that these decisions are translated into action, and the measures it takes must not be hampered by resistance from private interests or influenced by partisan pressure; once again we find the theme of the need for an independent public power subject only to the Law.

The administration of the State, the government of the State [said Gambetta in 1881], is neither sufficiently independent nor sufficiently free. It is subjected to a mixture of competition, pressures, influences and solicitations of every sort, so that the State and its various agencies are withering away before our eyes. The State and its agents must be given back their rightful prerogatives. . . . Public administrators are managers for democracy, and when we tamper with the administrators' prerogatives, we are undermining and destroying the very foundations of the house.

In this way there emerged an organizational model which imposed itself from above on to the nation after receiving the support of the majority. But the political majority won by the State was greeted with hostility by the hard core of traditional authorities: the aristocracy and the Church. This is the situation that lay behind the famous opposition, formulated by the theorist of royalist restoration, Charles Maurras,[8] between the two nations, real and legal: the real nation, with its trades, its provinces, its natural élites, and the legal nation with the centralized State based on the ballot box. State organization in itself therefore represented a political choice and thus administrative action inevitably appeared committed: the State was the triumphant, conquering Republic.

The Tools of Administrative Action: Prefects and Ministerial Cabinets

The political commitment of the State is manifested in various ways, the most direct and effective being the system of Prefects, in more than one way a significant institution. Firstly, it is an inheritance of the pre-1789 system of Intendants, of which Law[9] wrote:

It should be known that the kingdom of France is governed by Thirty Intendants. . . . These are thirty royal officials assigned each to a province, so that these provinces depend on them for their good or ill fortune, their plenty or their poverty.

8. Charles Maurras (1868–1952) was a writer and poet converted to monarchist doctrines. He was the editor of *L'Action Française*, a daily newspaper with considerable influence in traditionalist circles; in 1945 he was accused and convicted of collaboration.
9. In 1719 Law, a financier born in Edinburgh (1671), became Comptroller General (i.e. Minister) of Finance under the Regency, a post which he held for only one year.

In 1800 Napoleon Bonaparte provided successors to these Intendants, distributing them among the new territorial divisions which replaced the provinces: the Departments. 'Your mission', as the Minister of the Interior at the time wrote to the Prefects, 'extends into all branches of internal administration. Your attributions cover everything concerning the public fortune, national prosperity and the well-being of the citizens you administer.'

Throughout the nineteenth century the Prefects, as representatives of the Government in each Department, were used as public officials in charge of public order, the police and the preparation of elections. They particularly excelled in this role during the Second Empire. The Third Republic then made use of them to further the consolidation of the regime, as is confirmed by René Coty, who declared shortly after his election as President of the Republic:

Half a century ago, a young local councillor might have felt that his Sub-prefect[10] and his Prefect were engaged in politics in the narrowest sense of the term, that their main function was to uphold good and combat evil. I must confess that when one was on the side of the 'good' this seemed a perfectly natural state of affairs. It is only fair to point out that the Republic was only thirty years old then, and that it was incessantly under attack, and even endangered, overtly or covertly. And it had to stand up for itself.

This statement reveals the administrative version of the local political system mentioned in the context of party organization in the early years of the Third Republic, and also the link between government parties and electoral clientele.

The Prefects fostered the solid entrenchment of Republican Members of Parliament by giving them special access to the administration so that their constituents might reap the benefits. In this way, after conquering the State, the Republic managed to

10. The Sub-prefect is a subordinate of the Prefect, and is responsible for a sub-division of the *département*, the local *arrondissement*, which during the Third Republic was also the electoral constituency for Deputies and elected an assembly of its own, the *arrondissement* council, which was later abolished (cf. Appendix 1 to this chapter).

instal itself in a society partly hostile towards it, and protected itself against the attacks alluded to by René Coty.

As the Republic came less often under challenge, the action of the Prefects became more administrative and less political, and the extent of their direct commitment was further reduced by the multiplicity of political parties and the instability of Governments. The Prefect devoted himself more to his functions as a representative of Government in general, rather than of a particular set of Ministers; he then came to embody the continuity of central power throughout dangers and crises (in Chapter 7, devoted to centralization, we shall return to the role of the Prefect).

The State as a political force thus manifests itself directly through the activity of its Prefects. But the influence works both ways: the administration may also intervene independently. There was never any need to impose this system; generally it was enough for the administration to assume its responsibilities, which were seldom questioned, provided it was ready to resist interested pressure groups or tone down such interventions by Deputies as it judged over-fierce. The debates that have caught the enthusiasm of the political world have always been either extremely abstract or extremely precise and concrete. Secularism or State planning on the one hand, war-veterans' pensions or the special rights accorded to backyard distillers on the other hand, provided fuel for parliamentary polemic. Between the two extremes there survived, almost untouched, the part of State management to which the administration had attached itself, all the more effectively as the stability of its executive contrasted with the mobility of Ministers. When problems that could only be solved by a political decision arose, the appropriate machinery consisted, as we have seen, of a short, sharp jolt, the crisis, after which the ship of State had only to start up again on the same course.

It was rare for officials in the upper reaches of the administration to be changed, as on this point the prevailing political opinion converged with Napoleon's hope when he founded the Bank of France – that it would remain in the hands of the State, but not too much so. The same was felt about the top levels of the public service, which ensured the necessary continuity in the State's functioning. To exercise their influence on this independent body of men, Ministers called on personal collaborators, mainly recruited from the administration, to form what were to be known as their 'cabinets'. Members of these ministerial cabinets protect their 'boss' against the campaigns waged by various departments to persuade the Minister in question to accept their own solutions; if need be, they also supervise the enforcement of his instructions. The ministerial cabinet structure underwent a development paralleling that of the problems facing the Government.

Originally these cabinets were not very technically oriented, and took the form of a sort of enlarged political secretariat; they were composed of a few civil servants, as well as the friends and clients of the Minister, and were occupied mainly with constituency questions and lobby work in Parliament. But the need to master a machine as complicated as a ministerial department led the Minister to call on civil servants whose careers were linked to his own and who used their knowledge of administrative ways to counteract the natural tendency for large organizations to function in a vacuum and ignore the person momentarily placed at their head. Faced with departmental heads who not only had not been appointed by him but would also remain after his own departure, the Minister naturally felt the need of helpers attached to him personally, belonging to the 'home team' (or the team next door). The principle of rotation in office led to the practice of ministerial 'wills': on leaving his post, the Minister would arrange for some of his old collaborators to be appointed to influential positions, leaving his successor a set of modestly placed men accustomed to cabinet routine.

The link between the administrative machine and the political system in the narrow sense of the term was thus ensured, in particular by the network of top civil servants who constituted a sort of reserve from which Ministers drew their immediate advisers. For a long time Prefects provided a large proportion of cabinet recruits; as their role diminished in relation to local politics, their technical functions gained in importance; only 15% of

The Administrative Model

Prefects had served in cabinets in the period from 1876 to 1918; in the following period until 1940, the percentage rose to 41%, and under the Fourth Republic, 48%. In one of the last Governments of the Fourth Republic, under Guy Mollet, 46 'cabinet' members were drawn from the prefectoral corps, including 15 serving Prefects; about ten of these bodies were led by Prefects. But with the Fifth Republic a transformation took place, marked in particular by the promotion of members of the *grands corps* to State responsibilities.

New Directions

The legalistic, rationalist theory held by the Founding Fathers of the Third Republic could hardly fail to meet hard reality with a jolt, and in the end it succumbed, largely as the result of economic and social problems which were difficult to integrate into what was basically an abstract notion of the Republic. However, before this took place, the Republic had scored some noteworthy successes, the most significant of which was probably the introduction of free, compulsory education, which led to the rapid schooling of the illiterate masses. The State primary schoolteachers played a capital role in this process, as they were the main exponents of the ideal of progress through knowledge; no doubt this doctrine was excessively optimistic, but today its dominant characteristic seems only to have been that it was in advance of the state of society and the economy.

The rhythm of French political history, which is a succession of perplexed crises and confident bounds towards the future, does indeed seem to indicate that public servants had ideas ahead of their times, an advance which their successors later worked hard to overtake. Thus, the entire nineteenth century was spent in attempts to catch up on the head start taken by the 'great ancestors' of 1789; after 1875, the Republic outlined a model which fitted into this framework, but assumed that solutions had been found for a number of social and economic difficulties which had not yet made themselves fully felt. This led to the eclipse of the State, which, despite a century-old tradition of intervention, was ill-equipped to deal with questions of this magnitude, and indeed failed to come up with a new approach until just after the Second World War.

At the same time the political model had undergone several changes; this was the context of questioning and groping through which Gaullism blazed a trail for itself, by gathering together the principal themes inherited from the Monarchy, the Revolution and the Empire.

Firstly, the theme of direct contact with the people, as against the use of intermediary bodies. Under the Occupation, General de Gaulle had been struck by the attitudes of influential circles in society and the economy and even in the official intellectual world, the Academy, many members of which had gone over to Marshal Pétain. In a letter to Léon Blum, under whom he had served as Cabinet leader, Georges Boris, who was in England and had joined de Gaulle in June 1940 (and who until his death was the colleague and friend of Pierre Mendès-France), noted in 1942 that the General

did not naturally incline to democratic ideas. He came round to them, through reasoning and as a result of experience, because he despises the old élites, and has realized that all that is healthy in France is to be found in the mass of the people.

Immediately after his return to France, General de Gaulle attempted to draw his authority directly from the people at large, dispensing with any intermediate organization. 'More than ever,' he wrote in his memoirs, 'I had to seek support among the people rather than from the élites that tried to interpose themselves between the people and myself.'[11] Naturally these 'élites' included the parties, none of which, the General noted, was qualified to represent the general interest[12]; and which therefore could not build the 'strong, continuous power' the country needed. For these men, the General added,

the Republic had to be their private property, and the people existed as the holder of sovereign power only in order to delegate its rights and even its free will to the men presented to them.[13]

11. *Le Salut*, Paris, 1959, p. 8.　　12. *ibid.*, p. 239.　　13. *ibid.*, p. 258.

Fifteen years or so later, de Gaulle was often to return to this theme and show his irritation with what he called 'middle men':

The State will not tolerate any encroachment on its duties and responsibilities [he declared in October 1960]. It will not countenance that individuals, whether politicians, trade unionists, soldiers, journalists or others, should presume to influence the conduct of the affairs of France. Running the country is the prerogative of those designated by the nation. Consequently it belongs first and foremost to myself.

This theme of power based directly on a popular vote, using strong, if not actually authoritarian methods to ensure that the general interest should prevail over the private interests defended by intermediary bodies reveals the ambiguous relationship which has always existed in France between Caesarism and Jacobin democracy. It leads logically to the exaltation of the State as the privileged instrument and interpreter of the general interest:

Today, as always, it is the State's job to build up the nation's strength which, in present-day circumstances, depends on the economy. The economy must therefore be directed. . . . In my opinion this is the main reason underlying the measures for nationalization, modernization and control adopted by my government. [De Gaulle wrote of the 1944–5 period, adding] but this conception of a Government armed for cogent action in the economic field is directly linked to my notion of the State. I do not see the State as the parties do – a juxtaposition of private interests that can produce only feeble compromises, which is the situation to which the parties would like to see us return – but as a decisive, ambitious, active institution, expressing and serving only the national interest.[14]

'To bring this about,' the General concludes, 'first of all we must have a head, who needs subordinates recruited and trained so as to form a healthy, homogeneous corps running the whole of the public sector.' It was with this in mind that in October 1945 he founded the ÉNA (École Nationale d'Administration).

A New Instrument of Power: L'École Nationale d'Administration

The ÉNA is an institution as significant as was, in its time, the prefectoral corps. The idea of providing a common training for

14. *ibid.*, p. 98.

all higher civil servants goes back to the 1840s. Followers of Saint-Simon[15], whose 'industrialist' doctrine had considerable influence and inspired many of the Second Empire's enterprises, were the first to present, without success, projects along these lines. The *grands corps* of the State, i.e. the Inspectorate of Finances, the Council of State, the Court of Accounts and the Foreign Service still recruited their members through a set of separate competitive examinations, each branch clinging to its independence. More than once reforming spirits proposed unifying the upper échelons of the administration, but it was not until after the shock of war and occupation that General de Gaulle could harness the general wind of change in society, to impose a reform which, while not abolishing the old upper grades as such, replaced the old entrance examinations with a common recruitment system through the ÉNA. The main inspiration for the new institution came from M. Michel Debré, who expounded the strongly reformist conception of the State that is also found in the philosophy of de Gaulle. Concerning the ÉNA, the General wrote:

> Once the structure thus outlined has taken definitive shape, the new levers placed in the hands of the State will give it sufficient grip on the nation's activity for it to forge a stronger, more respected country.[16]

The ÉNA was to produce the men capable of carrying out a more coherent form of economic intervention; the Government was to call on them to replace the prefects, who had always been politically inclined rather than technically competent. The Fifth Republic has made wide use of these men, but it should be noted that their promotion took place at the time that personnel trained after 1946–7 would in any case have reached the level of responsible posts; none the less, this phenomenon has spectacularly affected the composition of ministerial cabinets, where the presence of this new blood coincided with an increase in ministerial stability. Ministerial cabinets have thus become, in a way,

15. Henri de Saint-Simon (1760–1825) hoped to replace 'government of men' by 'administration of things'.
16. *Le Salut*, p. 99.

depoliticized personal staffs, if not actually research units which recruit young, brilliant civil servants who are prepared to work hard in return for the prospect of an interesting career. Just before the March 1967 elections, there were ninety-two graduates of the ÉNA in ministerial cabinets. Of twenty-eight ministerial cabinets, more than half were led by ÉNA graduates: five were in the hands of members of the Court of Accounts and two were run by Inspectors of Finance; in addition one was run by an official from the Ministry of Foreign Affairs and two by general administrators. But only three were run by Prefects, as against ten in 1957. Where the main *grands corps* of the State are concerned, the preponderant role assumed by ÉNA graduates confirms the influence of the school: of the 19 Inspectors of Finance who belonged to ministerial cabinets (again in early 1967) 15 had been through the ÉNA, as had 15 out of the 17 members of the Court of Accounts and 11 out of the 17 members of the Council of State.

This transformation in the recruitment of ministerial cabinets indicates, firstly, the change undergone by relations between the bureaucracy and politics. In a sense the bureaucracy is more subordinate to political power than before, since the latter has become more stable, but at the same time the decrease in parliamentary influence frees the public service from limitations that until then it had had to accept; criteria of good management, as conceived by the civil service, now tend to take precedence over all other considerations. This strengthening of administrative independence has often taken on the appearance of relative isolation. A man to whom many of the younger administrators look as a leader, M. François Bloch-Lainé, remarked in 1961,

Under the Fifth Republic, the administration is left to its own devices with Ministers who take sides in its internal quarrels, because their own departments provide their main support: a situation which results in even greater immobility than under the Fourth Republic. It is becoming clear that pressures brought to bear from outside through political channels act more as stimulants than as brakes, even if they are the same as they used to be – and all the more so if they are now more intelligently planned.

It seems, then, that the Fifth Republic has pushed the system of State autonomy beyond the point of optimum returns. The divorce between membership of Parliament and ministerial functions, at first one of the most popular innovations, is now, seven years later, one of the most bitterly criticized features of the regime. For several years the main tendency was to appoint Ministers for their technical qualifications, but the regime has since reverted to choosing elected representatives, and, since the Constitution of 1958 states that the two posts are incompatible, Ministers are obliged to resign their seats. Now Ministers can only imperfectly see to the control of their respective departments – a mission they fulfilled, perhaps with excessive zeal, in preceding Republics – and Parliament serves little better as the interpreter of public opinion. This situation explains the complaints which have arisen continually since the earliest days of the Fifth Republic concerning a mythical figure – the technocrat – who has taken over from the penpusher who traditionally symbolized the administration.

The recent history of the central Government suggests two main observations.

Firstly, it underlines the complementary nature of the 'political' and 'administrative' models; the latter takes over part of the former's functions, although the political sector may occasionally challenge the administration's actions. Adjustments between the two systems have shaped the Government of France as a whole. However, the system is currently in a crisis.

Secondly, as the administration of the State could only function if its independence and continuity were protected, there have been constant efforts to centralize authority so as to allow an influence from above corresponding to the administration's particular style of action. These different tendencies have been carried to extremes through the diminished role of representative institutions characteristic of the Fifth Republic, and it is by no means impossible that they have now reached their limit.

Appendix 1 The Prefectoral System

The Prefect is the delegate and representative of the Government in a given *département*, within which he assumes, under the supervision of the appropriate Ministers, the overall direction of the activities of State officials, the representation of the national interest and the administrative control of local authorities.[1]

Prefects are the only officials whose career is not protected by the traditional civil service guarantees; their promotion is entirely a matter of choice and they may be transferred, suspended with or without salary or even permanently removed from office, all at the discretion of the State. Such extreme measures have, however, tended to become extremely rare: the last case was the suspension of the Prefect of Charente-Maritime in 1964, after the escape of a rebel ex-NCO condemned for his part in subversive activity in Algeria and imprisoned in that *département*; after a few months, the ex-Prefect was appointed to an obscure post in the Ministry of the Interior, which he left shortly after to go to a large private company.

For many years the appointment of Prefects was also at the discretion of the Government, but in practice they were generally chosen from among Sub-prefects (cf. below). Indeed, since 1959 there have been only two cases of discretionary appointments: MM. Guichard and Lefranc, both of whom had worked with General de Gaulle. Even then, M. Guichard was not given a *département* to administer, but was attached to the Prime Minister's Cabinet, before himself becoming a Minister in 1967. According to a decree of 29 July 1964, four fifths of Prefects have

1. The geographical side of national organization is examined in detail in Chapter 7.

to be recruited from among Sub-prefects; the remaining fifth is at the Government's discretion.

Sub-prefects are the assistants of Prefects. They are entrusted with administering an *arrondissement*, that is, a sub-division of the *département*. They may, alternatively, carry out the functions of General Secretary in a Prefecture, of cabinet director, of head of the prefectoral cabinet, etc. From this it is clear that Sub-prefects are the main executives in the prefectoral administration system. Recruitment procedure for Sub-prefects traditionally followed the same lines as for Prefects, and it has since undergone a similar transformation. From 1935 Sub-prefects were recruited through a special competitive examination, but since a decree of 14 March 1964 they have been recruited exclusively among graduates of the ÉNA, excepting a number of places reserved for officials in prefectures (one outsider for every nine ÉNA appointments). Provision is also made for the Government to appoint two Sub-prefects every two years; these may even be drawn from outside the civil service. The 1964 decrees were the practical translation of a wish to strengthen the technical side of prefectoral administration by giving the ÉNA a virtual monopoly of the appropriate training. A hundred or so former students of the ÉNA now work as Sub-prefects or General Secretaries, but in 1967 they boasted only four Prefects. Promotion is slow in the prefectoral system, by comparison with the other *grands corps*, and we shall no doubt have to wait for some time before the new generation makes its influence felt at full prefectoral level.

Appendix 2 L'École Nationale d'Administration

On 9 October 1945, an Ordinance of the Provisional Government presided over by General de Gaulle created the École Nationale d'Administration with a view to training 'officials for the Council of State, the Court of Accounts, diplomatic or prefectoral careers, the General Inspectorate of Finance, the corps of civil administrators and other corps or services,' i.e. all the upper échelons of the administration except for the technical grades.

(i) The ÉNA recruits its students through two separate competitive examinations: a so-called 'Students' examination' for candidates holding certain university qualifications, and an 'in-service examination' for civil servants who meet certain conditions. (The ratio is about seven students for every two officials.)

(ii) However, the higher up the scale one goes, the less crucially important the ÉNA monopoly becomes. Only General Inspectors of Finances are recruited exclusively from the ÉNA: for other bodies, there is an 'outside quota'.

We have already seen how this functions for the prefectoral corps; for the Council of State and the Court of Accounts, officials at the beginning of their career (*auditeurs*) are recruited entirely from ÉNA graduates; at the next grade up (*maîtres des requêtes et conseillers référendaires*), *auditeurs* account for three quarters of appointments; at the following grade (*Conseillers d'État* and *Conseillers-Maîtres*) two thirds of the appointments are made among officials already employed in the corps.

In the Foreign Service, nine ÉNA graduates are recruited for every official already belonging to the department; there is still a special examination for the 'Far Eastern corps' reserved for graduates of the School of Oriental Languages.

'Civil administrators' were regrouped into a single corps by a decree of 26 November 1964. Their brief, under the supervision of directors in the central administration, is 'to apply the Government's general directives in the conduct of administrative affairs, to prepare drafts of bills, regulations and ministerial decisions'. This corps, which is interdepartmental in character, was constituted in 1945 at the same time as the ÉNA, from which it is recruited, with an additional 'outside quota' fixed for every nine ÉNA graduates at:

TWO *attachés* from the central administration (executive grade);

ONE member of a department other than the central administration; preference is given to candidates from the external (non-Parisian) service of Ministries.

In 1966 the total strength of the corps of civil administrators was 2,947, 21.2% of whom were graduates of the ÉNA.

(iii) From its foundation until 1967, the ÉNA trained about 1,500 civil servants, about a hundred of whom left State employment. If we look only at appointments on graduation, i.e. setting aside those cases that left public service and also setting aside later changes (e.g. twelve ÉNA graduates were elected as Deputies in March 1967), we find the following distribution:

Council of State   102
Court of Accounts   111
Foreign Affairs   116
Inspectorate of Finance   136
Ministry of Finance   393
Ministry of the Interior
   (prefectoral corps and central administration)   181
Administrative Courts   45
Public Works   70
Education and Culture   69
Industry   39
Defence and War Veterans   37
Agriculture   25
Prime Minister's Office   5

6 The Autonomy of the State

'The administration's constitution has always remained standing among the ruins of political constitutions,' wrote Tocqueville.

The prince, or the forms of power might be changed, but the daily course of affairs was neither interrupted nor troubled; each individual remained, in the small affairs that interested him personally, subject to the rules and customs he knew; he depended on the same lower officials to whom he normally had recourse, and in general he dealt with the same agents of the State. Although with each revolution the administration was beheaded, its body remained untouched and alive; the same functions were fulfilled by the same officials, who carried their attitudes and methods throughout the succession of varying political laws. They judged and administered in the name of the King, then in the name of the Republic, and finally in the name of the Emperor. Then, fortune's wheel having turned again, they again set themselves to administering on behalf of the King, and in due course in the name of another Republic, and once more in the name of the Emperor. The men and their methods were always the same: what did the title of their master matter to them? Their business was not to act as citizens, but to be good administrators and wise judges.

Tocqueville wrote these words over a century ago, and time has given many more examples of the permanence he observed in the administrative system, a continuity which lasted through the 1789 Revolution, the *coup d'état* of 18 Brumaire, the 1815 royalist restoration, the 1830 and 1848 Revolutions and the *coup d'état* of 2 December 1851. This continuity implies a considerable degree of public connivance, a surprising fact as the general tendency of nineteenth-century revolutions was to limit the powers of authority. But this paradox may be explained in part by the fact that the public had had sufficient opportunities of measuring the practical drawbacks of unstable regimes and appreciating the advantages of an administrative system kept apart, in its essentials, from such adventures. History has scarcely changed since then and the grandchildren of Tocqueville's contemporaries have had occasion to make similar observations for themselves. With each upheaval, the country's officials dug their heels in and stood their ground, so that like Sieyès, when asked what he had done during the 1793 Terror, they could reply, 'I lived . . .'.[1] The old mayor of a village beside the Loire told me that, going through the town archives, he found a loyal address to the Emperor Napoleon III, followed by one to the Government of the Republic, voted by the same men in each case; he added that we should not be too ready to scoff, as we ourselves, he confessed, expressed our gratitude to Marshal Pétain in 1940, and to General de Gaulle a few years later. Another anecdote illustrates this continuity through the storms of history: when, shortly after the 1944 landings, General de Gaulle visited a small town in Normandy, he was asked to sign the visitors' book. At the last moment, however, the city fathers realized that the preceding page contained the signature of Marshal Pétain: to cover their embarrassment, they glued down the offending page so as to hide, but not destroy, a memento which in the circumstances they preferred to forget. History continually repeats itself and daily life continues. It was probably as much because of an awareness of the need for circumspection as because of any inherent tendency towards inertia that the administrative machine was able to function undisturbed throughout different regimes.

The Council of State, Cornerstone of the Administrative System

One institution in particular, the Council of State,[2] shows us the perseverance with which the administration has organized its own

1. The Abbé Sieyès, born in 1748, published a resounding pamphlet on the eve of the Revolution; he was elected Deputy and voted for the King's execution, but kept clear of the Terror. He later took part in setting up the Empire and was the inspiring force behind many of its institutions. Exiled in 1815 as a regicide, he returned to France in 1830 and died in 1836.
2. cf. Appendix 1 to this chapter.

independence, with more or less general approval. In order to understand the position of this body, we must bear in mind that the principle of rigorous separation of the administrative and judiciary authorities had been laid down in 1790. By virtue of this principle, the actions of the public authorities were not to be open to challenge in the courts, for the leaders of the Revolution remembered the judiciary branch's hostile attitude towards the royal administration, and hoped to protect the State against the sort of claims and encroachments by judges that had paralysed it in the past. 'Under pain of forfeiting their position, judges may not intervene in any way in the operations of the administration, nor may they subpoena administrators to appear in their official capacity,' to quote the law of 16–24 August 1790. But the Revolution had also laid down the principle of subordinating the executive's action to a respect for the law, so as to guarantee the country against arbitrary power. To provide individuals with means of challenging the actions of public authorities, Napoleon organized a system of appeals within the administration, designed to process complaints and prepare the decisions of the administrative authorities. To this end, he created a network of prefectoral councils which from the start acted as true courts empowered to deal with cases relating to public works, direct taxation and so on. Napoleon himself was advised by a council, the Council of State, which prepared drafts of Bills and regulations; it also considered appeals against decisions of prefectoral councils, and other matters which were beyond the scope of the prefectoral councils. The Council of State was consequently an auxiliary of the head of the executive; it succeeded the royal councils, keeping some of the Old Regime's terminology, for instance the title of *maître des requêtes*, but its power was only consultative: it provided the information on which the head of State based his decisions. However, in practice, the leader limited himself to ratifying the proposals of the Council of State, and this body rapidly acquired such authority and prestige that it became, to quote Cormenin, a lawyer of the time, 'the soul of the Administration'. It retained this role throughout the nineteenth century, and when the Republic was proclaimed in 1871, it was looked on as the symbol of the Napoleonic structure that was to be dismantled. It was therefore abolished. But it had become an indispensable part of the State, and as there could be no question of restoring power over administrative litigation to the 'ordinary' courts, which had been discredited by their subservience to the Empire, the Council of State was re-established in 1872. None the less, the National Assembly was suspicious of the Council and decided that from then on it should itself be responsible for appointing Council members. At this point the instinct for preserving the administration's independence emerged once more. Appointment of members of the Council of State by Deputies risked introducing political influence directly into the functioning of a body which was thought of as the regulator of the administration; to avoid this, the Constitutional Act of February 1875, which defined the power of the President of the Republic, restored to the head of State the right to appoint the members of the Council of State. The historian Daniel Halévy noticed with some surprise the existence of a clause which dealt only with the Council of State, which might well have been extended to cover all top-ranking officials. The answer, he concluded, was that the Council of State is the cornerstone of the administrative structure and

political history here brings us into contact with one of the permanent forces of the French State. By means of a last-minute amendment, the very constitutional laws that organize parliamentary power in France restore independence to our leading administrative body.

The Republican reforms of 1872 had brought, in addition to the rapidly discarded new recruitment procedures, official acceptance of the Council of State's role as a judge, and from then on the Council issued its decisions 'in the name of the French people' without submitting them to the approval of the executive. While this liberal development was taking place, the administration ensured its own independence of parliamentary influence and of the Government itself. By basing itself on the principles of the Republican tradition, the Council of State extended its control to cover all administrative actions by considering them in terms of their legality – legality interpreted in the widest sense of the term. This legalistic approach was intended to establish, beyond existing written formulae, the general rules for interpreting laws in accordance with the spirit of republican society: the equality of citizens before the law and before public responsibilities, equal access to public posts, the right to a fair hearing, etc. By virtue of these principles, the decisions of public authorities could be annulled, even if no text was applicable to the particular case.

Through the means of the appeal against the abuse of power, which was open to any citizen who could prove a genuine interest, the Council developed a system of control which extended over the entire field which ordinary courts could not cover, so that no decision, no regulation, no act of the executive could provide cause for grievance without the whole question being liable to review by the Council. By 1953 the number of appeals had reached 7,000 annually, and a reform had to be adopted to extend the jurisdiction of the old prefectoral councils and turn them into full administrative courts. The Council of State still deals with the most important cases, particularly with those concerning Government decrees, as well as with appeals against the decisions of the lower administrative courts.

The one limit set to this control is the law itself, which is by definition beyond appeal as it is the basis of legal practice and theory. This distinction is clearly marked where the law itself, i.e. the legal text as voted by Parliament, is concerned, but becomes less clear when we move into the purely political field. In order to avoid possible conflict, the Council of State has tried not to trespass on Government prerogatives, but the demarcation wisely laid down has gone through some difficult patches under the Fifth Republic, because of the more authoritarian character of this regime, with its tendency to submit Government actions directly to the electorate. One noteworthy incident took place in October 1962, when the Council of State annulled an ordinance based on the Presidential powers granted by the referendum over the Évian agreements which ratified Algerian Independence. Authorized to take every step necessary for the application of these agreements, General de Gaulle had set up a special military court to judge the rebel leaders of the French army in Algeria, but the Council considered that the organization of the court did not sufficiently uphold the rights of the defence, since the right to appeal was abolished in conditions and circumstances which, in the Council's opinion, did not justify such a measure. The Council's decision provoked violent reaction from de Gaulle, who promptly set up a committee instructed to prepare the re-organization of the Council of State, also obliging Parliament to validate the annulled ordinance retrospectively. This constituted a major blow against the extension of the Council's powers of control, although in the end the actual reorganization was limited to a few technical adjustments.

The Twofold Nature of the Council of State

Administrative courts provide a special form of protection for public servants and officials, as ordinary courts cannot hear cases relating to actions carried out by civil servants in the exercise of their duties, except when these actions are so arbitrary that they cease to qualify as administration. It is therefore the administrative judge who examines the case, who assesses the responsibility of the department and decides on the redress to be made, though disciplinary measures may be taken against officials who have been shown to have acted wrongly. At this stage of the process, however, civil servants enjoy guarantees which grew up over the years, becoming increasingly specific until, in 1945, a general civil service law was adopted. Since at the same time the formulation of rules governing recruitment and promotion had largely eliminated the possibility of arbitrary appointments, there is thus a complete system; and the Council of State, at the summit of the administrative pyramid, ensures that this system is respected.

These rules apply equally to heads of departments, Ministers and the President of the Republic himself. When an official is affected by a decision he considers unjustified he may appeal for it to be reversed. In this way many civil servants sanctioned after 1945 for collaboration with the Vichy regime were later taken back into the service, or failing that, received compensation and the restoration of their rights, particularly those affecting retirement pensions. In this way the administration limited the effects that political contingencies might have on its agents' circumstances, providing they had not wholly compromised themselves by unnecessary zeal; consequently the careers of a certain number of high-ranking officials, and prefects in particular, succeeded in spanning several regimes – a demonstration of the continuous nature of public service as much as of the virtues of individual prudence. The normal sanction for errors or negligence consists in being relegated to posts of low prestige or limited responsibility; dismissal is very exceptional.

For instance, in 1964, there were leaks of information from the central examination office, which enabled *baccalauréat* candidates to gain advance knowledge of the questions. After this episode the Minister of Education dismissed the official in charge, on grounds of negligence, but he appealed to the Council of State; the decision was reversed and the official was restored to his original post in January 1967 after he had proved himself innocent of the charge against him.

On the whole, despite these safeguards and guarantees, the system has not led to the formation of a privileged caste, as the civil service has been kept subordinate to the principle of 'public service' as upheld by the Council of State. This is in itself another characteristic feature of this institution, and explains why the Council has avoided the temptations of privilege which Parliaments under the Old Regime were unable to resist: the Council is not only a judge, but also a key element in the administration. We have seen how it served initially as Napoleon's adviser in the preparation of the drafts of laws and regulations, and while its legislative role later shrank with the emergence of representative assemblies, it has remained the Government's main legal adviser. Indeed, in certain cases it has to be consulted, particularly for the broader regulations implementing statutes.

Another of its functions is to look over draft Bills before they are passed by the Council of Ministers; generally its comments are accepted by the Government – for example, the reform of the municipal electoral system in towns of over 30,000 inhabitants was modified in spring 1964 after objections from the Council of

State. On the other hand, although it had expressed its disapproval of the procedure for revising the Constitution in October 1962, the President of the Republic brushed objections aside; but this was a purely political matter.

As it is associated in the daily functioning of the administration the Council is kept permanently abreast of the practical difficulties that arise. When, in its capacity as a judge, it has to decide on cases relating to administrative actions it attaches great importance to the circumstances leading up to and surrounding them. Legal theories, such as that of 'exceptional circumstances', were developed in order to meet the particular needs of the public service, which sometimes make it necessary for certain guarantees to be limited or even suspended. But each time such exceptions are admitted the Council of State accepts them only so far as they are inevitable: it was because the violation of the right to a fair hearing and the right to appeal did not seem justified by the circumstances of the case that it annulled the 1962 ordinance creating the special military court.

Evidently, it would be absurd to draw an idyllic portrait of the system. Despite its merits as far as arbitrary bureaucratic powers – which have been limited – are concerned, the system none the less implies a downgrading of the position of ordinary courts, a situation not without drawbacks. Because of continual distrust of judges in France, some individual guarantees (e.g. the right of *habeas corpus*) have never been ensured. The Republican tradition, dominated by the memory of the Parliaments' attempts to usurp authority under the Old Regime, has always shown itself wary of initiatives emanating from judges; the circumstances of history took care of the rest: it is difficult to give much authority to a body of judges whose very role forces it, according to the moment, to repress Republicans, Bonapartists and Royalists. After 1870, many judges compromised under the Empire or the MacMahon regime were dismissed; almost without exception, French judges took an oath of loyalty to Marshal Pétain in 1940, but this did not prevent them from presiding over the purge of collaborators in 1944. . . .

The Administrative Model

The failure of the Government to act forced the administration to carry out certain political functions; similarly the administration was led to assume some of the functions of the judiciary, setting up its own network of courts. This self-regulatory mechanism was developed with considerable prudence, as the need to safeguard not only individual, but also State interests had to be borne in mind. It has sometimes been accused of excessive timidity, but the contrary grievance was levelled against the Council of State by M. Debré (despite his membership of the very body he was accusing), who claimed that administrative courts tended to take an over-liberal line on individual cases. It is, none the less, a characteristic institution, illustrating the traditional independence of the administration, which is controlled first and foremost by itself. The French administration constitutes a complete system, with its own goals and its own set of criteria; while it is not capable of actually dispensing with political masters, at least it can extend its own scope as and when needs arise in the life of the nation. But it has also been able to subject itself to a discipline of its own. In this respect the Council acts as the conscience of the State.

Planning and Technocrats

We have seen how, through the Council of State, the administration assimilated the ideology of the winning side – the Republic – but it is equally clear that this conception of the State was subjected to certain limitations, stemming in particular from economic problems. The traditional order was essentially formal and legalistic; it found it difficult to come to terms with the problems that emerged after the First World War and, more acutely still, after the great Depression. In fact, the attitude of the administration remained on the whole liberal, and consequently passive, until the collapse of the country in 1940.

After the defeat of France, the question no longer presented itself in doctrinal terms. National shortages and the lack of organization in the economy had to be dealt with, available resources had to be distributed, the maintenance and renewal of equipment had to be planned – in short, a succession of concrete actions was imposed by circumstances. As this undertaking was carried out in a very special political context, it has often been interpreted as being no more than the application of the Vichy regime's corporatist principles; in reality, behind the hazy front of the outdated ideas held by the aged soldier and his grotesquely traditionalist advisers, it is possible to discern the shadowy but decisive figures of the first technocrats. General de Gaulle made an interesting observation about them when he wrote of the renovation of the economy:

> The Vichy regime had attempted to deal with the crisis. In the fields of finance and the economy its technocrats conducted themselves, despite hindrances, with undeniable skill.

Who were these technocrats? Engineers trained in the great State scientific schools, in particular, graduates of the École Polytechnique, who professed unquestioning faith in the benefits of rational organization. Their spiritual father was Saint-Simon, the great exponent of industrialist philosophy, whose influence throughout the nineteenth century has already been mentioned. From the outset Saint-Simon's ideas had particular appeal for the Polytechnicians, and it is among their descendants that we can see the first reactions to the economic decline of the Thirties, with the formation of a research group called 'X-crisis group' (X is the symbol of the Paris École Polytechnique, whose students are recruited on the basis of their high performance in mathematics). They were also to provide some of the leaders of the Vichy technocracy, the most important among them being Jean Bichelonne, who in August 1940 set up a network of committees aimed at 'organizing' and regulating each branch of the economy. The technocrats favoured what was later, in another political context, to be called a pluralistic economy, based on agreements between the representatives of State and industry designed to solve the problems highlighted by the great Depression and the ensuing national shortages. This type of pluralistic economy differs from the more authoritarian system of 'organizing committees' of the Vichy regime, by the importance it attaches to the association of trade unions into the process, and by its emphasis on open discussion; but with this politically crucial reservation, we can say that the modernization commissions set up after the Liberation and the Planning Commissariat itself are characterized by a manner of tackling problems that can be traced back to Bichelonne. The idea of a national economic plan itself appears in a law dated 17 December 1941, which envisages drawing up a general plan for the overall organization of production and the creation of a body controlling supply and development. De Gaulle's own Minister of Finance in 1944–5, Aimé Lepercq, had run one of the main 'organizing committees' under the Vichy regime before joining the Resistance. . . . Despite the political break that came with the Liberation, there was thus a degree of tactfully self-effacing continuity where direct State intervention in the economy was concerned, both in theory and in practice.[3]

Bichelonne, a former student of the Polytechnique and a mining engineer, had left public service for private industry before he was called on to reorganize the economy in 1940. Jean Monnet, who set up the French planning system in 1946, was even less closely linked to public service; how far can these two outsiders legitimately be included in an analysis of State autonomy? It seems that the administration, faced with economic challenges, managed to assimilate the ideas of these two innovators and grasped the opportunity to direct operations. Naturally, when we talk of 'the administration' this should not be taken to mean the body of civil servants as such, but rather the system itself, which was able to react dynamically to these transformations. Moreover, it had the necessary executants, largely thanks to the resources of the Inspectorate of Finances, whose members constituted a good proportion of leaders in private business, to which they often moved after spending a few years in State service. Apart from the men most compromised in the Vichy regime,

3. Bichelonne had been head of Cabinet under Raoul Dautry, who served as Minister of Armaments after reorganizing the railway system and arranged for the French reserves of 'heavy water' to be sent to Britain. In 1946 Dautry was the first administrator to head the French Atomic Energy Commission.

these inspectors continued their career, sometimes brilliantly: an under-director of the Bank of France, still in office in 1967, was the aide to the Secretary-General for Industrial Production in 1943, and the 1943 Secretary-General himself is now Inspector-General of Finance and comfortably represents the State on the board of some of the major insurance companies nationalized in 1945. There have been more surprising sequences of events: the 'Intendant' for Economic Affairs in the Limoges region in 1942 stepped into the post of Secretary-General for Economic Affairs in the same region in 1944, and the Orléans 'Intendant' was in 1946 appointed Inspector-General of the National Economy. ('Intendants' had been appointed by the Vichy regime to direct economic affairs alongside 'Regional Prefects'; they were abolished after the Liberation, and transformed into Inspectors of the National Economy; however, this corps of Inspectors did not succeed in imposing itself over the years and has tended to remain relatively unimportant.)

Created in 1946 in order 'to develop an overall plan for modernization and economic equipment' the Planning Commissariat, directed by Jean Monnet, soon managed to find a place for itself in the administrative system. It in no way encroached on the territory of other administrative departments as it did not compete with them, but tended rather to take the form of a research body, providing a convenient neutral platform for discussion.[4] In his report on the First Plan, Jean Monnet envisaged 'a permanent exchange of ideas between the administration and the country in a pluralistic economy, not a guided bureaucratic or corporatist economy'. The pluralistic nature of the economy was achieved by the 'modernization commissions' already mentioned, in which industrial leaders, trade-unionists and civil servants met together in an informal atmosphere inspired by Sir Stafford Cripps's working parties as much as by the work of the former organizing committees. The permanent team is small and does not constitute a special corps: members are

4. For further details about the Commissariat, see Appendix 2 to this chapter.

borrowed from the various administrative departments which give them leave for limited periods, a system which considerably simplifies communications.

The Commissariat, which is attached to the Prime Minister, has seen its influence on public opinion and the State grow increasingly. Although the Plan is now considered to be the normal channel for expressing Government policy, the Commissariat has managed to keep enough independence to win the confidence of its business or trade-union partners, under conditions that ensure its own moral authority. In this context, we may observe a phenomenon similar to the position won by the Council of State in another field: the Planning Commissariat is acknowledged to be objective; it is thus possible to call on it to undertake tasks which the more politically committed regular civil servants would never succeed in carrying out. At the time of the great pit strikes of spring 1963, the Government called on 'Three Wise Men', comprising the then General Commissioner, M. Pierre Massé, M. François Bloch-Lainé, then director of the Caisse des Dépôts et Consignations (an important State financial institution which acts as a bank for the public sector) and M. Masselin, a member of the Court of Accounts, to produce a report on pay conditions in the nationalized industries. The expression 'economic judiciary' which was used at that time and, later, the 'incomes conference' presided over by M. Pierre Massé, are in themselves indicative of the efforts made to introduce objective norms into economic life, and specifically to provide a frame of reference for State intervention.

In the ferment of ideas surrounding the French planning experiment, the administration's traditional conception of the public service gained new momentum. Despite the profound changes entailed by the transition from a basically legalistic, formalist approach, to a socio-economic analysis, we may say that the two are still related, given that the new conception is based equally on a rationalist, forward-looking view of society; the next step should be a better solution of conflicts by means of economic analysis and an increasingly precise knowledge of the mechanisms of society. The criterion of the general public interest has merely taken on a new colour by being defined in terms of planned growth instead of being conceived in terms of spontaneous progress in a static society. The role of the State has thus undergone a transformation, but none the less continues its tutelary mission.

The École Nationale d'Administration has contributed greatly to spreading this way of thinking among young public servants, by developing their versatility and by attaching greater importance to economic and social questions than to the traditional legalistic culture. Nowadays, these young men possess an overall view of administrative action, in all its aspects and with all its consequences. The considerations of form and accountancy which occupied their predecessors have given way to an almost obsessive attachment to the ideas of growth and modernization which has profoundly changed the climate of the upper reaches of public service by introducing a more positive, concrete attitude. But while its role has become more dynamic, the administration has still not abandoned the taste for regulation and guidance deplored by Tocqueville, but has extended and modernized it. The Gaullist conception of the independence of the State and the enforced hibernation of representative institutions have accentuated, especially among the youngest members of the administration, a superiority complex, of the type the public generally attacks in 'technocrats' along with their supposed indifference to the human aspects of technical problems.

The Limitations and Successes of the New Regime

Here we touch on one of the main weaknesses of a regime which otherwise possesses a coherent, progressive structure. Unlike the republican model of 1890–1900, the new doctrine has no political backing comparable to the movement that supported Gambetta, Ferry or Waldeck-Rousseau. It is also without a mouthpiece like the Masonic movement to spread the ideas of the technocracy and bring them support, albeit discriminating, demanding support.

Around 1960–61 the intellectual prestige of Pierre Massé, coupled with the desperate search for new ideas by a disorientated Opposition, ensured the success of economic planning and research. Until then only the movement led by Pierre Mendès-France had thought of tackling these problems in modern terms, but it had soon been overshadowed by the Algerian problem. About 1960 there was a series of debates and discussions among trade-unionists, high-ranking civil servants (in particular François Bloch-Lainé) and some politicians (Pierre Mendès-France), but these exchanges, although very stimulating, did not spread beyond the limited range of the political 'clubs' that were then making their appearance. For the most part these clubs were run by top civil servants dissatisfied with their limited scope for action and tending politically to the Left; their aim was to bring their ideas before a wider public. However, Gaullism produced a situation in which no political group could consider political problems in terms of ultimately reaching power. Until 1964–5, the political clubs had an unquestionable influence among intellectuals, but their impact on public opinion gradually diminished with the approach of the December 1965 presidential elections; this decline indicated the relative failure of an undertaking carried out in terms of the problems of government but outside the traditional political framework; despite the technocracy's hopes that the movement would lead to a trade-union revival, it has failed to reach the masses.

On the majority side, the situation was even sadder. Some Gaullists tended to think along lines approaching those of the clubs but they were totally overshadowed by the presence of the General, who left no opportunities for an independent line to develop inside the majority. Michel Debré, first as Prime Minister then, until 1966, as an ordinary Deputy, increasingly sang the praises of planning in an idiom consciously modelled on the style of Louis XIV's most famous servant, Colbert. This might have impressed the greenest young technocrats, but no more. Edgard Pisani, who served as Minister from 1961 to 1967 after proving an effective Prefect who got things done, took a boldly reformist position. Neither Debré nor Pisani managed, any more than other Gaullists, to attract sufficient following to translate this ideology into political terms, as each and every one inevitably settled into a system limited to the circumscribed field of administrative action. The State gave its approval to the ideas of growth and planned public investment, dear to technocrats, and even gave them its written blessing (implicitly during the Fourth Republic, and explicitly thereafter) but in reality the green light thus given to official action did nothing to set things moving. Despite the General's allusions to 'the Plan's burning obligations' this conviction failed to take shape within the political structure, and this was necessary before society could be spontaneously moved and become involved.

The fact remains that the technocrats' 'conspiracy' won over an important part of French élites to the cause of development between 1946 and 1966. This success probably played a far from negligible role in the transformations that took place during those two decades. The spread of the new ideas can be accounted for largely by the coordination achieved by the various modernization committees and by the part played by top officials in liaison with the universities. The study of national accounting was led by a former student of the École Polytechnique, M. Claude Gruson, an Inspector of Finance; his teams gave public action the necessary intellectual backbone. (Keynes' 'General Theory of Employment, Interest and Money' had in 1938 been translated by another Inspector of Finance; at that time it met with general hostility from academic economists.) The teaching dispensed by high-ranking civil servants in the Paris Institute of Political Studies doubtless influenced whole generations of students who in due course gradually changed the main ideas current in educated circles.

While favouring the evolution of the enlightened middle class, technocrats also worked to persuade political leaders of the need to continue with the reconstruction plans embarked on with the help of Treasury funds after the war. They succeeded in winning massive financial support for the nationalized industries, at the same time recruiting well-qualified, forward-looking staff for the public sector – which was no doubt a major reason for the economic success of the 1945 nationalizations, of coal and electricity in particular. These publicly owned undertakings proved a stimulant to private industry, and this greatly helped the economy to start up again after the war and continue its expansion. This continuity and convergence of effort is symbolized in the persons of men like François Bloch-Lainé, who ran the Treasury until 1952 and the Caisse des Dépôts et Consignations (which financed major building projects like the new town of Sarcelles) until 1967, or M. Massé, a deputy director general of the French electricity industry in 1948, and economic planning commissioner from 1959 to 1966, after which he returned to Electricité de France as President.

If we were to sum up the contribution made by the technocrats since 1946 we could say that that year marked a major innovation. This depended not so much on the techological fillip provided by state-employed engineers, as this body had always existed and had been responsible for the progress made in modernizing the railways and the postal system before the war; rather it stemmed from the thought given to the need for modernization and growth that would shake society out of its existing forms. The State's deliberate progress along this path can be attributed largely to what Alain Touraine calls a 'micro-society of liberal technocrats' who influenced collective action as much through the functions they exercised as by their powers of persuasion. Their independence made it possible to exert this twofold influence, based on a consciousness of the responsibilities of the State as instrument and driving force of society.

Appendix 1 The Council of State

In theory the Prime Minister presides over the Council of State, a survival from the time when he was the direct second in command of the head of the executive. In practice, however, the Council is headed by its vice-president. Its official payroll, i.e. the number of civil servants engaged officially on work connected with the Council, was 188 on 1 January 1967, but there are fifty more persons 'detached' from it to other posts (therefore paid out of the appropriate budgets), without counting members elected by Parliament. The real total strength of the Council is 242 members divided into four categories: 90 *conseillers*, 110 *maîtres des requêtes*, 30 *auditeurs* and 12 *conseillers en service extraordinaire* appointed for four years.

A. The Council's organization corresponds to its twofold role, as legal adviser to the Government, and as administrative judge.

(i) As *legal adviser* to the Government, it meets either in Plenary General Assembly (i.e. including all members of the Council of State) or in Ordinary General Assembly (i.e. with representatives of each 'section'). Other Council members are present only on a consultative basis, except for questions on which they must act as *rapporteurs*.

There is also a permanent commission which meets whenever a ruling is required urgently.

Rulings are normally prepared in one of the four administrative sections. Each of these comprises a chairman, at least seven council members, and *maîtres des requêtes* and *auditeurs*. These four bodies correspond to the four main fields of Government activity in which Council advice is sought: Interior, Finance, Public Works and Social Affairs.

The Administrative Model

Drafts of laws and administrative regulations are put before the General Assembly; the same holds for any important business.

(ii) As *administrative judge*, the Council of State includes a specialized legal section, which is itself divided into nine subsections (three dealing with tax matters). Each sub-section has three council members, as well as *maîtres des requêtes* and *auditeurs* who function as *rapporteurs*.

One *maître des requêtes* is designated to represent the Government, but he is not the mouthpiece of Ministers; he presents his own independent conclusions based on what he considers the general interest. Conclusions of this type have enabled the Council to develop an original, forward-looking body of case-law.

The sub-sections' main task is to prepare cases, which are then judged by larger bodies: for ordinary business, two sub-sections meeting together, with a council member from the administrative section; or the legal section with the chairman and vice-chairmen, the nine sub-section chairmen and two Council members from the administrative sections. The most important cases are handled by the Legal Assembly, which is presided over by the vice-president of the Council of State and includes the five section chairmen, the two vice-chairmen of the legal section and the chairman of the sub-section presenting the case. In each case the *rapporteur* takes part in deliberations.

B. The organization of the Council is designed to ensure liaison between its activities as Government adviser and as judge. This twofold function is reflected in the recruitment of members. All *auditeurs* are recruited from the National School of Administration; after eight years in office they provide three-quarters of the *maîtres des requêtes*. The remaining quarter is an outside quota, left to the discretion of the Government, which may appoint officials from other administrative departments providing they have served ten years in the public service.

At *conseiller* level, two thirds of the posts are filled from among *maîtres* who have already served for eight years. The remainder is again an outside quota, for which the one qualification is to be forty-five years old; candidates need not even belong to the civil service. Lastly, extraordinary councillors are individuals whose technical knowledge is likely to be useful to the Council. They are appointed for four years at a time and deal only with administrative matters, excluding legal cases.

The aim of this system is to keep the Council open to the realities of the administration and the country. Members are often delegated to outside missions; in 1966, seventeen of them belonged to ministerial cabinets. Of the fifty or so long-term detachments several concerned highly important posts: the Secretaries-General of the Government and of the Constitutional Council were members of the Council of State, as were the Permanent Secretary-General of the Ministry of Education, the chairmen of French Railways (SNCF), Air France and the Paris Transport authority (RATP), the permanent Secretary-General of the Ministry of Civil Aviation and the Commissioner for Tourism.

It is, however, a two-way process: clerks recruited from the ÉNA are lent to other departments (only one has held office as a Prefect, though) and after their tour of duty is over they return to the Council, while officials from other departments are promoted through the 'outside quota'.

c. Several major politicians were trained in or spent a period on the Council, among them Léon Blum, who excelled particularly in his summings-up as Government representative before 1914; Michel Debré became a member in 1935. Others have been appointed through the outside quota, e.g. M. Pompidou, who belonged to the Council from 1946 to 1952, and M. Lecanuet, who was appointed in 1956 after his defeat at the legislative elections.

Two members sit in the Senate and nine were elected as Deputies in March 1967. In case of defeat they return to the Council and resume their administrative functions: this is currently the case of five former Deputies.

Appendix 2 The General Planning Commissariat for
Equipment and Productivity

The Planning Commissariat came into existence with a decree
dated 3 January 1946. Its brief was to draw up national plans for
modernization and equipment, and to supervise their implementation.

Five Plans have been prepared since then; the first for 1947–53,
the second for 1954–7, the third for 1958–61 and the fourth for
1962–5, while the fifth covers the period 1966–70.

A. NATIONAL PLANNING AND PARLIAMENT.   The first and
third plans were approved by governmental decrees. The second
was ratified by Parliament, but only by a law dated 27 March
1956 – it was meant to cover the period from 1954 to 1957. The
fourth was passed by a law dated 4 August 1962, laying down the
conditions under which Parliament was to be consulted in future.
The new system was applied to the Fifth Plan, the broad lines of
which were submitted to Parliament in autumn 1964 while the
final text was ratified on 30 November 1965.

B. NATIONAL PLANNING AND THE GOVERNMENT.   At first
planning affected mainly the primary sectors of the economy, and
complemented other programmes concerning particular branches
of activity. The plans of different Ministries (Industry, Agriculture, Transport, Public Works, Housing, Education, etc.) were
progressively coordinated and their forecasts are now brought
together in a single framework. With the Fifth Plan, we may
consider that French planning has managed to formulate a
global middle-range policy covering the social, economic and
financial sectors. There is thus an increasing degree of coherence
between the plan and the Government's daily actions.

At present the Planning Commission has four main tasks.

(i) It functions as an administration geared to the future. It deals with long-term undertakings as well as middle-term projects.

(ii) It also makes sure the plan is carried out, whether by the public administration or by the private sector of the economy. With this in view it has been led to move closer to the machinery of Government and its officials play an increasingly important role in discussions between Ministries. This development has produced a certain measure of contradiction between the original idea of a consensus of opinion achieved through discussion, and the present tendency to consider the plan as the expression of one particular policy – Government policy.

(iii) As a result of its position and prestige, the Commissariat is equipped to carry out the tasks of research, confrontation and synthesis of views for which no other competent body exists. Whether the matter in hand concerns profits, employment, contracts for the steel industry or economic analysis for business, the Government calls on the Planning Commissariat. This side of its functions has become increasingly important since 1965.

(iv) Lastly, the Planning Commissariat forms a sort of uncommitted no-man's-land in the French administration, and so far it has managed to preserve its neutrality, although this is in contradiction with the closer relationship between Commissariat and Government that has emerged over the last few years. It therefore provides an irreplaceable platform for discussion and allows for confrontations that it would be difficult to conceive taking place elsewhere.

c. The General Commissariat, which is directly attached to the Prime Minister, employed a total of 166 (including chauffeurs and doormen) in 1967. Out of this total, 60 were commissariat staff in the strict sense. The Commissariat's interdepartmental nature can be seen from the varied sources from which it recruits; it employs, among others, officials from the *grands corps* (Inspection of Finance, Court of Accounts), civil administrators from various Ministries, statisticians and engineers.

D. The number of modernization commissions attached to the General Planning Commissariat has grown constantly. Under the first plan there were eight, while the fifth has thirty-two, with the participation of over 5,000 technicians, professionals and trade unionists. These commissions assemble information, hear opposing points of view and produce suggestions which are finally incorporated into the plan, after adjustments for purposes of coordination. The work of these commissions gives French economic planning some of the character of large-scale marketing research – a feature which has done much to dispel private industrial misgivings because of its utility to private firms.

E. Since 1946 there have been five men in charge of the Plan, beginning with Jean Monnet (1946–52) who had directed armaments, supplies and reconstruction in the National Liberation Committee in 1943, and later presided over the High Authority of the European Coal and Steel Community which, with Robert Schuman, he had helped to found. He was followed by Étienne Hirsch (1952–9), a mining engineer, who was assistant director of armaments for the Free French Forces from 1940 to 1944, joined the Planning Commissariat with Jean Monnet in 1946 and from 1959 to 1962 served as president of Euratom (the European organization for cooperation over the use of nuclear energy). Pierre Massé headed the Commissariat from 1959 to 1965; a graduate of the Polytechnique and state road-engineer, he made a career in the electricity industry and has since become chairman of the French electricity authority. François Ortoli (1966–7), a graduate of the National School of Administration and Inspector of Finance, led the Pompidou Cabinet from 1962 to 1966 and in 1967 was appointed Minister of Equipment; he was succeeded in 1964 by René Montjoie, a graduate of the Polytechnique and a mining engineer.

In April 1967 a Minister was put in charge of the overall supervision of the economic plan and national equipment. This was the third time this sector was entrusted to a member of the Government assisting the Prime Minister; previously the experiment had proved inconclusive, as the Planning Commission was difficult to deal with on a traditional administrative footing.

7 The Centralized State

Centralization is the indispensable complement to State independence as it is essential for orders to be communicated directly if there is to be any degree of autonomous action. When the Council of State came under fire in the early 1870s great pains were taken to keep the administration intact; in the same way, attempts at decentralization have met with fierce resistance. The most recent, most spectacular example of this came in 1946, with the non-implementation of Article 87 of the Constitution, according to which

local authorities will be self-administering with councils elected by universal suffrage. The decisions of these councils will be put into practice under the supervision of the mayor or president.

Despite these projected steps towards decentralization the Prefects remained the chief executives of *départements* and, as in the end the measures were never promulgated, supervised the communes. Thus the status quo continued, in spite of movements in favour of decentralization, and remained as vigorous as the administration's system of self-supervision – and for much the same reasons. It would be impossible, as well as unfair, to speak of routine or inertia opposing attempts at reform, as the existing system of government was in fact perfectly coherent, often more dynamic than the alternatives proposed, and responded to the demands of a history in the course of which national unity had more than once been in jeopardy.

Firstly, we shall study the geographical organization of this system and the machinery by which it operates, before outlining the balanced situation it helped to achieve.

The Geographical Organization of the State

The Revolution and Napoleon had completed the monarchy's projects for unification. By proclaiming the Republic 'one and indivisible' the Revolution provided a doctrinal justification for the form of the nation, and Napoleon implemented it on practical as much as ideological grounds.[1] By 1800 Napoleon had established the essential outlines of a system which has scarcely changed since, with as its cornerstone the principle that territorial units are an integral part of the State.

The two main territorial units of the French system, the *département* and the commune, might be compared with cells dependent on a larger organism which controls their functioning. The larger organism in question is the State, which represents the one complete, mature political and administrative reality, whereas other territorial units have no independent existence.

During the decentralization which marked the early years of the Third Republic – and was to continue in the Fourth – Waldeck-Rousseau objected that national sovereignty could not be fragmented. For him national unity represented 'the national will applied to the whole country'. Far from limiting freedom, this unitary conception of the State in fact constituted a guarantee of liberty as it made it impossible for a local majority representing only part of the country to thwart the wishes of the nation as a whole. Similarly, during the debate over the 1884 law on local and municipal government, Waldeck-Rousseau defended the tutelary right of the State to supervise local authorities, through the Deputy, and, for instance, the latter's right to take over control from an unsatisfactory mayor. To quote his actual words:

The commune is not a hermetically isolated compartment with its own life and interests distinct from those of the State; in given circumstances,

1. At that time national unity was constantly threatened from inside the country by the Royalist and Catholic rebellions in the Vendée, and from abroad by the intrigues of *émigrés* and the coalition of European monarchs against the Revolution, of which Napoleon was for many years considered the heir and defender.

events in a single commune may be so directly important to the country as a whole that it is inconceivable that above the mayor, who has only a limited jurisdiction, there should be no superior authority empowered to take the steps dictated by the general interest.

This hierarchical system, in which State authority applies to all decentralized units, had none the less to be reconciled with the principles of democracy. With this in view, the Napoleonic structure was modified by the laws of 1871 and 1884, which laid down the present-day characteristics of local units:

> each local government unit has a council elected by universal suffrage;
> the State is represented in each unit by an agent who acts as chief executive for these assemblies.

The *département* and the commune have thus a twofold nature: they are at one and the same time subdivisions of the central administration and decentralized communities. But this situation is not wholly symmetrical, in particular because of the number and diversity of communes.

In France there are 38,000 communes, of which 23,963 had less than 500 inhabitants and 9,767 between 501 and 1,500 inhabitants at the 1962 census, i.e. 11·7% and 16·9% respectively of the total population. At the other end of the scale, 32 communes of over 100,000 inhabitants contained a total of 8,751,220 inhabitants, or 18·4% of the population. All these communes have the same form of organization. They are administered by a municipal council which elects a mayor; he acts as head of the municipal administration, with extensive powers for governing the commune, but he is also the representative of the State and thus, for part of his functions, comes under the supervision of the Prefect's hierarchical authority. Moreover, the Prefect assumes supervision of municipal councils, some of whose decisions he may annul. In such cases, however, the municipality may take the matter to the administrative court, then, if need be, to the Council of State if it feels the Prefect has overreached his powers.

As an example of this procedure, on 10 August 1964 the Prefect of the Seine had cancelled a decision by the municipal council of Saint-Denis to organize a trip to Belgium for prize-winners in certain examinations. In the Prefect's opinion, 'the expense entailed by such a trip was not justified by any real need in the commune'. The (Communist) municipal council replied to this by going ahead with the trips as planned and placing the matter before the administrative court of the Seine which duly annulled the Prefect's decision as 'exceeding his powers'. But not, however, until December 1966.

The *département* may be compared roughly with the English county. At present there are 95 *départements* whose boundaries correspond very closely to the divisions made in 1789 by the Constituent Assembly, with the exception of the Paris region, where six new *départements* were created by law in 1964. As with the commune, the *département* is both a local authority and an administrative subdivision, but unlike the commune it has no elected executive; instead it has a Prefect.

The *département* assembly, known as the 'General Council', meets twice yearly to vote the budget prepared by the Prefect. In the intervals between these sessions, a permanent organ of the General Council, the *Commission départementale*, handles council business with the Prefect. The General Council is supervised essentially by the Ministry of the Interior and, to a great extent, by the Ministry of Finance; it has quite far-reaching powers concerning social assistance, communications and equipment.

Alongside the *département*'s activities as a local authority it also functions as an administrative area for the decentralized offices of Ministries. After a long period in which the General Councils gradually got rid of the burdens represented by some services by asking the State to take them over, in the last few years there has been a tendency in the other direction, with the State encouraging local authorities to bear a greater proportion of expenditure on equipment. In this connexion it should be noted that the local taxation system is not separate from the State system. The offices dealing with collecting taxes and making the payments decided on by Municipal and General Councils are part of the Ministry of Finance. Moreover, for many years local taxes were only an appendage to State taxation; *départements* and communes could only collect 'additional centimes' on national taxes. Later a local tax based on business turnover was introduced which provided one third of the resources of local units, but since 1968, when the local tax was abolished, the *département* or commune receives a State-administered tax (the wages tax, paid by employers).

These new resources have no longer any direct connexion with the local authority, as they are collected by the State and then redistributed proportionally according to the rate of one of the local taxes levied by the communities themselves; in this way, the amounts distributed depend on the taxes levied by local councils. The greater the contribution sought from local taxpayers, the more State aid they will receive. This ingenious system was devised to incite *départements* and communes to take a larger share in financing certain types of project, thereby easing pressure on the general State budget.

The division of expenditure between State and local contributions can be seen from the following figures taken from the national accounts (in millions of francs).

	1959	1966
State capital and recurrent grants	54,610	102,940
Local capital and recurrent grants	12,970	28,280

The current income of local authorities for the same purpose was as follows (in millions of francs):

	1959	1966
Taxes	7,840	17,500
Grants	2,830	6,620
Total	10,670	24,120

Between the *département* and the commune there are two other subdivisions, justified by the rural, dispersed nature of the country: the *canton*, which is among other things the electoral constituency for the General Council, and the *arrondissement*, which corresponds to the area of action of a Sub-prefect and represents an attempt to bring the administration closer to the citizens.

Local and National Politics

The State's presence at every level of local life and the mixture of State-appointed and elected representatives lead to a particular style of public life, in which local and national politics are not separated. This unity has its disadvantages – in particular it leads to excessive importance being given to parochial interests[2] in national debates, and to a degree of difficulty in recruiting young political workers, as in this situation a parliamentary mandate is looked on as the climax of a career begun on the municipal or general council; when a new Deputy has not worked his way up in this way, he quickly tries to catch up on the missing steps by angling for a post as mayor, or even for the chairmanship of a General Council, so as to ensure his influence at both ends of the power pipeline: Paris and the constituency. In the Assembly elected in March 1967, of 470 metropolitan Deputies there were no less than 264 mayors and 245 were members of General Councils (not always the same men, though the two posts are often held simultaneously). Of the 90 General Councils functioning at that time, 18 were chaired by Deputies, 26 by Senators and 13 by former Members of Parliament.

While the chairman of a General Council wields moral influence rather than concrete executive power, the same cannot be said of leaders in big towns. Despite their heavy responsibilities many mayors of major communes sit (or have sat) in Parliament. The 1962 census listed thirty-two towns with over 100,000 inhabitants; eleven of those had serving Deputies as mayors and seven others had former Deputies.

2. The fact that one is not a 'local boy' is considered a handicap for a parliamentary candidate. Most candidates do their best to create local links by exhuming some great-grand-parent in the region; failing blood ties, they buy a holiday house so that they can spend their summers in the region they hope to represent. This contrasts so completely with the British system that in the French edition of his book (*La Société politique britannique*, Paris, 1964, p. 132) Jean Blondel takes pains to stress that the concept of 'parachuting' candidates into constituencies has no pejorative overtones in Britain.

The Administrative Model

The demands of municipal government do, however, tend to discourage men from taking on several offices, all the more because local political issues are often an embarrassment for mayors in Parliament: they can become enslaved by the promises that won them their seats. For this reason M. Pierre Pflimlin (MRP), the mayor of Strasbourg, gave up his seat in 1967 to concentrate on his mayoral duties; M. Pradel, the mayor of Lyon, refused to stand as a Deputy, as did Senators like M. Morice, the mayor of Nantes, for fear of disturbing the balance of their municipal coalitions. Being mayor of Marseille at a time when the town council majority included Gaullists clearly proved as much a hindrance as a help to M. Defferre when he tried to stand for the Presidency of the Republic.

Generally speaking, there is no real break between local and national government, when we look at political representation. This is largely due to administrative centralization, in that electors tend to expect their elected representative to intervene effectively at the strategic levels of the administration: with Prefects at the level of the *département* and Ministers on the national plane.

In Chapter 5 we recalled how Prefects helped to establish the republican structure in the late nineteenth century. Their militant role naturally became eclipsed once the regime was no longer under serious attack, but Governments have never ceased to demand total loyalty from their Prefects. This particular requirement was complicated under the Fourth Republic by the existence of a number of different influences: the presence in office of Ministers belonging to different political parties and their rotation in office naturally led to a considerable degree of tolerance towards all shades of political opinions except Communism. The situation changed with the Fifth Republic, in that the concept of opposition now covered all the parties that had produced earlier leaders and retained solidly entrenched local positions. Prefects then found themselves in a very delicate position, as they were forced to reconcile loyalty to the Government with the requirements of their office, which obliged them to maintain good relations with influential local figures.

A Prefect who hopes to succeed in his *département* must

refrain from taking an overt political stand, as he would thereby risk losing his contact with local leaders who do not necessarily hold the same point of view as the Government. His influence depends entirely on his building up local confidence and a reputation for impartiality: in many ways his position is comparable with that of an ambassador. He is expected to take up his *département's* case with the administration in Paris and help realize projects concerning his region; at the same time, the central administration looks on him as a mouthpiece whose powers of persuasion are as important as his authority. In election periods this delicate balance is brutally put to the test as political positions stiffen and even the most diplomatic Prefect is forced to take steps in favour of Government-backed candidates – actions which later give rise to bitter recriminations. During the March 1967 elections it seems that in some *départements* in the Centre and South-West all discretion was thrown to the winds; the General Councils, solidly held by Socialists and Radicals, came out openly against their Prefects, criticizing their active, though often fruitless, support of the Gaullists.

The political mobilization of the Prefects was often requested by the Gaullist candidates, who had realized the weakness of their party infrastructure and were looking for help from the administration. This none the less goes against the main contemporary tendency to make the Prefect's tasks primarily technical, by turning him into a dynamic leader and coordinator, a role requiring complete impartiality on his part.

Regional Experiments

While the Government was trying to strengthen prefectoral qualifications by handing over the training of future Prefects to the National School of Administration, it embarked on a series of experiments in administrative decentralization and regional government which led to the reform of March 1964. This reform functioned on two levels:

(i) At the level of the *département*, the Prefect became more completely the representative of all serving Ministers. The

Ministries' offices in the *département* were now placed under the more direct and close control of the Prefect, with a view to coordinating their actions and avoiding decisions from Paris that did not take local circumstances into account. 'Deconcentration' is the name given to a move aimed at bringing the decision-making body closer to the place where the decision is put into action.

(ii) At the regional level, a new administrative grade was created corresponding to the twenty economic planning regions: the regional action zone, covering a number of *départements* with the Prefect of one of them at its head. He is known as the 'Regional Prefect' and is supposed to 'put into application government policies concerning the economic development and equipment of his area'.[3]

The regions formed in this way do not constitute a new local unit, but merely serve as a framework designed to facilitate the distribution of investment grants and the coordination of State action. However, as existing units had a direct interest in these matters (particularly because of their financial contribution to these projects), those responsible for the reforms also planned a consultative body: the Regional Economic Development Committee (CODER), which includes representatives of the General Councils, professional organizations and trade unions; mayors; and lastly 'qualified persons' appointed by the Government. The CODERs are consulted by Regional Prefects about the various phases of the Plan for their region. The hybrid composition of these bodies and the conditions in which they function have so far produced rather unsatisfactory results. The reform itself was a compromise between the demands of planning, regionalist aspirations and the nature of existing administrative structures.

Similarly there is a rather uneasy confusion between the traditional responsibilities of Prefects and their new economic role. The reform as a whole, though planned to meet a genuine need, seems to have underlined the State's dominance over

3. For a more detailed account, see Appendix 2 to this chapter.

elected representatives, so that Deputies attacked the authoritarian character and political implications of the new measures. The groping nature of this reform indicates the difficulty central and local authorities meet with in defining their new relationships, where the old network of contacts is being radically altered.

The Machinery of Centralization: the Role of the Ministry of Finance

We now come to the second aspect of centralization: the distance this type of organization maintains between the men who make decisions and those who carry them out. The degree to which the central administration can interfere in the smallest details of local affairs is a constant source of irritation to the public and never fails to astonish foreign observers. The obsession with uniform regulations and decisions taken in Paris has, indeed, been known to produce grotesque situations, but the system has stood up to criticism of this kind for over a century, largely because it possesses two highly functional features.

In the first place, centralization makes it possible for the regime to keep pace with a changing situation, which according to the sociologist Michel Crozier is still the main difficulty facing bureaucratic organizations; the isolation of the upper members of a hierarchy protects them from pressures brought by routine-bound subordinates and also from public reactions. It should not be forgotten that the French administrative system rose out of the ashes of the Old Regime, which had perished through its refusal to accept the reforms proposed by the ancestors of the men who founded the self-same new administration.

Secondly, the system is fundamentally egalitarian, as it is placed out of reach of social pressures: it is difficult to imagine anyone who could care less about the influence of local notables than an official from another part of the country, obeying direct orders from Paris and secure in the knowledge that he will continue his career elsewhere. This links up with the anti-Establishment character of the State in the early years of the Third Republic – which goes some way towards explaining why the right wing was then vociferously in favour of decentralization. When the Council of State was being debated, Gambetta justified its retention as an institution by saying: 'For administrative purposes the court's isolation guarantees the judge's authority and real impartiality.' A few decades later Alain pointed to the pair of gendarmes patrolling country roads as an example of the impersonal, objective nature of the State – yet another example of how Republican ideology contributed to the State's autonomous development.

How is the distance kept between those who make decisions and those who carry them out? Firstly, by the way the country is organized as a geographical unit, and by the system of supervision under which local units are placed. Furthermore, decisions within the direct scope of communes and *départements* pass along a line leading to the Ministries in Paris, where they are generally dealt with in financial terms. Herein lies the second key element in the system: this time it is not a person, like the Prefect, but an institution, the Ministry of Finance, which also wields its own supervisory power, often attacked but none the weaker for that, over all decisions involving finance.

At the preparatory level, the Budget Division of the Ministry of Finance collects requests from 'spending' Ministries and weighs up their respective proposals; this process is governed mainly by financial considerations, but inevitably it entails choices. It is often said that France is governed by the Ministry of Finance, and while the idea is somewhat exaggerated, it still contains a measure of truth. When disagreements persist, decisions are taken at the Matignon Palace by the Prime Minister or even, for the most important cases, at the Élysée, where the President of the Republic pronounces on the fundamental issues in the Budget. But most decisions are taken at a more modest level, strongly influenced by the Budget Division.

Each Ministry also contains finance officers, whose job is to control expenditure; they see that the Budget is respected by issuing visas of approval to all departmental decisions involving expenditure. When a particular item strikes them as doubtful, these officials consult the Budget Division. Similarly, when requests for payment relating to local expenditure reach the appropriate Minister, the controlling official examines the grounds, which are compulsorily stated; if in his opinion there is inadequate justification, no visa is forthcoming. Auditing is kept separate from the accounting side, which actually handles money; audit work is carried out by a special category of officials, with personal financial responsibility, supervised directly by the Court of Accounts.

This rigorously organized system, in which every item of expenditure must be justified in terms of an appropriate legal document, the whole based on a system separating 'accountants' and 'auditors', represents one of Napoleon's greatest achievements. The French monarchy had been beset by endless financial difficulties that placed it at the mercy of private moneylenders; memories of these difficulties (which had caused the summoning of the States General in 1789, and thus the Revolution) left their mark on the financial administration of the country. After the First World War the reappearance of financial crises and endemic budget deficits set off defence reactions, the most characteristic of which was the introduction of Ministry of Finance supervision of all State spending. The Ministry of Finance's isolated position placed it relatively apart from parliamentary pressures, which it was thus able to resist with reasonable success. Indeed its veto served as an alibi for Deputies committed to local interests; they could make the most impressive-sounding demands without completely sacrificing their consciences, because they knew in advance that their proposals would be resisted by the Minister of Finance, himself speaking on behalf of his Ministry. In this way everyone had a part to play in the game, which paralleled the relationship between Prefects and local notables and guaranteed the regime a certain degree of flexibility.

Here, as in other fields, the Fifth Republic introduced major changes by virtue of the restrictions imposed on parliamentary influence. At the same time the traditional pressure groups lost much of their power, as the interests of ex-servicemen, back-yard distillers, etc. were now defended by spokesmen without audiences. However, the Government was clearly still attentive to the demands of local authorities and tradesmen in connexion with the tax reforms voted in December 1965, since these measures were postponed until early 1968. While sometimes riding roughshod over local elected representatives, towards whom it tended to take an authoritarian line, in this instance the Government was none the less forced to withdraw in the face of their dissatisfaction. In any case, new pressure groups adapted to the new rules of the game have made their appearance. The best example of this strategy of applying pressure at the top is the CNJA (National Young Farmers' Organization), whose innovating approach was calculated to appeal to the technocrats. But this secretive character of the regime and the absence of parliamentary control have also favoured the development of a far less attractive rat-race, particularly in less well-structured sectors such as the building industry.

The Main Financial Controlling Bodies

The distance between the decision-makers and their subordinates shows not only in geographical and functional terms; it also stems from the preponderance of the major controlling bodies in the structure of the administration. We have already made several references to these bodies, and it is now necessary to consider their role as instruments of change.

These corps are characterized by a very demanding recruitment policy, which ensures successful candidates rapid promotion quite independent of the career prospects of lower grades. The most typical cases are those of the General Inspectorate of Finance and the Court of Accounts; between the ages of thirty-nve and forty, Inspectors General often take on virtually ministerial responsibilities and this feature, which has always existed, constitutes one of the most effective factors for administrative change. At thirty-five, M. Bloch-Lainé was Head of the Treasury Division, which is the key section of the Ministry of Finance, since all State financial projects pass through it. M. Ortoli, at forty, was General Commissioner for Economic Planning, and at the same age M. Saint-Geours was head of Budget Planning at the Ministry of Finance (his office includes the national accounts division).

The Finance Inspectorate was set up in 1816; for many years its powers were limited to controlling the State's financial departments, which were visited by inspectors on tours of duty, a system still in application. The inspectors' reports were then passed on to the agents affected, who had the right to reply; the argumentative true-to-life nature of these reports probably lies at the root of the system's success. The political upgrading of this particular corps dates from the end of the nineteenth century. Joseph Caillaux, who served ten years in the Inspectorate before moving into public life and, at the age of thirty-six,[4] becoming Minister of Finance, wrote that there were few professions

that subject young brains to as healthy a course of intellectual gymnastics. No other job obliges one to collect a more complete body of administrative knowledge in a few short years.

The versatility of the Finance Inspectorate is worth noting; it has produced the Paris region's first Prefect (M. Delouvrier), the Minister of Foreign Affairs (M. Couve de Murville) and the Secretary-General at the Quai d'Orsay (M. Alphand) as well as numerous political figures including M. Chaban-Delmas, the President of the National Assembly.

The Court of Accounts was founded by Napoleon in 1807, to supervise the regularity of transactions involving public funds; this gave it its original role as a court. The Court is composed of permanent judges who are entrusted with the function of enforcing the principles of public accountancy, according to which every transaction must be based on a precise legal decision. The absence of secrecy around State financial affairs eliminates the possibility of arbitrary decisions and while it does not in itself guarantee efficient management, it is still a fundamental condition for efficiency. The sole remaining fragment of the sovereign's old discretionary power lies in the existence of the 'secret fund',

4. This is also the age at which another member of the Inspectorate, M. Giscard d'Estaing, became Minister of Finance in 1962.

which is not controlled and constitutes on the financial plane the equivalent of the 'discretionary acts' which the Council of State does not investigate.

The upgrading of the Court of Accounts was more recent and less spectacular than that of the Finance Inspectorate; it resulted from the extension of State powers and its own newly introduced system of recruitment through the National School of Administration, which broadened the Court's traditional, rather formalist, outlook, so that in its turn it became a pool of talent from which Ministers choose their young assistants. These young men are happy enough to be seconded, as the rather boring file-oriented nature of their auditing work spurs them to aim at more attractive positions.

The preponderant role of the two major financial controlling bodies thus makes them, with the prefectoral network, key elements of the French system of centralized administration. In view of their guaranteed intellectual independence and their unchallenged authority within the civil service, they are able to act as a critical, reformist leavening which saves the French bureaucracy from degenerating into mere mandarin castes.

Paris and the Provinces

It has been seen that the administrative system continued functioning, in spite of criticisms, as the result of its functional aspects and its links with the political structure. In reality this affinity stems from the fact that the political structure as a whole adapted itself to the needs of society. Sociologists such as Michel Crozier have claimed that the French style of action represents the best possible solution to the problems inherent in governing people in a society dominated at one and the same time by an absolutist view of authority, a refusal of any dependence and a type of group action aimed essentially at protecting the individual's independence.

All this combined to produce a state of balance between central State power and society in general. We have already seen numerous instances of this equilibrium, which is also noticeable in the relations between Paris and the rest of France. By the nature of political and administrative organization, everything converges on the capital, which thus appears as the indispensable regulator of national life. This places Paris in a situation of unique prestige, but by the same token the city is singularly liable to infuriate the provinces. Paris is the incarnation of distant impersonal power, once symbolized by 'offices'. Now, however, the technocrats have become the traditional 'they' who, like some mammoth state conspiracy, include all the most influential figures in the administrative, political and business worlds. 'They' somehow control the everyday life of the provinces – nobody knows exactly how, but there is a general suspicion that 'they' are motivated by dubious appetites for power and wealth. The concentration of power in Paris in some ways magnifies the tendencies already inherent in the political and administrative systems, by elevating them to the level of myths.

With sixteen per cent of the total population at the 1962 census, the weight of Paris on the nation is greater than that of any other capital except London. After London it is the largest conurbation in Western Europe, but there is a far larger gap between it and the next largest urban complex than in Britain: the ratio is one to nine in France, as against one to four in Great Britain, and one to three and a half in the United States and Japan. In other terms, Paris exercises an almost irresistible attraction which drains manpower and resources from the provinces, none of which can combat this centripetal force. A statistical survey of the 'economic strength' of the various urban units, published in 1964, showed the enormous gap between the commanding role played by Paris, and that of Lyon, the French city which, by virtue of its regional influence, comes second; it also stressed the provinces' general dependence on the capital. 'Paris and the French Desert' is the title of a book[5] that indicates the frustration generated by a situation in which Paris is not only the political and administrative capital, but also the dominant centre of industry, finance and trade, the seat of the most important university and educational establishments and the intellectual

5. Jean-François Gravier, *Paris et le désert français*, Paris, 1947.

and artistic centre of the country. In the words of the poet Paul Valéry:

Being at once the capital of arts and science, finance and trade, pleasure and pageantry of a great nation, representing the country's entire history – this sets the city of Paris apart from all other giant towns.

The relative atrophy of the provinces, for which cures are currently being sought, can be traced originally to a deliberate policy adopted by Louis XIV when he attracted the élite of the French nobility to Paris in order to ensure the preponderance of his own central power. The social movement thus started duly spread to the economic and financial fields and influenced the form of the nation's infrastructure – for instance, the network of roads and railways that radiate out from the capital in an astonishingly regular star shape. We should also mention that while the rush to the capital stemmed from a desire for promotion of one sort or another, there were also other motives. In particular, Paris offered individual freedom from the restrictions and taboos of provincial society. Freed from pressures and prejudice, an independent, often subversive movement of opinion grew up, giving rise to the rebellious streak that can be traced throughout the history of the population of Paris. Thibaudet notes that Paris has always taken an opposition stand, thus going some way towards compensating for the centralization of power through the capital's general trend-setting role. This was true in the eighteenth century, when new ideas were spread first through aristocratic salons, which gave an enthusiastic welcome to the encyclopedists' critical approach and openly scoffed at the authorities. A similar situation emerged during the Third Republic, when the literary world, the press, the Academies and *salons* moved sharply right as soon as reactionary ideas had finally been defeated in the political field. After sparking off the Revolutions of 1789, 1830 and 1848, at the end of the century Paris was for General Boulanger, against Dreyfus, and anti-republican – precisely when the Republic was settling in permanently. Until then revolutions had been virtually monopolized by the capital, which had decided the fate of regimes, anticipating provincial opinion. However, the provinces grew tired of this situation, and the 1848 fiasco, followed by the failure of the Commune in 1871, resulted from provincial resistance. Indeed it was only once the Republic had acquired a provincial basis and character that it became firmly established – and Paris duly did an about turn, discarding advanced ideas and adopting the opposite line as a fashion.

The dialectic relationship between Paris and the provinces is mirrored by the reverse relationship between Paris and power, which seems to be a prerequisite of the traditional balance of power in France. The risks of oppression by a rigorously central-ized regime are counteracted by critical reactions so that the absolutist conception of authority is reconciled with freedom for the individual. In other words, authority is concentrated in Paris, but Paris itself is against authority, so that provincial distrust of the capital is twofold: provincial and republican. Alain's *Propos* provide a perfect illustration of middle-class republican thought in the early years of the twentieth century: provincial republicans were equally suspicious of the Paris 'offices' of Ministries and of the capital's *salons*, because of their possible influence on naïve Deputies newly arrived in town. This distrust was also found among the Parisian lower classes, whose reactions contrast with the slow spread of ideas in the rest of the country.

In this situation, the Third Republic maintained the capital's special statute: the municipal council is not headed by a mayor, but every year elects a chairman, who acts mainly as a decorative figurehead, while the real business of governing Paris is seen to by two permanent officials, the Prefect of the Seine and the Prefect of Police. Consequently the system of centralization culminates in the Government's super-tutelage over the capital. This system is motivated essentially by political considerations, but it has serious disadvantages, in that the municipal council's irrespons-ible position makes it a happy hunting ground for interest groups, and also because of the Prefecture of Police's disproportionate authority, as a result of which the Paris police has degenerated into a feudal empire. With the law of 10 July 1964 the Paris area was reorganized with the creation of six new *départements* and the disappearance of the *département* of Seine-et-Oise, but the status of Paris itself, which is administratively separated from the suburban communes and now constitutes a *département* on its own, was not affected by these reforms. The Prefect of the Seine simply became the Prefect of Paris. The Prefecture of Police has also been more closely controlled by the Ministry of the Interior since the outcry following the kidnapping and murder of Mehdi Ben Barka in 1965.

The conditions of the traditional equilibrium do, however, seem to be changing with a realization of the underdeveloped state of the provinces. The attempts at regional devolution contained in the March 1964 reforms are a first manifestation of the general tendency towards greater autonomy and a more direct share in decision-making. Morose resignation to Parisian leadership has given way to a more aggressive state of mind which has yet to find a satisfactory solution, but none the less indicates a reversal of the former tendency. In politics, the capital's behaviour remains perplexing: in 1962 Gaullists captured all thirty-one of the city's seats in the Chamber of Deputies, but in 1967 they lost ten of them again.

Appendix 1 *Départements* and Regions

The *département*, with its Prefect and General Council, remains the basic administrative unit in the French system. However, it has shown itself too small for some government departments, which have been obliged to reorganize their services in larger units. These units were originally set up in accordance with the internal needs of each department, so that in 1957 over fifty administrative or public bodies were headed in the provinces by agents responsible for several *départements*: but the respective areas of these various officials seldom coincided: a given *département* might well belong to different areas for Education, Public Health, and Justice.

The various specialized areas were reorganized and made uniform in January 1959 along the lines set out three years before by the General Planning Commissariat. It was therefore the needs created by the implementation of the Plan which gave rise to the new regional framework of twenty administrative regions in addition to the Paris region which has its own special organization.

(i) The decrees of 14 March 1964 followed up the logical implications of the new structure by defining the organization of State services in the twenty regional areas, each headed by a Regional Prefect, the Prefect of the *département* containing the main town of the area. Consequently the Regional Prefect adds his new regional responsibilities to his normal brief for the *département*; the existence of this accumulation of functions demonstrates that the region is not in itself a new administrative unit, but rather an intermediary stage between the *département* and central government. The Regional Prefect is not supposed to stand between the Government and the departmental Prefects – after all, he is one himself – but should only coordinate their activities.

(ii) The primary aim of these reforms is to foster economic development in the regions. To this end, the Regional Prefect presides over a meeting of *département* Prefects (the 'regional administrative conference') which assists him in drawing up public investment programmes which, before their adoption, the Regional Prefect submits to the Ministers involved. Each Regional Prefect is helped by a team of young higher civil servants, who are in charge of coordinating and promoting economic development.

(iii) The situation outlined above is purely internal to the central government, as the region is not a territorial unit, but simply a 'relay'. However, in order to meet the demands of local opinion, which for years had been asking for a voice in regional planning, on 14 March 1964 another decree set up Regional Economic Development Committees (CODERs). The CODER is required to give advice on regional development prospects and the aspects of the Plan relating to the region. It is consulted by the Regional Prefect, who fixes the dates of its meetings.

Each of the twenty CODERs has between forty and fifty members, of whom at least a quarter are mayors or members of General Councils, while half are nominated by Chambers of Commerce, Trade and Agriculture, trade unions and professional organizations, and the rest are chosen on grounds of personal qualification by the Prime Minister.

When the CODERs were established, in early 1964, their members included sixty-eight Deputies, fifty-three Senators and thirty-five former Members of Parliament, mainly drawn from among local representatives. Half the CODERs are presided over by Members of Parliament, who in this way have confirmed their influence in the regions.

(iv) At the beginning of 1967 a working party presided over by General de Gaulle drew up the balance sheet of regional activities. The meeting noted numerous criticisms, largely concerning the functioning and responsibilities of the CODERs, which were considered inefficient. Some modifications of detail were made, but the system is still experimental and there is still hesitation between straightforward improvement of the present system of consultation and the transformation of the regional divisions into full administrative units with their own elected organs of representation – a hope shared by a large proportion of provincial opinion. However, this development would create problems at the level of the *département*, which would inevitably lose its *raison d'être*, and it also meets with hostility from the Ministry of Finance. The question is therefore still open, especially as the original division of the country into twenty regions resulted from a compromise between local rivalries and the need for a structure better suited to planning needs, which would probably cut the number of regions to half the present total.

Appendix 2 The General Inspectorate of Finance

The General Inspectorate of Finance was created in 1816 and from 1847 on was recruited exclusively through a competitive examination. Since 1945 it has been one of the corps supplied by the National School of Administration.

It is part of the Ministry of Finance, directed by a departmental head, and is formed of Inspectors-General and Inspectors; Inspectors-General come directly under the control of the Minister: each is placed in charge of a territorial division, or a special division, and directs the work of the Inspectors placed under him.

The Inspectorate supervises the outside services of the Ministry of Finance, as well as savings and loan organizations, communes, hospitals and social security. It also takes part in a permanent operation of financial control and constitutes a pool of civil servants who are seconded to a wide variety of posts: to name one example, M. Jacques-Bernard Dupont was ambassador extraordinary to Dahomey before becoming Director-General of ORTF (French State Radio and Television).

At 1 January 1967 the Inspectorate had an official payroll of 103 (including members seconded to ministerial cabinets); in addition, 100 Inspectors of Finance were on secondment.

Appendix 3 The Court of Accounts

The Court of Accounts was created in 1807 and is organized along the same lines as an ordinary court. It is composed of permanent magistrates who since 1945 have been recruited from the National School of Administration; they are divided into five specialized Chambers, a sixth being devoted to publicly owned industries.

The Court examines the balance sheets of public accountants. It checks the regularity of transactions and makes sure that all the forms have been observed, in particular that 'visas' have been obtained from the controllers. The procedure takes place in three phases:

1. the case, which is made by a *rapporteur*;
2. the conclusions of the prosecution, composed of a Procurator-General and two Advocates-General;
3. the judgement, pronounced by one of the five chambers.

The Court of Accounts also exercises an administrative control, assessing not only the regularity of activities but also the standards of management. Each year it submits a report to the President of the Republic, containing observations based on inspections and rich in often picturesque examples of waste or abuse.

The magistrates of the Court are divided into *auditeurs*, *maîtres des requêtes* and *conseillers maîtres*. At 1 January 1967 the Court had an official payroll of 205, including about twenty belonging to ministerial cabinets ; thirty-eight of its members were on secondment to administrative posts.

8 The Civil Servants' Republic

The model of the State as the driving force in a centralized society may be considered either as a successful undertaking or as a hangover from the past. It is successful in so far as it provides an example of pragmatic adaptation to conditions laid down by history itself and by the nature of political life in France. On the other hand, it appears archaic if we consider its inherent rules, which are foreign to the spirit of an industrial society, and are surely bound to hinder the more fundamental changes that could at last bring France into step with a competitive, developing world.

A system of such complexity cannot, however, be assessed solely in terms of the immediate present. If we are to gauge its strengths and weaknesses, we must consider the system in a historical context, in terms of the process that gradually shaped it. Indeed, its shortcomings often turn out to be former good points that have got out of hand – in the same way that, as Chesterton said, the errors of modern times are merely Christian truths that have grown into Christian folly. In its traditional form, the political and administrative system had succeeded in pragmatically creating a kind of balance between aristocracy and democracy, between centralization and pluralism, between the imposition and the limitation of State power.

The main pattern of authority which was to assert itself after the irremediable decline of the aristocracy was that of public service. Children of the old nobility who were forced to earn their living went into the army or the diplomatic corps; the upper middle classes continued the tradition set by the educated classes, by bringing up their sons for the liberal professions or the *grands corps* of the civil service; the lower middle classes saw promotion and advancement opened up to them through public service, which was also the first rung up the ladder for the working class. The closed, family character of most commercial firms offered outsiders few prospects in business life, and class barriers were still so strong that the only way to succeed was provided by the Republic: public administration. Equality of opportunity, although still existing only in theory, first became a reality – for the most gifted – with the spread of education.

When in 1830 Stendhal published his famous novel *Scarlet and Black*, the title symbolized the two ways open to ambitious children of poor families: scarlet for the Army, black for the Church. By the 1880s the State had replaced the Church as a stepping-stone, offering three parallel, often closely linked routes to success: politics, Freemasonry and public administration. Social advancement took place in clearly defined stages, each corresponding to a generation. The peasant's son left the land, not for industry, but for the public service which, since the spread of free, compulsory primary education, was now open to him; he became a schoolmaster or a *gendarme*, or worked for the Post Office or as a Treasury clerk. His children in due course went on to secondary education, culminating in the École Normale Supérieure, an establishment training teachers for secondary and higher education, but also offering other prospects: it was to produce a good proportion of the leading political personnel, mainly during the first decades of the century (at the time Thibaudet spoke of a 'Republic of Teachers'), but also in our own time: M. Pompidou, appointed Prime Minister in 1962, is a graduate of the 'rue d'Ulm'.

'Vertical Federalism'

Selection through competitive examinations provided chances of rapid promotion in addition to the normal progress of careers; the most favourable ground for this was the still brand-new and welcoming Ministry of Public Education. The Third Republic had, basically, adapted existing institutions, thus winning itself the loyalty of the army and the diplomatic corps, although these were recruited essentially from the old aristocracy; it has also created some new structures, including the public education system, with the result that in spite of extreme geographical centralization, the system incorporated an element of functional decentralization: a pluralist distribution of influence and authority, which Daniel Halévy summed up as 'vertical federalism'.

The solid framework linking an egalitarian political society and a stratified civilian society was provided by various types of aristocracy or élites, i.e. the intermediary bodies, the common characteristic of which was excellence as shown in competitive examinations. This type of selection procedure was perfectly compatible with Republican principles; at the same time the individuality, independence and superior prestige attached to these élites were congenial to upper middle class modes of thought. It might be said that this reconciliation of democracy and traditional social values enabled the regime to settle in, by avoiding the misadventures of preceding republics; its performance may be analysed in sociological terms as a practical adjustment between the violent desire for equality and the no less deep-rooted atavistic taste for hierarchies that are characteristic of the French temperament.

Daniel Halévy, who was one of the most perspicacious historians of the Third Republic, called these intermediary bodies 'fragments of the State', remarking that the pluralism guaranteed by their existence tempers the potentially intolerable side of administrative centralization, but without the risks that geographical federation would entail in so varied a country. Moreover, they allow the social machine to function more or less regularly in times of political crisis, as can also be said of the independent position of the State.

One idea recurs frequently, referring to the cornerstone of this edifice: the competitive examination. From the most modest job to the most brilliant career, the competitive examination is the preferred mode of recruitment as it alone ensures perfect (although largely theoretical) equality, and it alone perpetuates a feeling that promotion is bound to go to the most able. Standing midway between open-market conditions and the arcane ways of the Establishment, it constitutes a third channel, which was officially adopted by the Republic when it was faced with responsibility for a society ignorant of capitalist values and hostile to tradition. Every day the *Journal Officiel* carries advertisements along the lines of the following, which appeared on 10 December 1966:

Authorized in the three months following publication of the present notice, a competition for the recruitment of two cabinet-makers for the national establishment at Sèvres.

The successful candidate in a competitive examination acquires statutory rights which are more than mere legalities, in that they are not limited to guarantees but also carry with them elements of social prestige and promises of success, depending on the difficulty of the test. We have already mentioned the National School of Administration (ÉNA), the École Normale Supérieure and the École Polytechnique; to this list we should add institutions linked to the Polytechnique (Schools of Mining, Public Works, etc.) and the École Centrale des Arts et Manufactures, which gives the country the greater part of its upper technical staff and also many of its managers.

These institutions produce bodies of men who, without any written rule, show such a degree of solidarity that, for instance, a student of engineering who graduates with a good degree can move straight into a managerial post where he will be welcomed by his elders. As we mentioned in connexion with the Plan, Polytechnicians have played an active part in economic organization: the arcane nature of their world and its mysterious prestige caught the public imagination and gave rise to the popular belief in the 'synarchy', a rather novelettish conspiracy of technocrats, a myth which had its hour of glory just before the Second World War. By inflating and distorting facts, myths of this type indicate a confused awareness of the key role these carefully selected, homogeneous élites play in the life of the nation.

The existence of these leading State higher education institutions has resulted in constant communication between upper executives in business and in State service – a situation which can have its disadvantages, in view of the influence of private interests in the running of certain ministries, particularly those concerned with technology. However, the administration's structure limits the possible consequences of over-close relations between private employers and high-ranking civil servants. The main Ministries constitute relatively autonomous bodies, with their own identity and traditions, in more or less open rivalry with other departments. For instance, the Ministry of Finance may feel that the Ministries of Industry or Public Works tend to deal with branches of activity that are properly Finance's province, and it will subject the others' projects to pitiless scrutiny. Apart from possible direct intervention by the Minister, it is difficult to envisage excessive favouritism developing inside such a system, as it would almost inevitably be pounced on and exposed by related departments.

The Internal Pluralism of the Administration

The actual character of the Ministries is one manifestation of Halévy's 'vertical pluralism': it takes the form of a sort of self-government which varies in extent but is quite considerable in the larger Ministries. There is no need to stress further the independence of the Ministry of Finance; however, the Ministries of the Interior, Armed Forces, Foreign Affairs, Public Works or Education could be cited as so many individual bodies, each with its own particular administrative ethos that raises invisible barriers against arbitrary political decisions and thus tempers the apparently monolithic nature of the State. This situation was indeed deliberately fostered by some statesmen under the Third Republic, as we can see from this curious declaration made by Jules Ferry in 1880:

As I understand it, the administration of public education must aim essentially at marshalling the energies of teachers and bringing their initiative and responsibility into play. This is why we call on teachers, why we try to consult them. It is, if you like, a form of self-government in public education.

The independent nature of Ministries shows very clearly in their political leanings, which until very recently made it virtually impossible to appoint Ministers not associated with the appropriate political colour. In this way Education and the Interior are, as a result of the anti-clerical struggles of the early days of the Republic, 'citadels of free-thinking', to quote the French specialist J.-F. Kesler; neither of these Ministries was ever given to a Christian Democrat, and when General de Gaulle chose his Ministers of Education, he called first on Socialists, such as Boulloche and Paye, or on well-known secularists like Joxe and Sudreau.

This political identity may even be found between the main divisions of ministries; in this way, the Division of Public Health, tending towards Radicalism and Socialism, was particularly receptive to the influence of Freemasonry, whereas the conservative or Christian Democrat Division of Population was more amenable to Catholic overtures. The Ministry of Finance's long-range planning section includes a particularly high proportion of civil servants holding advanced left-wing opinions.

Another characteristic of the system is the political freedom of civil servants. They are entitled to leave for the duration of their campaign if they stand as parliamentary candidates. If elected, they are automatically placed on long leave for as long as they are in Parliament; if defeated, they return to their posts immediately the result is announced. In 1962 the Government showed itself unwilling to reinstate three *maîtres des requêtes* of the Council of State, who had lost their seats in Parliament; all three were violently opposed to General de Gaulle's Algerian policy. But the Government's breach of faith aroused such indignation in the Council of State, including those members least sympathetic to the views of the three former Deputies, that they were finally reinstated.

This freedom is also seen in the expression of opinions, although naturally this varies with rank and functions: while it is total among the lower ranks, it naturally becomes more reserved as one rises up the hierarchy. Nothing prevents a civil servant from belonging to a political party, whether supporting Government or Opposition, but no official in a position of authority may publicly criticize the Government whose decisions he is there to carry out, nor may he figure officially among the leaders of any political party. These unwritten rules are interpreted pragmatically by the corps itself, which aims at protecting its own independence and avoiding ministerial reprimands. Save in exceptional cases, the Government applies far less political pressure than does the corps itself: what a civil servant may do and say is governed, ultimately, by the influence of his colleagues and immediate superiors. Up to the present this influence has not produced political conformism, by virtue of the multiplicity of parties and the instability of Governments, and on the whole the Fifth Republic does not seem to have tampered with the rules of the game. In any case, the administration is far too subtle and complex an organization to risk being dragooned into conformism; furthermore the practical drawbacks of weakening its critical spirit outweigh the personal satisfaction a Minister might draw from silencing his subordinates. These principles, which have been respected up to now, may none the less undergo changes if the current political stability turns out to be lasting.

It should be added that civil servants generally tend to hold left-wing persuasions, particularly in the middle and lower grades, while employees and executives of similar status in the private sector usually hold far more conservative views. Michel Crozier, who has studied this question, considers that it corresponds to a difference in background linked, on one side, to the secular public education system, and on the other, to religious private schools. In this context he provides interesting confirmation of what we have said about the significance of the republican State, itself an anti-Establishment:

As a result of the influence exercised on the French administration for fifty years or so by the parties of the Left, the working-class and peasant masses have been able to send their children into public service without having to conform to conservative criteria; the traditional way up through conservative patronage, usually dependent on religious observance, has been circumvented by a secular route to promotion.

On the other hand, the Right has traditionally held certain sectors as its fief, particularly the army, the diplomatic corps, the judiciary and the *grands corps*. This was another sign of the subtle balance maintained within the administration; despite their members' lack of sympathy for left-wing Governments, these bodies were so well integrated into the State system that their collective loyalty was above suspicion. The army itself, for which the 1940 defeat had provided an opportunity of venting its feelings about the Republic, only slowly recovered from the blow of General de Gaulle's dissidence when he invoked a national legitimacy greater than the formal regularity of the Vichy regime, and thus broke with the rule of absolute obedience to the civilian branch.

'Young Masters' and Mandarins

In order to survive, the traditional balance called for continual efforts at adaptation. In Chapter 6 we mentioned the positive side of this adjustment to growth and the needs of the modern world. But over the last few years, difficulties have emerged inside the system itself.

Firstly, the stratified, hierarchical model of the Republic of civil servants was justified only as long as it ensured the existence of a leaven of criticism in the upper reaches of public service. There is, however, one field in which these spurs, built into the administration itself, have lost their sharpness: the Ministry of Education. Once quoted as the greatest achievement of the Third Republic, it has since then rather tended to rest on its laurels. At present the French educational system is having serious difficulty in modernizing its ideas and methods so as to cope with the problems of population growth and the duration of studies. Ferry's 'self-government' of 1880 has degenerated into a conservative aristocracy with as its prototype the Société des Agrégés.[1] With its ferocious attachment to the privileges that

1. The *agrégation* is the highly restrictive competitive examination traditionally considered as the peak of academic achievement; it is generally prepared for in the École Normale Supérieure; and was originally designed as an entrance qualification for teaching in secondary and higher education. It is set and administered by an association of holders of this qualification, the Société des Agrégés.

accompany success in the *agrégation* and admission to the circle of members, the association looks on reform with suspicion, if not with downright hostility, although the examination no longer has any relevance in an age of mass education. In this way an immobile, uncooperative mandarin caste stubbornly blocks the way to innovation, and the present educational crisis in France takes on a certain symbolic value in that it attacks the Republican model. Admittedly the problems stem also from the general changes undergone by French society, as we shall see in the last chapter, but they can also be explained by the disfunction of the regulating mechanisms present in other administrations. The hierarchy of competitive examinations concerns the appointment of teachers and it is not, as in the case of the *grands corps*, related to the selection of leading managers; it could be that this particular type of structure carries in itself the germ of its own paralysis.

In any case it is significant that the Ministry of Education remained aloof from the general movement of rejuvenation sparked off by the opening of the ÉNA (École Nationale d'Administration). While the Ministry of Education employs half the total force of civil servants, the ÉNA has supplied it with only 57 officials, as against 393 in the Ministry of Finance and 181 in the Ministry of the Interior, and it is felt that this under-administration is largely responsible for the shortcomings of this particular Ministry.

The transformations brought about by the ÉNA are themselves beginning to be examined in a more critical light. It is stressed that the decrease in parliamentary influence is fostering the emergence of a governing clique which is taking over the machinery of State and that graduates of the ÉNA are succumbing to the temptation to join the club. In particular, the early hope that the School would lead to democratizing the system does not seem to have been fulfilled. The selection of the most talented is justified only as long as it is open to all and ensures a constant turnover of élites. As it happens, the student intake of the ÉNA, which is one of the most prestigious short-cuts to high office in existence, tends to be exclusively middle-class. Promotion through a competitive in-service examination reserved for lower-grade civil servants has been a failure; in the early years almost as many candidates were recruited in this way as through the student entrance examination, but this proportion has fallen to one third since 1959 and even these places are not always filled. In 1966 only twenty-two places out of 112 went to serving civil servants. The students themselves are drawn mainly from the families of members of the liberal professions or high-ranking civil servants. No students with working-class or peasant backgrounds were admitted in 1963, and in 1964 only one working-class student and two farmers' sons entered the school.

Similar observations have been made of the other competitive examinations, particularly in connexion with the École Polytechnique. It is as if a hereditary monopoly had grown up, held by a few families who only grudgingly admit new blood. No doubt the proportions have not varied much since the early years of the Third Republic, but what was then a spectacular advance has become an increasingly intolerable procedure as the level of education in all sections of French society continues to rise.

Over the last two decades we have seen the emergence of the contradiction between new conditions and the time-honoured mechanisms that regulated traditional republican society. The process of legal selection entitling the lucky candidate to a stable legal and social situation is hardly compatible with the mobility demanded by modern economic conditions. A propensity for reconciling an obsession with hierarchy and a desire for equality has sometimes led to ludicrous situations: one case was the reform, immediately after the Second World War, which placed the whole personnel of the public service on a single grid for the purposes of calculating pay scales; this was aimed at providing a legal means of measuring differences in salary and thus giving a rational explanation of discrepancies so that they would be more tolerable. But the system has often led to mutual spying among the various corps, which suspected one another of not obeying the rules; in reality, the desire to attract high-calibre staff spurred central offices to offer their employees bonuses and various other attractions. The complexity of salaries in the public and nationalized sectors is so great that, as has been seen, it was necessary in 1963 to engage three 'Wise Men' to carry out a comparative survey of salaries.

Moreover, as the State was earlier than the private sector in giving its employees certain advantages, particularly security of tenure, retirement pensions, etc., salaries in the public sector tended to be lower than in private employment, where the law of supply and demand held sway. When social security benefits and unemployment insurance extended these privileges to the greater part of wage-earners, the public service's statutory guarantees lost much of their original appeal. At the same time, salary discrepancies were felt all the more acutely because Governments, in their fight against inflation, tended to start off by pegging the salaries they could control directly. State employees consequently felt they were losing both ways, and clung on to their established rights, while demanding parity with the private sector. This situation explains why the public service and the nationalized industries played so important a part in agitation over salaries and wages.

The influence of civil servants in French trade unionism contributed to giving the movement a particular outlook which has spread to employees in the private sector. Workers' organizations prefer to address their demands directly to the State, instead of embarking on negotiations with their employers. The concept of a legal code imposed by the Government takes precedence over negotiated contracts: agreements, which in other countries are reached by collective bargaining, are often handled in France by regulations, while labour relations, which are weak and disorganized at factory level, tend to be acted out on the national plane. The measures taken may be the same in each case, but the difference in procedure is significant, given the dynamic nature of these problems.

Consequently, it seems that the system is forced to struggle constantly against its own inherent tendencies towards rigid, stratified structures defined basically by rights established legally *vis-à-vis* the state. In one sense the spontaneous reactions of twentieth-century Frenchmen seem to reveal an unconscious nostalgia for a bygone order: the Old Regime, which in its last days, according to Herbert Lüthy, was 'no more than a system for dividing and distributing income'. The concept of established rights had by then extended to all social categories, who expected the State to preserve the status quo, in the economic field as in everything else.

A Rentier Society

In his *Discourse on Free Trade*, the liberal economist Frédéric Passy tells that in 1825 the inhabitants of Lille complained that the linseed oil used for lighting was facing competition from a new product: coal gas.

For which reason [Passy continues] they humbly crave that His Majesty, as natural protector of their labour, should see fit to preserve their established rights against attack, by suppressing this new product which was putting their livelihood in jeopardy.

Their pleas fell on deaf ears, yet the bourgeoisie's rise to power, confirmed five years later by the 1830 Revolution, did not lead to a transformation of French society along capitalist lines. The new leading class simply took control of the State without justifying its right to govern by any dynamic activity. As Tocqueville wrote in his *Souvenirs*, the middle class

was thus not only the sole directing force in society, but also, as one might say, it lived off it. It settled in every position of power, prodigiously multiplying such posts, and acquired the habit of living as much on the public Treasury as on its own industry.

The desire to use the State as a source of personal profit, and to look to it for help and protection, reveals a permanent feature in social attitudes which is closely linked to the State's image of itself as driving force. It spotlights a particular feature of French society: a persistent indifference to the capitalist system of values. It was only later that industry began to make genuine progress, thanks to the existence of a totally different system: the Napoleon III regime which, as we have noted, was inspired by Saint-Simon's doctrines and bent on turning France into the most advanced industrial society of the time. This approach, even then technocratic in nature, and the openings offered to competition in 1861 by the free-trade agreement with Great Britain, strike an oddly evocative chord a century later. . . . However, the great industrial undertakings which were launched, much later than in Britain, were almost always the creations of individuals isolated in a predominantly rural society; the motives moving these industrialists seem to have been largely foreign to the normal driving forces of capitalism, the profit motive. The public acclaim given to Ferdinand de Lesseps (himself a Saint-Simonian) for his exceptional feat in raising the loan for building the Suez Canal, was explained by admiration for technical prowess and a taste for the exotic as much as by economic interest. French investments indicated reactions closer to those of property-holders under the Old Regime than of capitalist stockholders, as Government bonds and foreign government loans were the favourite investments.

Until fairly recently, French capitalism could be divided roughly into two clearly distinct categories. On one hand, there was producer-based capitalism, embracing family firms still steeped in the traditions of the better-off peasantry; it was more important to keep the family name going than to expand the business by going public as a limited company. On the other, there was the capitalism of the financiers, who were mainly Jewish and Protestant, so that the key people in this field occupied a marginal position in society. Jewish finance became thought of as the symbol of foreign, corrupting power, with an influence in political milieux that was exposed by the Panama scandal in 1892. In order to obtain authorization to raise a premium bond-type loan, the directors of the Panama Company (which had already constructed the Suez Canal) bribed a number of Members of Parliament, through the intermediary of Baron Jacques de Reinach, a Jewish businessman, whose activities were denounced by the Right. The political antagonism between pro- and anti-clericalists was aggravated by jealousy of the success and growth of Jewish banks; this resentment crystallized in the form of a violent antisemitic movement a few years later, with the Dreyfus Case – all the more virulently as most Jews were also Republicans.

For many years the influence of industrial employers remained extremely weak because of their traditionalist politics, which placed them in the defeated camp. The employers' class was Catholic and conservative; it kept its distance from the Republic which, it is true, had to reckon with the economic force the employers represented, although this force never expressed itself collectively.[2] The steel industry was one of the few organized sectors, thanks to the efforts of the famous Comité des Forges (Iron and Steel Works Committee), which controlled *Le Temps*, the most influential newspaper of the Third Republic.

The early years of the century saw a *rapprochement* between small and medium-scale employers and the Left, through the Republican Committee for Commerce and Industry, better known, after its founder, as the 'Mascuraud Committee'; this organization was designed to raise election campaign funds. The relationship between economic leaders and politicians remained marked by a degree of strain which cleared only after the First World War, with the arrival of a new right-wing generation. New men such as Tardieu and Flandin were attentive to the interests of large employers, and professed Malthusian protectionist doctrines which echoed the industrialists' basic wishes. Apart from pressure for the defence of the status quo and raising election funds, relations between businessmen and political leaders still continued to be rather formal and fragmentary: capitalist circles remained outside the main movements in French political life, which in its turn stayed unaware of the questions that concerned capitalists. This reciprocal ignorance was not substantially modified when the problem broke through the surface in 1936.

The one sector that held the attention of Parliament was agriculture, partly because of the importance of the farming vote,

2. See Chapter 9, Appendix 1.

but also for deeper reasons. The Republican leaders of the 1870s had realized that they could give their Republic solid foundations only by rallying the support of all those who feared the working-class movement: first and foremost, the peasants, whom the Republicans wooed away from their Royalist, Catholic allegiances. This strategy entailed standing still on the social question; the unspectacular way they handled this issue, a course of action rendered easier by the weakness of the anarchist-dominated working-class movement, won the Republicans the loyalty of the lower middle classes and the tolerance of the interest groups. In other words, the Third Republic chose to ignore the problems raised by industrialization[3] in order to pursue its own political ends. It counted on achieving the progressive objectives laid down by its very principles, through the play of political democracy, as the result of the combined development of scientific and industrial progress and the spread of public education, to which it devoted its energies to good effect.

'Pantouflage' and the Defence of the Little Man

While the ideology of public life did not take economic matters into account, public servants themselves maintained a rather ambiguous relationship with the business world; this showed itself most often in the way higher civil servants moved, or were enticed over from the public sector to managerial posts in private industry. This practice, which went by the evocative name of *pantouflage* (from *pantoufles*, carpet-slippers, implying an undemanding, comfortable situation), was very widespread, and can be explained up to a point by the absence of specialized training for businessmen. It is only in the last few years that the

3. The one statesman to give his attention to this question was Waldeck-Rousseau. By pushing through, in 1884, the law recognizing the legal existence of trade unions, then by proposing they should be entitled to acquire and possess property, he hoped that the French working-class movement would be steered along a path similar to the one followed by British trade unions. However, the influence of revolutionary elements channelled it into quite another direction.

Paris Chamber of Commerce's school of advanced business studies, the École des Hautes Études Commerciales (HÉC), has attempted to train managers of the same calibre as higher civil servants. Until then, the administrative and financial management of private business had been carried out either by engineers trained in the *grandes écoles* or by Inspectors of Finance who had decided that industry offered more lucrative openings than State employment. This movement seems to have been checked, largely due to the extension of public and para-public sectors which offer higher civil servants more glowing prospects than does government service proper, without their having to leave State employment. It has already been pointed out that of 1,500 graduates of the ÉNA, less than ten per cent have left public service.

The cruder type of Marxist analysis has laid great stress on the relationships and alliances between captains of industry and top civil servants, taking them as confirmation of the theory that the State serves the interests of capitalist monopolies. There can indeed be no doubt that the upper classes assimilated the members of the *grands corps*, but the significance of the phenomenon is not so straightforward as it may seem. In many ways the State was more dynamic and enjoyed higher status than private management. The fact that the managers themselves were recruited from among former civil servants helped to build up an image of private business as a parasite, which fell back on State help and protection rather than work at winning new markets; it could therefore be said that the movement was caused by the capitalist world's shortcomings as much as by its attractiveness. The civil servants recruited by industry were indifferent, if not downright hostile to the profit motive: this was instilled into them by their early training, and they took these principles with them when they moved to private management – not a situation calculated to produce bold action.

The confluence of this attitude of mind and the political preoccupations we have described provides an explanation of the protectionist tariff devised by Méline: at the end of the nineteenth century a system of customs barriers fenced in French agriculture, and allowed it to survive almost without change until the end of the Second World War.[4] Naturally industry followed suit, and even commerce contrived to obtain protectionist measures for small traders against competition from department and chain stores. However, as these interest groups spent their time negotiating for safeguards, they turned out to be of little use for imposing any positive action policies. When Jean Monnet and Robert Schuman proposed a European Coal and Steel Community, the steel industry, which had always been one of the best-organized sectors of French industry, opposed the project violently – but to no avail, as, despite all the industry's efforts, the plan was ratified by Parliament.

In other words, pressure groups had power only as far as they insisted on the State's responsibility to protect the interests of little men: wine-growers, ex-servicemen, tenants or backyard distillers. Naturally, others followed in their wake, and spokesmen for interests with less sentimental appeal played on the belief that political democracy meant the protection of the traditional way of life and avoidance of the inhuman consequences of capitalism. In this connexion it is not without significance that the revolt of small shopkeepers led by Pierre Poujade in 1955 borrowed some of its battle-cries from the most time-honoured Republican repertory: in the Poujadists' view, liberty and equality were frustrated by the workings of the economy and the State's role was to ensure their peaceful enjoyment of their vested interests, as their ancestors had put it in 1825.

Only the industrial proletariat failed to profit by a system which had been set up without taking the workers into account. As it was, their influence came to be felt only through occasional sudden explosions, as in 1936 with the Popular Front, or in special circumstances as when, just after the Liberation in 1944, they obliged the State to pass general measures which owed much

4. Jules Méline, Conservative Deputy for the Vosges, founded the Order of Agricultural Merit and fostered *rapprochements* between protectionists and farmers, who were worried by American competition; this led in 1892 to the reorganization of the customs system, in order to reserve the home market for national produce.

to the system of adjustment through crises mentioned in connexion with the political model. Normallly matters were dealt with through decisions taken inside the politico-administrative system, which was dominated by the middle classes.

While the Poujadist revolt in 1955 was theoretically sparked off by more efficient tax inspection, it was in reality the consequence of a transformation of the economy which had been fostered deliberately after the Second World War. The policies of modernization and expansion embarked on at that time had brought into question the traditional balance of the politico-administrative system, which was becoming more and more top-heavy. The appearance of Gaullism in 1958 and its consolidation after 1962 seem in this context to have a far greater meaning than the mishaps of decolonization that brought the movement into existence.

Part Three 'Immutable and Changing'

Part Three 'Immutable and Changing'

Changes in French politics since 1958 have been interpreted in two main ways. For one school of thought the Fifth Republic is identified with the power of one man – General de Gaulle – whose accession to power in 1958 fits into the logical sequence of events of the traditional political model. The Algerian war had blocked the parliamentary machinery; the laws of the model were that only a Government crisis could set things going again. However, unlike preceding crises, the 1958 crisis did not stop after the downfall of a Cabinet; instead, the whole regime collapsed. De Gaulle himself had hinted at this outcome in the press conference he gave in July 1955 to announce his temporary retirement from politics after the failure of his RPF party:

In its inmost depths our country is building up new strength. The troubles of the world beat against our shores. While we cannot yet foresee what event will provoke a change of regime, we may be confident that one day the blow will fall.

The traditional French political class has never managed to regain the power it was forced to delegate to the General to deal with the Algerian question, for the new President of the Republic quickly set up a counter-system of his own, which served initially to ensure the ratification of his Algerian policy, but which he later used to have his authority backed directly by the electorate. The revision of the Constitution in October 1962 institutionalized this procedure by legislating that the President should be elected by universal suffrage. Thus the Fifth Republic emerges as the outcome of a process which in the late 1870s had become diverted towards a Deputy-centred Republic; by reversing the process the regime has moved back on to its original lines. While in one way it represents a culminating point, it may also be the start of a new development.

Opinions concerning the future are divided at this stage. According to some, the crisis system will continue to apply but on a larger scale than before, at regime level rather than Government level, and the present regime will disappear with its leader; it will have been no more than a parenthesis – longer than most, admittedly – and the nation will duly return to a parliamentary system which, while modified, will no doubt conform basically to French political traditions. For others, the break has been so sudden and complete, and it has set off reactions so new, that the system is bound to be permanently changed even if the specific legacies of Gaullism are discarded.

While the first interpretation stresses the element of 'upheaval', the second takes its cue from the image of a nation gathering strength 'in its inmost depths'. This second school sees the new regime as the result of the economic and social changes of the last two decades. De Gaulle has liquidated not only the Algerian problem, but also, and above all, the old system; according to the journalist Serge Mallet, he has been responsible for 'the birth of a new political system, corresponding at institutional level to the role of the modern capitalist State'. The traditional parliamentary system had shown itself incapable of guiding economic development because of the built-in preponderance of socially conservative (albeit perhaps politically left-wing) elements, and as a result, through its failure to meet the needs of a new type of society, it was swept aside at the earliest opportunity. In these terms the Fifth Republic marks the end of a regime based on notables and the middle classes, and the rise of most social groups connected with industrial development.

Here again opinion is divided over the future; some foresee the abolition of the Napoleonic State after entry into a vast capitalist market, whereas others predict that this state-model will be strengthened by a closer association between state technocrats and private managers.

We have no intention of making a choice between these two interpretations, as it would be absurd to limit oneself to a single set of explanations in an attempt to assimilate so complex a set of phenomena, especially as these theories stand or fall by the future – over which there are differences of opinion in both camps. It seems more useful to detail the main changes in French society which influence the Government of France; some of these affect economic and demographic structures, while others are more sociological; finally others affect institutions. It should be added that government is not only the product of the country's structure; the problems it faces also contribute much to determining the actual form and method of government adopted.

9 Mutations

The most immediately striking transformations that have affected
France since the Second World War concern the country's economy and the growth of its population. We have already mentioned them several times, but without describing them; they
should now be examined in some detail – as, even though their
influence on the form of government in a given society is less
direct than is sometimes imagined, they are still by no means
without importance. In order to find out how France has
altered over the last twenty years, we would do well to begin with
the most easily observed data: material changes.

Basic Data 1: Economic Growth

Between 1946 and 1964 France's economy showed an unprece-
dented rate of six per cent annually. Never since 1896 had
expansion been so rapid over so long a period. Naturally a
phenomenon of this order is bound to have political implications,
although the conclusions to be drawn are more complex than
conventional thinking generally admits.

Firstly, if we set aside the immediate post-war reconstruction
period, the growth rate of the gross domestic product was 4·9%
between 1951 and 1964. While this is in itself a remarkable figure
it is not far removed from the 1920–29 growth rate of 4·8%; that
period too was characterized by a dramatic rise in exports and
investments, brutally interrupted by the Great Depression. The
generally accepted idea that the growth of the French economy
after 1945 represents a revolution by comparison with the inter-
war period is thus inaccurate but significant: significant because
its exaggeration camouflages the dismay caused by the realization

that the 1929 production level was not reached again until 1938 and only in 1948 did the country return to the 1938 (i.e. 1929) level. In other words, France had made no progress in twenty years, and for the first time in modern history a generation came of age with no greater material resources than its parents had had. The French élites were shaken by these facts, which led to a prolonged change in their attitudes towards economic problems, at the same time provoking harsh judgements on the preceding period. A more rigorous study does not temper the severity of these judgements, but it does state their limits. French failure to expand emerges as a relatively recent phenomenon resulting from the Great Depression; however, the Depression affected the whole world and on the face of it France's case would seem to have been in no way exceptional. In fact the real cause for lack of expansion was the country's inability to make a cool assessment of the situation: until 1936 Governments and élites clung grimly to the irrational hope that the previous state of balance, and in particular the unshakeable nature of the currency, might be preserved. Refusal to devalue the franc was literally stifling the economy until events obliged France to abandon both the gold standard and old rates of exchange. The difficulties from which the parliamentary regime could not disentangle itself were caused by this error of judgement, which was primarily an intellectual one but at the same time reflected a desperate reaction by traditional elements in society, determined to use all means possible to protect its way of life, its values and its organization; although these had been put under great strain by the war, it was thought that they had been saved by the sacrifice of devaluation under Poincaré in 1928. In 1936 the Popular Front expressed the revolt of public opinion faced with a situation which it analysed no better than the conservatives had done. For instance, the Communist Party was furiously hostile to devaluation, which was postponed for as long as possible; moreover devaluation's stimulant effect was largely cancelled out by the Government's restrictive measures. As a result, the country moved without transition from depression into inflation and did not emerge from the vicious circle until 1952–3.

Memories of this period of confusion thus explain the judgement condemning the inter-war period, and erroneously applied to the whole of the Third Republic, which is generally presented as one long period of stagnation. This view is, in fact, totally false. Between 1900 and 1913, industrial production per inhabitant rose by more than fifty per cent, at that time the highest rate in Europe; if we consider the whole of the period from 1896 to the present, it becomes clear that the rapid development following the Second World War could be thought of, in terms of the overall tendency, as catching up on the lag from 1929 to 1945.[1]

The performance of the traditional French system was therefore no worse than that of other organizational models – a conclusion which goes against that which might be drawn from oversimplified arguments. On the other hand, it is true that contemporary changes have increasingly shown the contradiction between the pursuit of expansion and the preservation of the balance set up in the Third Republic.

There again, though, we must be cautious in our judgements, for the arrival of the Fifth Republic has brought no noticeable change in the rate of progress. As might reasonably be thought, the crises of the traditional political model have repercussions on economic growth, but there is no striking correlation between the assertion of the new regime and continuing expansion. It seems, in fact, that the machinery of growth has become relatively independent of institutional structures. It is often claimed, in current polemic debate, that without the Fifth Republic progress would have come to a halt, the Common Market would have been an impossibility, or inflation would have put a brake on the national economy, but these unverifiable assertions leave one sceptical when one remembers that Italy beat all European expansion records under a political regime not particularly different from that of the Fourth Republic in France.

1. Paul Dubois, 'La Croissance en question', in Darras, *Le Partage des bénéfices*, Paris, 1966.

Basic Data 2: The Population Revolution

There is, however, one field in which the contrast between the supposedly static nature of pre-war France and the dynamic expansion of the country since 1945 holds good: population growth. When this is taken into account, it is easier to understand why the country could happily denounce Malthusianism proper, yet apply Malthusian doctrines to the national economy; as Alfred Sauvy[2] pointed out, the two attitudes are closely linked. The atmosphere created by the renewal of economic growth was one of the main factors in the recovery of the national birth-rate after the war.

Between 1896 and 1946, the population of France remained completely static, at forty million. In 1821 the population had been thirty-one million, which shows that low population was no new phenomenon: indeed the tendency certainly pre-dated the Third Republic, which managed to survive with it until the last-minute realization that if steps were not taken the country faced inevitable decline. In 1939 the Government accordingly adopted the essential measures that were to help recovery after 1945, by promulgating the 'Family Code', which included an important innovation: family allowances. It had suddenly been realized, with the approach of war, that the French birth-rate was the lowest in Europe, at 14·9%. In 1946, France climbed to seventh place in Europe, with 20·6% (beating the United Kingdom's 20·2%): a spectacular rise in the birth-rate accompanied the end of the war in most of the nations involved, but the French case was more marked, and above all, the rise continued, profoundly modifying the structure of the population. France is no longer a country of 40,000,000 inhabitants: in 1967 it reached 50,000,000, and will probably reach 60,000,000 in 1985. At the same time, the overall population structure was transformed, as we can see if we compare the distribution of age-groups in 1946 and in 1965.

2. Alfred Sauvy, an economist and a demographer, played a considerable role in creating an awareness of France's decline in the 1930s.

'Immutable and Changing'

	1946	1965
Under 20	29·5%	33·9%
20 to 59	54·5%	48·7%
Over 60	16·0%	17·4%

The numbers of the old and the young have both increased with the higher birth-rate and increased life-expectancy, so that the proportion of intermediate age-groups has gradually decreased. One turning-point was reached in 1965, with the coming-of-age of the immediate post-war bulge generation, but the proportion of elderly people will continue to rise until 1975; it will then begin to decline with the progressive entry into this group of the 'lean years' that correspond to the generations born in 1915–19.

Demographic structure is important for the economy by virtue of the degree to which young people and old depend on adults; it also has psychological and political side-effects, though these are more difficult to evaluate. It is probably not without significance that electors over the age of 65, who represented 15% of the electorate in 1936, topped 19% in 1967, although development is so slow that any prospect of revolutionary change is ruled out. Population changes are essentially long-term, so that their direct impact is negligible from one election to the next, at least by comparison with the influence of other factors.

The Fifth Plan envisages the following increase in population (including immigration) for the 1965–70 period:

TABLE 16.

Age group	Strength in thousands		Percentage of total population	
	1965	1970	1965	1970
Under 20	16,535	16,799	33·9	32·7
20 to 59	23,853	25,205	48·6	49·2
60 and over	8,561	9,286	17·5	18·1
Total	48,949	51,280	100	100

If we limit ourselves to the active population, we see that in the last fifteen years it too has undergone considerable change. The last census published, which dates from 1962, gave the following distribution by occupations:

Agriculture   20·6%
Industry   38·6%
Services (including transport)   40·8%

The active population as a whole had not progressed by comparison with the preceding census in 1954, but the way it broke down by occupations revealed movements which surprised even the statisticians. The agricultural population had shrunk by a quarter, losing 1,300,000 active members. In 1906, almost half the active population was employed in agriculture, and this proportion had declined very slowly, reaching 26·7% in 1954; we can thus appreciate the speed with which the figure dropped over the following eight years. The Plan forecasts that agriculture will employ only 14·5% of the active population in 1970.

Parallel to this, the wage-earning sector increased by 1,360,000 between 1954 and 1962. The division between wage-earners and non-wage-earners was one of the typical traits of traditional French society, and goes far towards explaining some of its political features. In 1954, wage-earners still represented only 64·9% of the active population; in 1962, they had grown to 71·7% and the figure forecast for 1985 is 85%.

Basic Data 3: Migration to Towns

The other important structural change concerns the slow rate of urbanization in modern France. While in Great Britain town-dwellers were in the majority by 1830, a similar situation did not occur in France until a century later. Even then, the development only took place at the price of increasing the imbalance that already existed between Paris and the provinces. Between 1901 and 1936, the population of France grew by 930,000, while the Paris conurbation alone grew by nearly two million. Demographic trends changed after that and the tendency was – relatively at least – slowed down. Between 1936 and 1962 the

'Immutable and Changing'

French population grew by over four and a half millions, but the Paris conurbation only acquired about 1,300,000 new residents. However, the larger cities did not benefit by this change, as migration now tended to be channelled towards medium-sized towns. When countries are classified in order of the percentage of total population living in towns of over 100,000 inhabitants, France figures at the foot of the list, along with Canada and the USSR. It is almost as if the country found some particular difficulty in moving away from the old structure, characterized by the dominance of Paris over the scattered communes, towards a better articulated framework in which the regional metropolis (of which eight have been chosen) would share the prestige and attraction currently monopolized by the capital.

In other terms, the significant change that must be grasped before all else is the noticeable rise in urban population, defined as people living in towns and cities of more than 2,000 inhabitants: the percentage remained stationary at 57% between 1936 and 1946, but rose to 59% in 1954 and 63·3% in 1962, while it is predicted that the 1971 figure will be 67%. The urban population increased by about seven million between 1913 and 1954, and by a further 7,400,000 between 1954 and 1966, i.e. more in twelve years than in the preceding forty. In 1985, out of a total population of 60 million, 44 million (73%) will probably live in towns. At present, then, the shape of the country is undergoing a profound transformation, which is taking place relatively fast by comparison with previous development; this trend should lead to a proportion of town-dwellers identical to that in the neighbouring major industrial countries.

However, the old-established structures put up a surprisingly lively fight against this new tendency. The 38,000 communes still in existence are the heirs to the Old Regime's 44,000 parishes, and reformers are unable to make consolidation acceptable. Plans to amalgamate small communes into larger, more viable administrative units must reckon with opposition based on a wealth of tradition and memories, so that in the three years up to early 1965 only 176 amalgamations involving 376 communes took place. Half-way solutions, like joint local authority boards, are only palliatives. The institutional elements of traditional French society show considerable resilience, which cannot be analysed solely in terms of habit, routine or resistance to progress. The obstinacy with which the smaller communes fight for independent survival, in the face of all reasonable arguments, doubtless expresses an instinctive attachment to a balanced social life which is today threatened without there being a really satisfactory alternative to offer in its place. As if progress was conceded only regretfully, medium-sized towns have shown the greatest growth, while the largest cities have failed to catch the imagination – or, incidentally, to develop the forms of government appropriate to their own administrative needs.

Alongside the survival of dispersed local cells, signs appeared of a contrast between regions caught up in the trend towards modernization and those in which traditional elements survived. At the 1962 census, it was observed that in sixteen *départements* in the west and south of the country, the active population included over 45% employed in agriculture, a percentage comparable to that found in Greece or Spain. Could it be that there are two Frances, which coexist with some degree of harmony, one attached to the past and the other in the throes of modernization?

Two Frances?

The idea of a France composed of two separate countries is often quoted to explain the spectacular contradictions between the two images of the nation: one of them, abundantly described in the early 1950s, is summed up by the French title of Herbert Lüthy's book *À l'heure de son clocher* (literally: In time with the church clock). The other is based on the economic and technical exploits of the 'French miracle', and as both may be backed by observation, it is tempting to try to interpret this dualism in terms of a conflict between old and new. Political commentators have seized on this as an opportunity to rationalize clashes, in particular between Gaullists and anti-Gaullists, in terms of objective social and economic factors. For instance, just after the 1965 presidential elections, the theme of two French nations was put to polemic use by the Gaullists, who claimed to be the voice of modern France. But however attractive the simplicity of this version may appear, neither geographical nor sociological facts provide any confirmation.

It is amusing to note that the same characteristics used to explain away the backwardness of traditional France were duly pressed into service to explain the country's transformation. The authors of the already quoted (p. 224) *Le Partage des bénéfices* point ironically to the fact that American studies attached primary importance to the supremacy of the authoritarian technocrat, who was generally a graduate of the Polytechnique, imbued with a prudence and a lack of energy derived from the Napoleonic model, a hierarchical system which discouraged initiative by sharply defining the personal responsibility of each agent. Later observers were struck by the extent of change, in which the same polytechnicians, previously held responsible for national stagnation, have opportunely become 'the heirs of the Saint-Simonians, committed to progress and economic rationality . . .'.

It is, to say the least, difficult to equate realities as ambiguous as these with conflicts defined in regional terms, any more than with a new class struggle, or even with the competition between two forms of social organization, despite the fact that all these elements indisputably come into play. However, none of them on its own provides the key to the problem. One must therefore make a choice, without abandoning the attempt to clarify the pressures at present bearing on the traditional model. We can quote two examples: the current transformation of the education system, and the arguments surrounding the traditional role of the State; these should help us to see the nature of the challenges this model must face.

The challenge shows itself in two ways – in terms both of quality and of quantity – where education is concerned. The sheer scale of the change that has taken place since the end of the Second World War has led to doubts about the general efficiency of a system based on the selection of élites, and consequently the basis of traditional society is brought under scrutiny. The competitive examination system severely limited recruitment, in accordance with the principles of a static society. There was little promotion as such, but rather élites were successively creamed off, as in this connexion equality was interpreted in a restrictive sense: the most gifted could, in theory, reach the highest positions, while the rest were guaranteed the minimum education necessary to the ordinary citizen. The Third Republic had committed itself to realize this aim, and we may say that it had largely succeeded by 1914. The modifications that should then have followed in order to ensure the gradual improvement of this minimum turned out to be very inadequate, despite attempts at increasing the length and accessibility of education, by Édouard Herriot in the 1920s, then by Jean Zay,[3] whose ideas are still the inspiration of reformers. But when it moved beyond primary to secondary education the reform met with resistance, exacerbated by the fact that the spread of education was shaking one of the pillars of the existing social order, by attempting to open up what had until then been a jealously guarded cultural preserve.

The growth of secondary education continued in a rather haphazard way, contrasting with the deliberately planned primary education system organized at the end of the nineteenth century. The trend to raise the school-leaving age beyond fourteen began slowly and then gained in numbers and momentum, to judge from the following figures, which give the percentage of each age-group receiving full-time education.

Age group	1953	1963
14–15 year-olds	56%	72%
15–16	39%	57%
16–17	30%	49%
17–18	19%	35%

3. Édouard Herriot and Jean Zay tried to bridge the gap separating primary education, which was proletarian in character, from secondary education, the preserve of the middle classes. Jean Zay, a Deputy of the Radical left wing, was Minister of Education from June 1936 to March 1940; he raised the school-leaving age to fourteen and placed *lycée* primary classes under the auspices of the primary system, as a move to end the segregation of teaching staff. He was arrested and murdered in 1942 by French collaborators.

'Immutable and Changing'

In 1900, approximately 2% of the corresponding age groups (16–18 year-old) held a school-leaving certificate at *baccalauréat* level; in 1960 the figure was 11·5%, and it is forecast that it will reach 23·5% by 1970. Moreover, the movement was accelerated by the post-war 'bulge' which overloaded the Ministry's organization to the point of collapse. In 1900 there were barely 100,000 pupils receiving secondary education in public establishments (*lycées* and *collèges*); there were about 150,000 in 1920 and 250,000 in 1940. Today there are over a million. The corresponding figures for private, usually religious, establishments are less than 200,000 in 1940, as against 400,000 in 1965. The conflict between public and private education, a hangover from the secularist quarrels of the beginning of the century, further complicated the problem by making education a political issue, with the supporters of public education in a defensive position. They themselves were divided into reformist and orthodox camps, the latter attached to a middle-class view of secondary education with the *baccalauréat* as its culmination and symbol. As more and more people came to hold this diploma, the *baccalauréat* lost its old social and cultural meaning, without acquiring a new value; about 5,700 candidates passed in 1900, just over 10,000 in 1920, and 27,000 in 1939 – a fairly slow increase. In 1955, there were still only 40,000 passes (out of 60,000 candidates) but the figure reached 105,000 in 1966 (out of 212,000 candidates). This spectacular rise explains the deep-seated malaise from which the Ministry of Education has yet to recover.

Similar observations may be made concerning higher education, which had reached less than 30,000 students in 1900, and just over double that figure in 1939; but in 1967 514,000 students were registered at universities. The forecast for 1972 is close on 800,000 students.

This phenomenon, in itself normal and healthy, cannot be thought of as a mere speeding-up of an existing trend, under the influence of the spontaneous spread of culture and population growth, for it puts massive, lasting pressure on the structure of society, in which balance had until then depended on slow progress. A new, more dynamic equilibrium must be found, one in

232

which the old selection machinery is replaced by collective advance; the values of a stratified society will have to be adapted to the conditions of a mass civilization which refuses to fit into the traditional moulds.

An Opening on the World

This internal pressure corresponds, in a way, to an opening towards the outside world, manifested symbolically by membership of the Common Market, which was founded in 1958 and ten years later had abolished all restrictions between member countries. The most obvious consequences of this free-trade policy can be seen in foreign trade figures: the annual growth rate (in volume) of imports rose from 6·4% in the 1952–8 period to 8·8% in the 1959–65 period. France's entry into the world of international competition implies a rethinking of the role of the State in a closed society, and also of the initiatory role played by the State since the end of the Second World War.

After 1945 the State proceeded to reappraise its economic ideas. The system of legalistic and technical management which had been applied until then had welcomed progress without measuring it against the criteria of profit and competition that characterize capitalism. We could say, with only slight exaggeration, that traditional France appreciated technical innovations in much the same way the Chinese used their own invention, gunpowder – for fireworks. For instance, the spread of the railways was sponsored and financed by the State, which in this way enabled even the most isolated rural communities to benefit from this new means of transport. A slow method of communications was replaced by a faster one, which made life more pleasant but which often entailed financial burdens that were not met by revenue.

Similar observations could be made concerning other public services, like the postal system. Basically, there was a hangover from the psychology of conspicuous consumption, which had been the prerogative of the upper classes under the monarchy, and which the Republic was able to bring within the reach of the entire population. After the Second World War the demands of reconstruction entailed restrictions, and obliged the State to supervise and guide collective development. At that time the main preoccupations were of an economic order, but only within the relatively limited context of the nation: private activity followed the lead of the Plan and was carried along by the dynamic example of the public sector.

From now on the nation is entering a new phase. Initiative is becoming more outward-directed and the centres of activity are tending to move outside the country, so that the State will ultimately lose its monopoly of decision-making. Moreover it is deprived by the regulations of the Common Market (prohibition of subsidies and the principle of non-discrimination) of some of its economic tools. The Fifth Plan has already attempted to prepare a strategy corresponding to this new situation,[4] but the decentralization of key decisions towards which it is moving does not only imply a readjustment of the tools at the disposal of the Government; it also presupposes a strengthening of economic structures in the private sector. Industry will find itself dealing with foreign customers, suppliers and competitors, and the State will be unable to interpose its protection, so that the firms will have to take on the independent responsibility that has thus far been dealt with by the central government.

The significance of the privately owned firm, which had become rather devalued as a result of a general indifference to the values of capitalism, as well as the importance of the public sector, will probably make a comeback; indeed, the first signs of this new mood are already showing. The influence of a wide market dominated by competition will force existing élites to make a place on the status ladder for men who devote themselves to profit and commercial ventures. Paradoxically, these values are only half-heartedly recognized by employers themselves, who hesitate between moralistic, slightly shame-faced justifications (there is a vast literature on the social responsibility of the factory-owner), and the outdated recriminations of liberals nostalgic for the days of *laisser faire* and *laisser aller*. In the few cases

4. Jean-Jacques Bonnaud, *Le Ve Plan, une stratégie de l'expansion*, Paris, 1967.

where the conditions of modern economic life are accepted without reservations for what they are, this appears to be the choice made by strong personalities, rather than a characteristic expression of the psychology of industrial employers, who on the whole have tended to remain dependent on the State, which is expected to provide subsidies and guarantees, on condition the beneficiaries may occasionally declare a quasi-religious fervour for Manchester-style capitalism. For instance, in January 1965 the Comité National du Patronat Français published a kind of manifesto in which, alluding to 'natural economic laws', they affirmed the need to limit the role of the State, which they accused of 'progressive incursions' into the employers' prerogatives, and claimed undivided authority for the employer.

This manifesto did provoke considerable surprise in most milieux, including managerial circles – in itself a significant fact. Firstly, while the French employers implicitly professed most of the theses propounded in their name, they were not used to taking sensational stands. From experience, they knew how suspicious public opinion can be of anything emanating from captains of industry, and consequently tended to avoid publicizing their actions. Furthermore, the allusion to 'natural laws' of economics seemed as incongruous as a bishop standing up to defend divine order in political matters. Incompetence was aggravated by stupidity: it was common knowledge that State intervention had been crucial in post-war recovery and development. Ideas in this context have changed so markedly in the last decade that the controversy between liberals and *dirigistes*, a burning issue a few years ago, no longer arouses the slightest reaction.

The competence of employers is thus much questioned; at the same time it is essential for the nation that the idea of business should be taken more seriously. However, although the State is able to – and does – put considerable pressure on industrial structures to foster concentration and modernization, it cannot take the place of private directors, nor conjure up a new generation of tough and dynamic managers.

In other words, present conditions demand that active, well-

235

organized intermediaries should themselves take charge of tasks originally dealt with by the State. This is true not only for employers, but also for trade-unionists.[5] It is essential that there be discussions between social partners capable of resolving between themselves the problems attendant on adapting the economy to outside competition, a situation which leads to unemployment problems and redeployment of labour. Because of the importance of State intervention, labour relations have remained rudimentary. Trade-unionists have regularly called on the State to impose by law the improvements which employers refused to negotiate, a fact which explains why collective bargaining plays only a marginal part in the solution of social conflicts.

Higher management as a whole has remained attached to an outmoded conception of authority, sometimes known as 'divine-right management', as we see from the manifesto issued by the Comité National du Patronat Français; consequently managers and employers have never really come to accept trade unions as possible partners in discussion. It is true, admittedly, that the working-class movement suffers from weaknesses due to its own division, and tends to prefer anti-capitalist declarations to concrete negotiations; its more tangible efforts are hampered by the persistence of a polemical and ineffectual anarcho-syndicalist tradition. The ideological character of the French working-class movement, which has often been contrasted with English pragmatism, did not deter leaders from cooperating in relative trust with the experts working on the Plan; it may even have been because of a distaste for corporate activity that the movement did not oppose productivity drives with the customary resistance and restrictive practices applied elsewhere by the craft unions.

The integration into the system of a strengthened, modernized trade-union movement seems essential for the balance which is at present being achieved, if only because of the relative weakening (or rather, the increased self-effacement) of the State. In the last few years there have been attempts at modernization, the most successful of which was the transformation of the French Confederation of Christian Workers (CFTC) into the French

5. In this connexion, see Appendix 1 to this chapter.

Democratic Labour Confederation (CFDT); the CFTC (Confédération Française des Travailleurs Chrétiens), which was not influenced by the revolutionary tradition, thus moved away from its original Catholic inspiration and today groups together the most responsible, best-trained working-class militants. But division persists, even among the non-Communist unions, which are proving extremely difficult to amalgamate.

In this connexion, there is a striking time-lag between trade unions and political life, which explains the minimal results so far shown by the simplification of the party system and the regrouping of the Left. The hostility between Communists and non-Communists, which was overcome on the electoral level, remains far stronger in the trade-union movement, particularly within Force Ouvrière, a breakaway movement of the Confédération Générale du Travail, which is still far more opposed to the latter than is the Confédération Française Démocratique du Travail.

Here again, the State is unable to take the place of inadequate interest groups, especially as trade unionism is essentially an opposition movement, and it would hardly be in the Government's interests to back up its own adversaries. The problem would still remain, however, even if political power were to change hands and it must therefore be borne in mind as an element in serious need of adaptation.

The Perplexed Intelligentsia

The pressures straining the French model have not spared the 'intellectuals' – by which we mean the body of writers, journalists and academics who have played a major role in the country's political life. These people have always tended to act as a group, and their influence fostered certain characteristics of French political life, for instance, the tendency to give debates a radical turn. In the context of society as a whole this group functioned like a selective magnifying glass, bringing political conflicts into the public eye, but in a filtered, artificial and sophisticated form.

Intellectuals gained their modern status once the Republic was finally established and left-wing ideas prevailed in the circles of power. The intellectuals then moved over into opposition, perhaps because of the characteristic tendencies towards equilibrium already noted in the relationship between Paris and the provinces. However, the opposition they put up varied according to whether, with Barrès and Maurras, they were rediscovering the charms of traditionalism and the value of bygone years, or simply dissociating themselves from the abuses of power, even if it were held by friends. With the Dreyfus Case, they realized, to use the words of Charles Péguy,[6] how the 'mystique', the disinterested commitment to truth and justice, could become degraded into 'politics', manipulation and exploitation. It was at this time that the term 'intellectuals' began to appear, used pejoratively to refer to the writers – Émile Zola among them – and academics who campaigned for the rehabilitation of Captain Dreyfus. At the same time the intellectuals acquired a position comparable to that held by churchmen under the Old Regime; their critical and moral functions made them the guardians of the principles which society revered, whether observing them in everyday life or not. Their potential authority was not due only to the fame surrounding some of their members, but rather expressed the respect in which literature and science were generally held.

After the Dreyfus Case, French intellectuals often intervened in political life. Their most effective action undoubtedly came after the riots of 6 February 1934, when they created an 'Anti-Fascist Vigilante Committee', which was to grow into the Popular Front. There were originally three men behind this committee: the radical philosopher Alain, the socialist physicist Paul Langevin and the ethnologist and Communist sympathizer Paul Rivet. Paul Langevin himself presided over the meeting on 8 June 1935 at which the left-wing parties decided to band together as the Rassemblement Populaire.

Consequently French intellectuals formed an avant-garde which often decisively influenced the behaviour of the Left. Despite divergences, they subscribed to the same set of convictions acknowledged by left-wing opinion in general. It is true that

6. A Catholic poet with a wide following, he was killed in action in the first days of the First World War.

the Soviet Revolution provoked a split in so far as October 1917 began to compete with 14 July 1789 as the starting-point in the liberation of mankind; the struggle against Fascism masked this schism, but it still marked the beginnings of a kind of moral exile for the intelligentsia; this was to show itself fully in the post-war period, when the intellectuals were withdrawing, not only from society, but also from their own left-wing parties, Communists included. Sartre's stormy relations with the Communist Party and the short-lived experiment of the 'RDR' (Rassemblement Démocratique Révolutionnaire) which he founded in 1947, formalized the total divorce between the intellectual leaders and organized politics. The intellectuals accused politicians of cowardice as well as opportunism in handling the colonial wars which were then beginning. The disillusionments of the Cold War exacerbated their scorn for political compromises and spurred them to even greater intransigence.

The ensuing years saw the emergence of a dialectical relationship between the giddy esoteric arguments of the intellectuals, who applied themselves heart and soul to rationalizing the Left's defeats, and the idea-free pragmatism practised by the politicians. The disclosure of Stalin's atrocities, Soviet action in Hungary and the embourgeoisement of the Khrushchev period finally stripped the intellectuals of their last vestiges of certainty, and they set about searching for replacement myths. For a time they thought that a new incarnation of the Revolution had presented itself in the form of the colonial liberation movements. They expected denunciation of the atrocities committed in Algeria to spark off a new Dreyfus controversy,[7] but the '121 Manifesto' in 1961, which justified refusal of conscription, met with general apathy. At the same time it became clear that the leaders of the Third World had problems of their own and were not prepared to wait for their old

7. A special place should be set aside for Catholic intellectuals like Mauriac, Pierre-Henri Simon, or the teams of the magazine *Esprit* or the weekly *Témoignage Chrétien*. Their indignation and concern over the Algerian war and the methods used by the French in Algeria reflected genuine moral uneasiness; but there was nothing in common between them and the revolutionary hopes of Marxist intellectuals. (The Communist Party kept remarkably quiet all through this development.)

Parisian masters to tell them the solutions. 'We have no longer anything to say to the young,' said Sartre, adding, 'It is degrading to have lived fifty years in the backward province that France has become.'[8]

The foreign policy of General de Gaulle finally broke the ranks of the intellectuals, who were inclined to interpret world events as a struggle between forces 'moving with the tide of history' and the retrograde powers of capitalism and imperialism. For them, any left-wing success in France must go hand in hand with the defeat of the Western bloc, symbolized by its leading member, the United States. While they abhorred Gaullist tactics on the national level, they found themselves led, through the varieties of anti-Americanism, to take a line similar to the General's on the international plane. The contradiction thus created was intolerable.

Sartre was right. Intellectuals have nothing more to tell the young. They predicted economic failure in the West and the gradual running-down of European impetus, and the last few years have given proof of the opposite. They are caught unprepared by the serious and difficult questions raised by the development of scientific societies. After having surrendered to the head-turning attraction of ideologies, they have suddenly realized that they have no ideas for their own times. In the last ten years, the only stimulating new ideas have been launched by top technicians like François Bloch-Lainé or Pierre Massé, or by nonconformists like Bertrand de Jouvenel or Raymond Aron, whose disturbing questions contrast with the peremptory chatter of the intellectuals; as a result, the latter have fallen silent.

In this contest the astonishing vogue for structuralism and the popularity of ethnology take on their real significance as an anti-historical about-turn; intellectuals have turned aside from politics for other research.[9] Admittedly they still occupy a respected position in society. When General de Gaulle wrote to Sartre to tell him that the Russell Tribunal would not be allowed to sit in

8. Foreword to the reprint of Paul Nizan, *Aden Arabie*, Paris, 1960.
9. François Furet, 'Les Intellectuels français et le structuralisme', *Preuves*, February 1967; English version in *Survey*, January 1967.

Paris, he began his letter, '*Mon cher Maître . . .*'. The presence of André Malraux in the Government fosters the illusion of a Republic well disposed towards arts and letters. But intellectuals are now no more than frills on public life. Political leaders once wooed or cursed them, but now pay them scarcely any attention. At most, the Communist Party keeps a decorative role for Louis Aragon and, for the purposes of public relations, tolerates the esoteric research of Althusser in his attempts to reconcile Marxism and structuralism.

French political life has become an intellectual desert. The times are gone when intellectuals took part in politics; this fact is in itself significant of a change which is probably worth remembering in order to understand French electoral behaviour, which we now have to analyse.

Appendix 1 Economic Organizations, Trade Unions and Pressure Groups

Economic and social organizations reveal characteristics very similar to those of political parties.

Like political parties, they are divided, generally without much authority over their members, and with scanty means at their disposal. They also find considerable difficulty in defining their exact position and their acknowledged role in society. Their relations with the political world give signs of a malaise that indicates the uncomplimentary overtones attached to the idea of 'pressure groups', and also of the low esteem in which politics are held in these circles.

Employers

There was no national organization of employers until Clémentel (Ministry of Industry and Trade) encouraged the foundation, in 1919, of the Confédération Générale de la Production Française.

This body was dissolved in 1940, and it was not reconstituted in 1944. Employers were then very unpopular because of their lack of participation in the Resistance, and at the end of 1945 they formed a new organization, the CNPF (Conseil National du Patronat Français); M. Georges Villiers, who had been deported to Dachau during the war, served as president until June 1966, when he was succeeded by M. Paul Huvelin.

The CNPF is a flexible organization, gathering together about 3,000 groups and federations, and representing both industry and commerce. It functions in both the economic and the social fields, and covers a rather heterogeneous range of bodies, as it takes in organizations representing powerful industries (e.g. the Union of the Metal and Mining Industries, the Union of Chemical Industries, the National Building Federation and the Union of Textile Industries) as well as hordes of small industries represented by the General Confederation of Small and Medium Enterprises (CGPME), whose Secretary-General, M. Gingembre, claims 700,000 member firms.

Declared interests and methods of action naturally differ greatly according to the members: the CGPME are inclined to show suspicion of their larger brothers and 'trusts'. They issue frequent, vociferous declarations, contrasting in this with the reserve of the Conseil National du Patronat Français. They were precursors of the movement of agitation led by Pierre Poujade, who in 1955 founded the Union for the Defence of Shopkeepers and Artisans, which won 52 seats in Parliament (since then the Union pour la Défense des Commerçants et des Artisans has been somnolent, and Poujade himself went over to Gaullism in 1966).

Particular mention should be made of the Centre of Young Employers; at its foundation in 1938 it was basically a Catholic organization, but during the fifties it moved towards a progressive position. The Young Employers, favouring the idea of a pluralist economy and a measure of planning (largely due to the efforts of José Bidegain who was their president from 1961 to 1964), command an audience out of all proportion to their small membership (3,650 in 1965). Until 1965 they were represented in the Conseil National du Patronat Français, but the CNPF then adopted a tougher attitude and preached a more aggressive orthodox liberalism. This change in the CNPF's policy reflected the increase in competition within the Common Market and the difficulties firms had to face with the 'Stabilization Plan' issued by the Government in 1963.

To sum up the political role of employers, it is necessary to distinguish between collective action cordinated by the CNPF and moves initiated by its various branches.

(i) As has been said, the Conseil National du Patronat Français aims at avoiding publicity. With the exception of the first years of the Third Republic, when a few bankers and industrialists sat in Parliament, employers have seldom been candidates in elections: in March 1967, only 157 employers or company directors stood; about fifty of them were elected; moreover, some were politicians who had moved over to private business, rather than the reverse. The CNPF therefore intervenes firstly with a view to ensuring the sympathy of future Deputies by distributing electoral subsidies. This financial assistance seems to benefit all parties except the Communists. Sometimes one party is more favoured than the other: Henry W. Ehrmann points out that by abandoning the Gaullists for M. Pinay's Independents the employers hastened the decline of the Rassemblement du Peuple Français after 1952.[1] According to unverifiable sources, the same fate overtook M. Lecanuet's Democratic Centre in 1966.

The CNPF's actions can for the most part be thought of as public relations; it subsidizes various publications and, under the Fourth Republic, often appeared to be particularly anxious to make sure that it had friends in Parliament, whatever their political affiliations. This type of infiltration at individual level was made easier by the weak structure of French parties.

(ii) More direct action usually emanated from specialized organizations, which often made their presence insistently felt during electoral campaigns. (To the Small and Medium Enterprises (CGPME) already mentioned should be added road transport, the distilling industry, shipbuilding and naval dockyards.) At parliamentary level, they put pressure on committees by distributing slanted documentation, or by more direct approaches, and generally tended to try to counter Government action rather than fight for the adoption of new legislation.

The changes introduced by the Fifth Republic have modified the nature of interest group activity; the tendency is now to disregard Parliament, and aim rather at influencing the Administration, and since they now operate directly on the Ministries, lobbies have become far less visible. Pressure on individual Deputies becomes less important than well-timed lunch-parties

1. H. W. Ehrmann, *Organized Business in France*, Princeton, 1957.

in this new type of strategy, based on personal contacts. Lastly, new bodies have appeared on the scene (the electronics and nuclear industries) while others (e.g. the Small and Medium Enterprises) are phasing out, and yet others (road transport, public works and construction) are adapting themselves to the new situation.

As for the Conseil National du Patronat Français itself, it has maintained good, though not particularly warm relations with the Fifth Republic. The employers are politically embarrassed, as they are becoming thoroughly tired of Gaullism, and find increasing difficulty in formulating an economic doctrine capable of satisfying both their avant-garde and the mass of their members. It keeps to a position of discretion and reserve, and since the incident of the January 1965 neo-liberal manifesto it has limited itself to 'technical' pronouncements.

Working-class Trade Unions

When the Confédération Générale du Travail (General Confederation of Labour) was constituted in 1895, there were about 400,000 union members; just before the First World War, membership had risen to over a million.

At the 1906 Conference, the Confédération Générale du Travail adopted a resolution known as the Amiens Charter, which declared that confederated organizations had no right, as trade unions, to have anything to do with political parties. The CGT looked to the Revolution to destroy the State apparatus, and refused to have any part in dealings with Parliament. The Amiens Charter thus shows an attitude based on anarchy and hostile to organized politics, rather than a truly apolitical position.

Later, the working-class movement underwent several splits. In 1921 a schism occurred similar to the one that had divided the Socialist party at Tours in the preceding year, but this time the dissident minority was composed of Communists and their sympathizers, who founded a separate organization. The alliance between the parties of the Left in 1936 led to a reunification which lasted until 1939; in the interests of the Resistance, a second reconciliation was arranged in 1943, but did not last beyond 1947. Thus, despite the principles of the Amiens Charter, political events have directly influenced the trade-union movement, and it could be said that the relationships between working-class organizations are parallel to those between left-wing parties.

The Confédération Générale du Travail

Since the 1947 split, when Communists were in the majority, the CGT has been controlled by the Communist Party. Its Secretary-General, M. Benoît Frachon, followed in 1967 by M. Georges Séguy, is also a member of the Communist Party politburo. It follows the Party line and takes part in its campaigns, though occasionally with reservations (e.g. when Soviet forces invaded Hungary in 1956). It also admits the existence of a minority which expresses its points of view in CGT congresses.

The Confédération Générale du Travail – Force Ouvrière

After the 1947 split, the non-Communist minority founded the CGT–Force Ouvrière in April 1948. While this movement is fairly close to the Socialist Party (its Secretary-General since 1963, M. André Bergeron belongs to the Socialist party), Force Ouvrière takes pains to stress its independence, and its links with the Socialist Party could not be compared even remotely with those between the CGT and the Communists. This organization has never really recovered from the original schism, and is character-ized by a pronounced anti-Communist line. It is particularly strong among civil servants and employees of the nationalized industries, with about 600,000 declared members in 1966.

The Confédération Française Démocratique du Travail

Alongside the traditional working-class trade-unionism incar-nated by the CGT, there has also, since 1919, been a Catholic-inspired organization which recruits its membership mainly among white-collar workers: the Confédération Française des Travailleurs Chrétiens. During the war, several of its leaders and militants were associated with the Christian Democrats, which gave birth to the Mouvement Républicain Populaire in 1944, but after 1946 the CFTC made sure its independence was clearly recognized.

In 1947 the Confédération Française des Travailleurs Chrétiens adopted a similar attitude towards the Church. This development can be explained by increased working-class recruitment, which has transformed the old, rather paternalistic white-collar organization into something more along the lines of a modern trade union. The climax of this tendency was the victory of the movement's left wing (the 'Reconstruction' movement) and the election in 1961 of M. Eugène Descamps, a former leader of the metal-workers' trade union, as Secretary-General. In 1964 the CFTC became completely secular when it was transformed in the Confédération Française Démocratique du Travail.

However, a minority refused to accept this move and formed an organization which remains attached to the religious element of the old movement; it is said to number about 80,000 members.

Since then the CFDT has pursued a boldly trade-unionist policy, not hesitating to cooperate with the Confédération Générale du Travail; despite the schism, its membership is slightly higher than that of Force Ouvrière.

Lastly, there are some independent unions, such as the Fédération de l'Éducation Nationale, which was not affected by the 1947 split (400,000 members), and the Confédération Générale des Cadres (CGC), which exists as a group mainly to defend the interests of executives (about 200,000 members).

The French trade-union movement appears numerically weak by comparison with movements in neighbouring countries: it is suggested that between twenty and twenty-five per cent of all wage-earners are union members.[2] The movement is deeply divided into rival organizations, which continue to suffer from the repercussions of political conflicts. Attempts at reunification

2. Jean-Daniel Reynaud, *Les Syndicats en France*, Paris, 1963.

are fraught with insuperable antagonisms, firstly because of the Communist control of the Confédération Générale du Travail, and also, where non-Communist unions are concerned, because of their attachment to other traditions: the mutual distrust of secularists and clericalists can be seen among the leaders of Force Ouvrière, even after the Confédération Française Démocratique du Travail became secularized. Apart from this, the CFDT has embarked on original research concerning the democratic or political planning of wage-levels, and this is being watched suspiciously by the Movement's possible partners.

In the 1963–5 period, attempts at forming pacts between political parties and trade unions on the occasion of the Presidential elections came to nothing because of differences of traditions. This particular aspect of the situation does not seem to have improved since 1965.

Agricultural Organizations

Before the Second World War, agricultural organizations were dominated by two main ideological tendencies: one was basically conservative, and was reflected in particular in the Chambers of Agriculture (*département* bodies grouping agricultural interests, on the lines of Chambers of Commerce for employers and Chambers of Trade for artisans) and in associations like the Société des Agriculteurs de France (SAF).

The other movement was a radical, secular movement, based particularly on the institutions specializing in agricultural loans, mutual-aid schemes and cooperation. Lastly there were a few groups oriented towards direct action, such as the extreme right-wing 'greenshirts' led by Henri Dorgères.

In 1940 the Vichy regime instituted a compulsory organization, the Peasant Corporation; traces of this experiment, which left its mark on most professional leaders, can still be seen, although the institution was swept aside after the Liberation, when the Socialist Minister of Agriculture, M. Tanguy-Prigent, encouraged the foundation of the Confédération Générale de l'Agriculture (CGA) which grouped together trade unions as such

– the Fédération Nationale des Syndicats d'Exploitants Agricoles (FNSEA) – and loan, aid and cooperative organizations.

The Socialist-led Confédération Générale de l'Agriculture lost its authority as the FNSEA gradually stabilized its independence. In 1949, M. Blondelle, who had been a member of Pétain's National Council (the Vichy regime's consultative chamber), became President of the FNSEA, and by 1953 the CGA had become no more than a liaison organ. This division accentuated the opposition between Socialists and the Right, and a Socialist agricultural leader, Roland Viel, launched what was to become the Guéret Committee (a group comprising the agricultural organizations of seventeen *départements* in central France), although remaining within the Fédération Nationale des Syndicats d'Exploitants Agricoles.

This political rivalry camouflaged an opposition of interests between the large farmers of the Paris area (wheat and sugarbeet), who had taken over the control of the FNSEA, and the small farmers of the centre and south.

Alongside this political and professional rivalry, a conflict between generations made its appearance after 1954, with the emergence of the Young Farmers' Movement (in some ways analogous to the Young Employers).

The teams of the Centre National des Jeunes Agriculteurs (CNJA), led by M. Michel Debâtisse, had been trained by a Catholic educational movement, Jeunesse Agricole Chrétienne; the CNJA defended modernist ideas which were opposed to their elders' conservatism. In particular, the CNJA came out in favour of structural reforms, whereas traditionalist leaders were worried only about defending price levels; conservative demands were voiced through organizations specializing in particular types of produce (vine and wine-growers, cereals, beet-growers, meat and dairy products, etc.). As these leaders were linked to the Fourth Republic's parties and their specialized organizations played an active part as parliamentary pressure groups, they distrusted Gaullism. Consequently, the Government was more disposed to listen to the young farmers and to encourage their influence, which ran along the same lines as Government policy.

'Immutable and Changing'

As they grew older, the Young Farmers' representatives entered
the directing bodies of the Fédération Nationale des Syndicats
d'Exploitants Agricoles, of which M. Debâtisse was elected
Secretary-General Adjoint in 1964. Their ideas gained in popularity, but the presidency and control of the FNSEA have been
retained by the large farmers of the Paris region. M. de Caffarelli,
elected in 1963, sums up in himself the two processes of rejuvenation and regional domination. The abyss that separates small and
large farmers had become deeper with time, since after a period
of violent agitation, the large operators have tried to tidy up their
relations with the Government, while the small men oppose this
collaboration.

Politics became involved in agriculture again when the Communist Party contrived the foundation of the Mouvement de Défense des Exploitations Familiales (MODEF) to protest against
the concessions granted to the FNSEA and use this issue as a
basis for agitation. The MODEF acquired a large audience because of its systematic defence of small farms doomed by
economic developments. Since the demise of Parliament in 1958,
direct-action movements, which had first appeared at the end of
the Fourth Republic, have sprung up sporadically in declining
areas or in regions, such as Brittany, which are going through
difficult times. The present tendency is therefore towards the
division of the industry into two geographical groups which
correspond to two different economic situations and, but less
consistently, two political attitudes.

Appendix 2 The Official Representation of Interests

Professional trade-union organizations are associations subject to private law, and the State is not concerned with their creation or functioning. There is also, however, an institutionally organized system of interest representation, which was envisaged at first on the local scale and, since 1924, at national level.

(i) *Chambers of Commerce, Trade and Agriculture*

The first professional institutions, in the form we know today, were the *Chambers of Commerce*. Their organization dates from 1898, but it has been modified since, and in 1960 the title became *Chambers of Commerce and Industry*.

These Chambers are semi-public institutions, whose members are elected by the tradesmen, industrialists and firms of the town or region. There is at least one of these Chambers in each *département*, but there may be more (there were 155 in 1965). Chambers of Commerce have a threefold mission:

1. They are consultative, and keep the Government informed of professional problems.
2. They are representative bodies, the official expression of commercial and industrial activity *vis-à-vis* the administration.
3. They are administrative organizations, entrusted with various functions, particularly with the management of some public services, such as warehouses and docks, and also of certain educational institutions, e.g. the École des Hautes Études Commerciales (HÉC), which was founded in 1881 by the Paris Chamber of Commerce.

'Immutable and Changing'

Chambers of Agriculture were first created in 1924, along the same lines as Chambers of Commerce, but with more limited powers, so as to provide the administration with 'consultative and professional organizations representing the agricultural interests of their region'. They too are distributed so that there is at least one in each *département*.

Chambers of Trades were instituted in 1925 to provide artisans with representation. They have a consultative role, and have a certain importance in the field of vocational training.

(ii) *The Social and Economic Council*

The first attempts to set up a national organ to represent socio-economic groups date from 1924; after changes in 1936, 1948 and 1958, the need was finally met by the Social and Economic Council. This body must be consulted over any proposed economic plan or other legislative proposal which has economic implications. Optionally, it may be consulted over drafts which the Government sees fit to send to it, except that taxation and finance Bills are excluded from its competence.

The desire to represent all socio-professional categories resulted in the Social and Economic Council having a rather disparate character. It comprises:

> 45 representatives of workers, employees, civil servants, technicians, engineers and executives designated by the main trade-union organizations (CGT, CGT–FO, CFDT, CFTC, CGC, FÉN and independent unions);
> 41 representatives of industrial, commercial and craft firms, among which are 16 representatives of private industrial firms, 6 representatives from nationalized industries, 9 representatives from commercial firms and 10 representatives of artisans. All these are designated by trade unions or organizations, except that those from the nationalized industries are chosen by the boards of these bodies.
> 40 representatives selected by the most important agricultural organizations, 8 nominated by Chambers of Agriculture, 12 by the FNSEA, etc.;

15 persons with qualifications in the economic, social, scientific or cultural fields, appointed by the Government;

15 representatives of social activities, 8 chosen by family associations, 2 by consumer cooperatives, and the five others by the Government (housing, savings, health, etc.);

7 representatives from miscellaneous activities (tourist trade, exports, regional economy, etc.) mostly appointed by the Government;

2 representatives of the middle classes, selected by the Middle Class Liaison Committee;

25 persons qualified by their knowledge of the economic and social problems of overseas France and the franc area and 10 representatives of the social and economic activity of overseas territories and departments. The last two categories are nominated by the Government.

Apart from these members, a number of experts chosen because of personal qualifications are appointed by the Government.

Hardly anyone has been left out. . . . But the spectacularly mixed recruitment of this Council, bringing together political figures appointed by the Government after they have been defeated at elections, representatives of large organizations and swarms of debatably representative spokesmen, as well as the arbitrary weighting of its various elements, makes it very difficult for the body actually to take decisive action. As a result, the Council's opinions are virtually meaningless, and its influence is only slight.

10 The French and Politics

It is clear that the changes mentioned up to now must have a bearing on political life, as they radically change the general climate as well as the precise issues at stake. On the other hand research has failed to show any significant relationship between these changes and French voting behaviour. The one unquestionable instance of a link is, as we pointed out, Pierre Poujade's movement, founded in 1955, defending the interests of small tradesmen and artisans. The Poujadist movement came to symbolize anti-modernist reaction, so that its leader's name has been turned into an adjective which is nowadays used almost as currently as the term 'Malthusian' once was; we even hear references to 'left-wing Poujadism' when the Communist Party takes up the defence of the small family farm but the term is more generally used to refer slightingly to an excessive attachment to old-fashioned habits. However, the expression 'left-wing Poujadism' implies an important new fact: there is no longer any connexion between attitudes towards progress and political persuasions, and retrogressive and forward-looking views are to be found in roughly the same proportions from end to end of the political spectrum. It may well be that the Left has sometimes greater difficulty in shaking free from its traditions than does the Right, as Gaullism relieved the Right of many of its more reactionary officials, who sank without trace along with the *Algérie française* policy on which they had pinned their political hopes.

The ideas of innovation and expansion have not failed to arouse positive reactions, but they have still to find a political form. One of the most significant recent advances was the young farmers' movement, a protest by energetic, untrained new men against their elders' attachment to outdated battle-cries. Realizing that it was inevitable that agriculture would be transformed, and that there would be a spectacular drop in the number of farmers, the younger members of the farming community tried to turn this change into a positive incentive, instead of opposing it in vain; without becoming associated with any precise political leaning, they largely succeeded in spreading their ideas. Similar observations may be made about the political clubs mentioned earlier. In short, between 1958 and 1965, it seems that innovating theories inspired more or less disinterested pressure groups, which set out to persuade public opinion (and often succeeded when they were backed by an administrative élite), but only in exceptional cases has their influence had any real political significance. The opposition between 'old and new believers' has been a constantly recurring theme for journalists, rather than an electoral reality.

In a certain sense, this spreading of ideas above party level has been a good thing, as it made it possible to convince Right and Left alike of the need to break with some of the myths that had been clogging up French public life. In this way, new elements were introduced into the political organizations, inside which the traditional pressure groups were in any case losing ground. But these new elements throw no light on the changes in voting behaviour that have emerged since the end of the Second World War: doubtless this field is governed by laws of its own, and reflects the inertia that characterizes matters political. At this point, we should turn to the precise political data, considering them in relation to outside determining factors.

From Stability to Instability

There were two main characteristics in the electoral structure of France before 1945: geographical stability and the lack of any spectacular swings in voting patterns. André Siegfried, who was the founding father of election analysis in France, noted that the same tendency could be seen in a *département*, or even a *canton*, over a period of half a century, and sometimes longer. He discovered certain laws, for instance that in the west of France granite-rock areas voted Right, whereas chalky areas voted Left. In point of fact, the physical nature of the terrain determined the type of agriculture practised and whether farms were scattered over an area or grouped together in villages – a point that was not without consequences during the Revolution, where the spread of the Royalist and Catholic resistance (the Chouans) was concerned. In these cases geology plays only a secondary determining role, for the main factor is essentially a historical one. There is the well-known case of a village in the Haut-Doubs, a region in the east of France close to the Jura mountains, which still has some remnants of a feudal system; this village, in the middle of a Catholic, reactionary area, has always had a left-wing majority. The only explanation that has been advanced for this strange fact hinges on the fact that the village priest went over to the revolutionary side when the civil 'constitution' for the clergy was promulgated. All the other priests in the surrounding area refused to swear the oath, and went underground; only this priest swore loyalty to the Republic. Whatever the truth of this story, the time-scale involved underlines the unbelievable stability, in isolated areas, of voting behaviour inherited from a distant past.

The other trait concerns the constant balance of strength between the two main camps up to 1945. François Goguel, currently the most eminent French authority on voting behaviour, has suggested grouping the various opposing tendencies under the Third Republic into two main 'parties', which he calls Order and Progress. This is obviously an extreme simplification but it does take account of the fundamental attitudes towards the evolution of society in this period; it also fits well with the mechanics of the electoral system,[1] since after the expression of preferences in the first ballot, the second ballot calls for a more general choice: according to a traditional saying, 'At the first ballot you choose, at the second you eliminate.' Consequently there had to be criteria enabling one to define the adversary without any ambiguity, and the negative attitudes thus revealed help us to discern the two opposing camps. François Goguel observes that their

1. For the electoral system, see Appendix 4 to Chapter 2.

respective strengths developed very slowly. For instance, from 1877 to 1928, the swing never rose above one per cent of votes cast. If we look at the last election under the Third Republic, which brought the Popular Front (i.e. the coalition of Radicals, Socialists and Communists) into power in 1936, we can see that the overall Popular Front candidates gained only 288,560 votes, while the Right lost about forty seats, with a voting swing of about three per cent against it. The reason for the discrepancy between losses of votes and losses of seats was the disciplined withdrawal of left-wing candidates and the barrage consequently directed against right-wingers.

Throughout the Third Republic the stability of public opinion is in striking contrast with Government instability and the fluid nature of political organizations. After 1945, however, things were no longer the same. Firstly, women were given the vote, and their voting behaviour turned out to be very different from that of men, as we shall see; moreover, traditional structures and the old balance of power had been swept away by the war. Finally, the abolition of the single-member two-ballot majority system and its replacement by proportional representation tended to magnify new trends. Each election from 1946 to 1958 was marked by the appearance of a new party, which expanded rapidly and subsided no less quickly. In 1946, the MRP won 5,500,000 votes, of which it kept less than half in the following elections in 1951; in 1951 the RPF (Rassemblement du Peuple Français) founded by General de Gaulle shot into prominence, with over 4,000,000 votes, but it had practically disappeared by 1956, when the Poujadists won over 2,500,000 only to disappear two years later. The two-ballot majority system, which was restored in 1958, exaggerated the success of the Gaullist movement and further increased its majority in 1962.

Parallel to these erratic movements, the traditional left-wing parties found their share of the votes subsiding, while the Communist Party developed on its own and, after a setback in 1958, gradually won back its position, though without regaining its immediate post-war percentages. The following table enables us to gauge the importance of the disorderly jolts that punctuated

French politics after 1946. Figures are given as percentages of votes cast for the main political groupings.

TABLE 17.

	November 1946	June 1951	January 1956	November 1958	November 1962	March 1967
Communist	*28·60*	25·67	25·74	18·90	21·78	22·46
Socialist	*17·90*	15·00	17·00	17·30	15·10 }	
Radical	12·40	11·04	*13·50*	8·30	7·56 }	21·05
MRP	*26·40*	12·80	11·10	11·70	8·92 }	
Moderate	12·80	12·30	14·40	*20·10*	13·42 }	17.87
Gaullist	1·60	20·40	4·40	17·50	31·90	*37·75*
Extreme Right			*11·50*	3·20	0·87	0·87
Others	0·30	2·40	2·20	3·00	0·45	

Figures in italic show the peak achievement of each party. For March 1967, the Socialists and Radicals are conflated in the Federation of the Left (Fédération de la Gauche Démocrate et Socialiste), also including the votes cast for the small PSU (Parti Socialiste Unifié).

Some of the candidates previously counted as Radicals now stand further to the Right; the MRP (Mouvement Républicain Populaire) and conservatives are grouped together to form the Democratic Centre, which also included sundry other candidates of the same leanings; however, part of the Independents and some MRP candidates were backed by the Committee for the Fifth Republic, whose voting figures now include all votes cast for these parties, whereas in 1958 and 1962 the heading 'Gaullist' covered only the UNR (Union pour la Nouvelle République). These movements from one category to another partly explain the decline of movements other than Communism and Gaullism, but the essential factor is the appearance since 1946 of a floating vote of from ten to fifteen per cent of the electorate. The term should, however, be defined a little more closely. In France, unlike Britain or America, the 'floating vote' does not correspond to a part of public opinion which hesitates between the two main parties, as France does not have a two-party system; secondly, the French floating vote is a residual concept, not a tangible body of electors. It does not follow in the least that the electors who, election after election, ensured the success of the MRP, the RPF (Rassemblement du Peuple Français), the Poujadists and finally the UNR were the same each time. Some abstained, while some voted for the first time; moreover the areas from which these parties drew their brief support coincide only occasionally (and in the case of the Poujadistes not at all). These percentages should consequently be thought of as the net results of infinitely more complex operations.

Despite the erosion of traditional political structures, which principally affects left-wing parties, the last elections, i.e. the Presidential election in December 1965 and the parliamentary election of March 1967, revealed the persistence of certain reflexes, as well as the first signs of new groupings (see the last column of the table on p. 258).

The theme of the 'two Frances', already mentioned, was copiously exploited after the presidential elections, because of the success of M. Mitterrand in twenty-four *départements* in the south and centre. Jacques Fauvet, the editor of *Le Monde*, then pointed out that as far as the Left was concerned, the map of France for the 1849 elections was virtually unchanged today: the bastions of the Progress party of a hundred years ago may have been won over here and there, but for the most part they remain in the same hands as before, strikingly demonstrating the staying-power of left-wing traditions.

In view of this, efforts were made to establish a relationship between M. Mitterrand's success and the economic situation: for some analysts, the left-wing regions had cast a protest vote complaining about their backwardness by comparison with the rest of the country, while the more prosperous part of France voted for General de Gaulle. The results were not convincing, however: as the political scientist Alain Lancelot pointed out, M. Mitterrand won more than his national average at the first ballot in the twenty *départements* where the average net wage in industry, commerce and the service industry is the highest. In fact, some under-developed *départements* in the west voted for de Gaulle, while other under-developed *départements* in the south gave M. Mitterrand a majority. . . . On the other hand, at the 1967 parliamentary elections the Gaullist setback in the Paris area, the north and certain *départements* of eastern France was linked with economic considerations such as insecurity over employment, but this may be only coincidence.

A more important factor in future development may be the weakening of the Centre electors' traditional aversion to the Left, although we cannot yet be sure of the significance of this trend. The votes cast for M. Mitterrand at the second ballot in 1965, or for a Federation (sometimes even a Communist) candidate at the second ballot in 1967 may be due to the absolute hostility to Gaullism of certain right-wing elements, but it might equally be explained by the adhesion of a part of Catholic opinion, no longer frightened of the Communist bogeymen. Both theories have their enthusiasts; time will tell.

Electors and Parties: Who Votes for Whom?

We now leave geography and pass to public opinion polls, the most complete of which was carried out by the Institut Français d'Opinion Publique (IFOP) between February and May 1965, with a sample of 12,000 informants who were asked whom they would vote for if there was a legislative election. This poll produced interesting results concerning attitudes in terms of age, sex and social background.

Firstly, it emerges that the Communist Party has the youngest voters, and Gaullism the oldest. This in itself tends to refute claims that Gaullism represents the new emergent France whereas the traditional parties reflect the old social and economic structures. Of a hundred electors declaring their intention to vote for each given party, the proportion of under-35s is as follows: 33% of Communist voters, 32% of Giscard d'Estaing's Independent Republicans (which belongs to the majority), 29% of MRP supporters (the Democratic Centre was not then in existence), 27%

of Socialist voters (again, at the time there was no Federation), 26% of CNIP (independent, later allied to the Democratic Centre), 25% of Radicals, and only 24% of UNR voters.

In the 35–49 age-group, the Communist party still leads, followed by the Independent Republicans, but here the UNR overtakes the Radicals.

If we look at the figures for older voters, we see that of a hundred people declaring their intention to vote for a given party, there are 22% of over-65s among UNR supporters, 18% for the MRP, the Socialists and the Democratic Centre, 17% of Radicals, 14% of Independent Republican supporters and only 12% of Communist voters. In the 50–64 group, the Radicals lead the field, followed by the CNIP, then the UNR; Communists come at the foot of the list.

Distribution by sex is interesting in view of the large vote represented by women. Three parties have a majority of women voters: the MRP (53%), the UNR (52%) and the Independent Republicans (51%); in contrast the Radicals have the highest proportion of male voters (64%), followed by the Socialists and the Communists. This information can be used in conjunction with another poll carried out by the IFOP in May 1966, concerning the influence of religious practice in the December 1965 presidential election: General de Gaulle obtained four times more votes among practising Catholics than among people who considered themselves without religious affiliations. In contrast M. Mitterrand received nine times more votes from agnostics and atheists than from practising Catholics. However, the proportion of women who practise religion regularly is far higher (43%) than among men (27%), so that religion is perhaps not the determining factor it at first appears, and the influence of division by sex probably subsumes much of the apparent importance of the split between Catholics and non-Catholics.

If we examine social and professional categories, we notice that, not unexpectedly, more than half of the declared Communist voters are working-class (51%), but a quarter still belong to the middle classes, a percentage already observed in 1952; a third of the Socialist electorate is working-class, and seems fairly constant, to judge from the 1952 polls, while the working class supplies a quarter of the Radical voters. The working-class proportion of UNR is only 27%, lower than the national average, but this percentage still represents an appreciable number of followers: although more than a third of the working class votes Communist, a quarter of them support the UNR, i.e. more than the total working class support of the Socialist Party and the Radicals.

The farmers constitute a quarter of the MRP vote, noticeably more than the national average, and this proportion has risen appreciably, while at the same time falling in the Radical and Independent electorates by comparison with the 1952 figures. Wage-earners and middle-rank executives are fairly equally spread through the parties, with a maximum voting for the UNR just as in 1952 a maximum voted for the RPF. Industrialists and tradesmen are thin on the ground among Communist and Socialist voters, and tend to vote Radical or Independent; the Independents head the list for upper executives and the liberal professions. Lastly, the proportion of electors with no declared occupation is highest for the UNR and the Independents; the same holds good for the most wealthy sections of the population. However, one of the unexpected facts revealed by this poll was the relatively high average income of Communist voters – higher than that of MRP, Radical or Socialist voters. Alain Duhamel,[2] commenting on these results, points out that they are probably explained by the low representation of rural voters (the least well served as far as nominal income is concerned) while the Communist Party presumably attracts the support of a working-class aristocracy, better paid than the white-collar Socialist voters.

A Fragmented Political Community

The opinion polls we have just quoted give a general impression of dispersion and lack of cohesion. While it is true that the Communist Party draws most of its support from among the

2. This information is extracted from *Sondages*, Institut Français d'Opinion Publique, 1966, no. 2.

workers, it is still supported only by a minority of the working class. The upper classes generally tend to vote right-wing, but there is no overwhelming correspondence between social and occupational position and political preferences. Indeed, far from decreasing, this incoherence is tending to become more pronounced. Consequently it is clear that this approach will provide few clues to help us to a meaningful interpretation of French political behaviour.

If we try to give a rough summing-up of developments over the last decades, we could say that there was, initially, a dislocation of party structures, during which time the issues at stake became increasingly difficult to grasp: since 1958, Gaullism has imposed a new framework on society, forcing public opinion to pronounce first and foremost about the regime itself; in this way a certain logic has been introduced into the system. However, this logic coincides only very imperfectly with the spontaneous movements within society. The question is to discover whether Gaullism's present system will succeed in bringing about a new articulation and new reflexes in public life, or if it will turn out only to have added to the confusion.

The heart of the matter depends on the emergence of the floating vote which, by its erratic shifts of allegiance, upset the functioning of the French political system. It is worth asking whether this spectacular post-war trend is continuing. A survey carried out between June 1964 and May 1966 by the French opinion-poll firm SOFRES (Société Française d'Enquêtes par Sondage) produced interesting results in this connexion.[3] According to the authors, the dominant trait of the French electorate is the existence of an amorphous mass, consisting of about a third of registered voters; they represent an undecided element with unforeseeable reactions. They, in fact, are the floating voters who, by abandoning General de Gaulle, made a second ballot necessary in the Presidential elections, although most commentators expected the General to be re-elected at the first vote.

3. Results published in E. Deutsch, D. Lindon, and P. Weill, *Les Familles politiques aujourd'hui en France*, Paris, 1966.

'Immutable and Changing'

Over and above this, the informants who declared a chosen political position by defining themselves as right- or left-wing still showed considerable variation in their replies to questions. Whether the matter discussed was a time-honoured problem like the authority of the Government, secularism or the nationalization of private industry, or a contemporary question such as decolonization or relations with the USA, it was impossible to judge from replies whether the elector belonged to the Right or the Left. For many years this could also have been said for some simple questions, like secularism, which generally corresponded to a genuine split cutting across political divisions. But now the identikit of the French elector is unclear, impossible to identify at first sight. Even under the Fourth Republic, surveys had begun to show the dispersion of opinions which was undoubtedly one of the main causes for the general lack of cohesion in political life. The traditional choice between Right and Left which for generations had been sufficient to classify opinions, was joined by contradictory options dealing with concrete questions. German rearmament and the planned European Defence Community, to name only two examples, caused a diagonal split which affected all shades of public opinion with the exception of the Communists. Colonial affairs, and particularly the Algerian problem, created deep divisions in all parties (including, as far as we can tell, the Communist Party), and led to rifts in the Socialist, Radical and, later, Independent parties. The traditional terms of Right and Left which, for the sake of convenience (or perhaps through force of habit) were still being bandied about, must, in such a situation, become pure formalities, without any precise meaning. It must, none the less, be admitted that right-wing electors tend to form a more homogeneous body than do left-wingers, who are fundamentally divided into Communists and non-Communists.

The geography of French politics could be interpreted as a single original land-mass, whose relief has been eroded away with time, while the old watersheds have been disrupted by more recent splits and upheavals. The old demarcation lines remain, but they are now overshadowed by new peaks or cut by ravines, so that they are far less simple than in the past: at most, 'Right' and

'Left' can be taken as referring to temperaments, for the precise content they once had is no more.

It is, however, permissible to examine the past significance of these categories, and to wonder if an opinion poll might not have revealed a similar lack of cohesion fifty years ago, with the exception, of course, of the secular question. Dispersal of opinions is probably a spontaneous phenomenon, recognizable either by the simplicity of the questions actually raised, or by the simplification required by institutions and, in particular, the party system. In the case of France, from the First World War onwards the political regime had to face problems which had nothing in common with those facing the Third Republic before 1914. Since 1945, the question of former colonies and the consequences of the Cold War, aggravated by the existence of a strong and flourishing Communist Party, piled up on top of the old difficulties, so that each issue entailed its own independent split of opinion. A vigorous institutional system could no doubt have brought some order into the responses, but, as we know, this was not to be the case. The delicate machinery which kept the balance between the demands and claims of various groups could be suspended for a short period of truce in order to deal with an urgent problem, but it could not cope with the endless difficulties that presented themselves from day to day.

As we have seen, the Third Republic functioned in accordance with the logic of refusal, corresponding to the two-ballot system. In the final analysis, the electors voted against the candidates they disapproved of, rather than choosing one by whom they positively hoped to be governed. This was the famous 'Republican discipline' as it was known on the Left or, for the Right, the 'national vote'. All that was needed was a handful of simple issues to reduce the complexity of the situation and ensure the continued functioning of the whole. But in due course the system got out of hand and unleashed its centrifugal forces at the precise moment when what was needed was positive pressure by a united majority. The Communist vote provides a typical example: in a way the progress of the extreme Left concentrated all the

265

negative aspects of traditional left-wing opinions, and this negative nature turned back on to the extreme Left itself; consequently, only in ten per cent of cases does a vote cast for the Communists express the real hope of seeing a Communist regime in France; for the vast majority it is a protest vote, expressing opposition to all other parties. If we limit ourselves to concrete aims, the aspirations of extreme left-wing voters correspond roughly to those of the Labour Left in Britain, but as the restraints of a majority system do not exist, the extreme Left's driving force deteriorates into pure opposition.

The more disturbing aspects of the Communist Party were accentuated by the brutality and Stalinist allegiance of its leaders, leading to an increase in existing hostility towards the party and causing a split almost as metaphysical and deep-rooted as the old controversy over secularism. Until 1962 everyone from the Socialists to the extreme Right agreed on the need to keep the Communists out at all costs. As a result, political society acquired a sort of moral ghetto, in which Communist militants and voters huddled together, acutely aware of their separateness. Polls conducted between 1947 and 1962 show the remarkable constancy of the Communist vote, which forms a solid block distinct from the rest of public opinion. For instance, in 1950, between 77% and 89% of subjects interviewed were in favour of a united western Europe, but only 19% of Communist voters shared this opinion. In 1954, when 60% to 85% of the electorate was satisfied with Pierre Mendès-France as President of Council, the Communist figure was only 40% in favour. In 1957, while 10% to 30% of voters as a whole considered that it was impossible to raise wages without affecting prices, 60% of Communists expressed the opposite conviction. Pierre Fougeyrollas, who has studied the results of these polls, has observed that in almost all cases the majority was inverted between Communist and non-Communists.[4]

In reaction to this state of affairs, the general feeling of hostility became crystallized. In 1953, 54% of subjects interviewed felt that

4. Pierre Fougeyrollas, *La Conscience politique dans la France contemporaine*, Paris, 1963.

Communism was a danger: this figure included 59% of Socialist voters, only 45% of whom mentioned Fascism. . . . More recently, the SOFRES survey established a 'sympathy quotient' according to groupings: the most homogeneous sector is the extreme Left, which broadly accepted the Federation of the Left presided over by M. François Mitterrand, and massively rejected the Centre and Right; on the other hand, the moderate Left showed itself almost as well disposed towards the Centre, and even the Gaullists, as towards the Communist Party.

More recent polls, however, have shown changes in the electorate's opinions. According to a survey carried out by the IFOP at the request of the Communist Party and published in January 1967, half the subjects interviewed considered that the Communist Party's role since 1945 had been 'useful' and 40% claimed to be in favour of the Party's participation in the Government, whereas 24% were hostile. Moreover, the scale of this thaw in opinion is confirmed by the ease with which supporters of the Centre and the Federation of the Left transferred their votes to Communist candidates at the second ballot in the March 1967 elections.[5] None the less, the thaw still depends on fluctuations of international tension, and can be jeopardized by mistakes on the part of the Communist leaders, as when they promptly adopted the Soviet line in June 1967, at the time of the Israeli–Arab war.

A Tormented Conscience?

The distribution of political opinions on both sides of a major line of cleavage was made impossible by the existence of two main splits in opinion, each of which had claims to be the supreme division in French politics. Firstly, we have the antagonism between Left and Right, which concerned not only varying degrees of preference for order or, on the contrary, for progress (or justice), but which also resulted from a far more fundamental conflict, in which the State itself had been at stake. M. Mitterrand spontaneously revived the language of this struggle when he declared himself the 'candidate for Republicans'. While the Right

5. Raymond Barrillon, *La Gauche en mouvement*, Paris, 1967.

had resigned itself to accepting the Republic, the Left had always considered the regime menaced; at times this fear was not unfounded, but sometimes it was rather exaggerated, aimed at welding the regime's supporters into a solid front and imposing 'Republican discipline' on voters and candidates alike. Despite many setbacks, this system of classification still functions, as was proved by the 1965 presidential elections and the 1967 legislative elections; an appeal to the Left triggers off a response in public opinion that is immediate and massive, albeit relatively weaker and, perhaps, less enthusiastic than in past years. It was widely thought that this division was dead and buried, in particular because the proportional representation system did away with the need for a super-criterion, but the readoption of the majority system soon revived it.

The other explanation for the temporary disappearance of the Right–Left division stems from the concurrent antagonism between Communists and non-Communists which, from 1947 to 1962, took on all the characteristics of an absolute dogma. This situation was largely responsible for the paralysis of the regime, which was no longer able to launch any positive lines that might have attracted the electorate's support.

But could there not be some deeper, more long-standing cause for unease? Pierre Fougeyrollas, in the work already quoted, suggests that the political consciousness of the French, whatever their political allegiance, is itself divided between nostalgia for national unity and a tendency towards ideological individuality. In this way he puts forward a general explanation based on the fragmentation of a conscience that is unable to become reconciled with itself. Some authors trace this state of affairs back to the 1789 Revolution: since the execution of Louis XVI, they claim, the French nation has been an orphan affirming its independence through the diversity of its citizens' political leanings, although still regretting the disappearance of the old unity personified by the monarch.

This frustration, nurtured by the anonymity and instability of regimes, explains the explosions of enthusiasm for individual personalities who deliberately set themselves up as arbiters above party politics, and speak in the name of the national interest. The latest example of this to date is, of course, General de Gaulle, of whom honest citizens naïvely declare that, 'At least he isn't a politician.' . . . All sectors of opinion, including the Communists, are infected; in the referendum of 28 September 1958, which in reality was a Gaullist plebiscite, 66·42% of registered electors voted in favour (79·25% of votes cast), while only 17·38% voted against. Communist candidates had received over a quarter of the votes cast in the 1956 elections (in November 1958 they received 18·9%), and the real number of Communists voting in favour of General de Gaulle in 1958 was clearly greater than one would at first conclude from the difference between these two figures. In some regions, such as the south-west, the percentage of negative votes was greater than those previously won by the Communist Party: the traditional republican electorate, expressed by the influential daily *La Dépêche du Midi*, backed the Communists and camouflaged voting shifts that are without doubt more striking than the raw figures would lead one to believe. Similar observations were made at the presidential elections, particularly in the communes of the Paris area, where de Gaulle definitely received part of the old Communist vote.

However, the conception of a unitary 'national consciousness' probably covers two distinct phenomena: on the one hand, the need for a dynamic, personal leadership which had only occasionally been satisfied, explaining, perhaps, the popularity of M. Mendès-France among sections of public opinion far removed from the Radical Party; and on the other, the desire for a type of unanimity above party level, i.e. an apolitical tendency, which is one of the Right's favourite masks. This unsatisfied longing to be governed was only too liable to deteriorate into hankering after a unity rendered even more desirable by the dispersal of the parties, and the nation was thus caught in a psychological vicious circle, for the absence of any direct relationship between voting and the real choice of Governments under the Fourth Republic favoured a feeling of irresponsibility which ultimately accentuated the divisions between parties and the fragmentation of political trends.

269

11 Towards a Mass Democracy

The instability and divisions that have left deep scars on French political life may not have been inevitably preordained, but they do none the less reflect a marked propensity to individualism and overdramatized quarrels, despite the fact that these tendencies exist alongside a deep-rooted opportunism and a longing for unity which have had at least as many chances of showing themselves. If in 1879 Marshal MacMahon's successor had simply appointed the main Republican leader head of the Government, this might have been enough to establish a different set of customs and traditions. But this, as we know, he did not do.

At the end of the nineteenth century political structures, like soft wax, were easily moulded by events. With the passage of time they set stiff, and in due course this inflexibility itself played a part in the way the system functioned; instead of being determined by outside forces, the structures became determining factors in their own right, as the result of decisions made at institutional level at the beginning of the regime – decisions that committed the regime to following the current of the national character instead of counteracting its more extreme leanings. But why were these choices made at all? Not because of ignorance on the part of the protagonists, for we know that Adolphe Thiers[1] and, it is said, Gambetta himself were convinced in their heart of hearts that the best solution would have been a presidential system. If they followed another line in practice, this reflected a series of pragmatic adjustments rather than any ideological preferences. In other words, the regime then instituted owed less to constitutional ideals than to a tentative adaptation to the realities of French society.

1. See Chapter 4.

'Immutable and Changing'

It should be borne in mind that two previous attempts at setting up Republican regimes had misfired, and the third succeeded only in so far as it managed to avoid creating a gulf between the preceding monarchies and the new democratic State. The new Republic's main achievements were that it established a Senate and invested the President with powers similar to those enjoyed by a constitutional monarch – in short, it contrived to break with the past while maintaining important links with the old order. Essentially a compromise between moderates from both camps, the Third Republic managed the transition from the monarchical legitimacy, now repudiated once and for all (albeit a restoration appeared possible until the last minute), and the new democratic legitimacy which was quietly consolidating its positions. The new Republican leaders were well aware that by following these tactics they would have history on their side; first, however, they had to play for time, in particular by taking care not to let the regime appear to break too brutally with the past, for the public, however satisfied in appearance, would certainly have found this disturbing. This policy, in many ways akin to the slow infiltration of enemy ranks, ruled out any spectacular action, particularly where power itself was concerned. Accordingly, quiet, self-effacing men were placed at the head of the State, and in due course they chose their Government leaders from among men not deeply involved in the polemics of the hustings; consequently it was impossible for the enemies of the Republic to lay hands on any clear issue to use as pretext for a showdown.

The Price of the Republic

Under these conditions, a set of 'rules of the game' grew up – the 'game' in question being democracy. Universal suffrage had a part in this system only so long as it was channelled, filtered and diluted by a series of intermediary bodies such as the Senate. We have not so far devoted much space to the Senate, although in itself this institution provides an excellent example of the merits and demerits of this type of procedure. To begin with its merits: in all probability it was due to the existence of the Senate that the regime survived repeated attacks from the Right at the time of General Boulanger's abortive uprising or during the Dreyfus Case. Yet Republicans had looked on the Senate as a sort of bogeyman, a paradoxical situation recorded by Joseph Caillaux in his memoirs: if the moderate monarchists had not made the creation of an Upper House a condition to their acceptance of the compromise constitution, it is very likely that the left-wingers would have had their way with a single-chamber Assembly; a regime organized along these lines would certainly have succumbed at the first major crisis, for the Republic could have been crushed by anyone gaining control of the sole body competent to exercise power. This type of move was, however, ruled out by the existence of the Senate which, with members elected on nine-year mandates, one third of them resigning every three years, provided a virtually insuperable obstacle, all the more so as it was elected by local and municipal councils and therefore reflected long-standing traditions of local feeling.

In this way the Senate took the Republic into the remotest, most unchanging corners of rural France, thus clinching the establishment on solid, broad-based foundations. But at what cost? At this point we begin to see the drawbacks of the system, which made themselves felt most strongly after the First World War, when the Senate began to act as a hindrance to new policies; from being a stabilizing force, it had set hard into a stumbling-block, which the Left tried to do away with in 1946. But such is the irony of history that in 1958 General de Gaulle gave the Senate back part of its old prerogatives – and the Senate forthwith became the most deeply entrenched bastion of opposition to him.

Through the 38,000 communes that elect its members, the Senate represents the traditional currents of French political life, so that it is rather an ambivalent institution, reflecting the most doggedly enduring aspects of the nation, and by the same token the most conservative forces. Although it can no longer hope to reverse decisions taken by the National Assembly when the latter is asked for a final pronouncement, its resistance still has a symbolic value: it is like the tip of an iceberg, which for all its apparent smallness tells us that far more lies submerged, and in wait. The Senate may be reformed or even abolished, but this will not affect the real situation it expresses: it is not the tip of the iceberg that must be modernized, but the mass.

In the form it took under the Third Republic, when it enjoyed an acknowledged right to overthrow governments, the Senate functioned as a typical cog in the delicate machinery of the State. It seemed to be accepted that democratic action should not develop through open political channels, but should operate indirectly through the State. By taking over the State, the Republic could make its influence felt and began to play the part of an anti-Establishment, with the political system proper functioning as a regulator. Under these conditions the process – and practice – of adaptation through crises took on added significance, for the crisis mechanism was no longer aimed only at resolving disagreements at parliamentary level: it had also become a sort of general safety valve. When there was a risk that the social groups on which the regime was founded might become so discontented as to endanger the Republic, the situation was saved in the nick of time by the fall of a government. Parliamentary leaders used this procedure in frequent, small doses to keep Government action in line with the reactions of public opinion. This obviously implied that groups which opposed one another while campaigning were forced of necessity to disband once elected to Parliament, giving way to more moderate formations which could work out a synthesis acceptable to the country as a whole. Since it was unable to bring about peaceful coexistence between majority and opposition factions, the Third Republic was forced to try to find an empirical means of persuading the French to live together in harmony, at the same time giving some measure of satisfaction, often more apparent than real, to the dominant trend.

Radicalism embodied the essentials of this political outlook, which ensured that the country never went too far in any direction. 'France is a Radical nation', Barrès had observed at the beginning of the century, and in 1939 the left-wing Catholic monthly *Esprit* remarked that the existence of a party on the lines of the French Radical movement would have spared Spain its

Civil War. ... Such considerations cannot simply be brushed aside. However, like the Senate, this regulating system had its disadvantages. First, it made it impossible for the electors to have any direct influence in choosing the men who were to govern them; it also fostered a sense of frustration and an alienation of responsibility since, whatever the election results, the policies followed by the Government changed only slightly. Finally, the Radical approach made it impossible for the Government to count on large-scale popular support. Indeed, for many years massive support of this kind seemed positively undesirable, as the anti-Republican camp might have taken this as a provocation; it was essential to screen around the main lines along which power was transmitted. Moreover, the Republican attitude towards the masses was not without reservations, motivated by an awareness of how in the past mass movements had swept away the very regimes they had carried to power. Had it not been stifled in 1871, the patriotic and social insurrections of the Paris Commune would without doubt have turned the Senate, and with it the sectors of France it represented, against the Republic; the crucial fact was that the Republic could survive only if it was accepted as the legitimate regime by the Senate-oriented part of the nation. In the long run, the Republic was also obliged to turn itself into a regime designed for the Commune's heirs, the industrial proletariat. In order to achieve this it was necessary to integrate the working classes into the system, by remodelling the decision-making procedures along more collective lines. But this was never done, and as a result a substantial Communist vote survived on the fringe of the political system, while the social classes which originally supported the regime gradually declined and the newcomers became increasingly impatient with the instability of the Republic.

Some Consequences of a Majority System

Going beyond the institutional upheavals of 1958 and 1962, the Fifth Republic has reopened the whole question of this traditional state of balance. The situation had come under heavy fire from critics after the Second World War, and with this in mind the founders of the Fourth Republic thought up a system opened up to the electorate through a rigid grouping of parties. But this proved impossible to put into practice, as the groupings promptly dissolved when candidates reached the Assembly, so that the new system's effect on Government leadership turned out to be nil. The Cabinet's task was thus made rather more difficult than before, without its receiving any of the increased authority it needed, and the old system soon reappeared, although it was by then even less suited to the needs of the society it was supposed to run. In 1958 it was duly pushed aside, amid general apathy.

The main innovatory feature of the Gaullist regime has been its systematic recourse to collective, majority-based procedures to strengthen the regime's power; the first referendum, in September 1958, was followed by three others between then and October 1962; the last of the series gave regular institutional status to the election of the President by direct universal suffrage, until then an exceptional measure. In historical terms, the 1958–62 period shows up in a rather ambiguous light. The referendum procedure was interpreted at first as a return to the Bonapartist practice of calling on the people to oppose Parliament; such tactics had indeed been used by the two Napoleons. However, this view of things failed to make allowance for the fact that the two societies concerned in the comparison were very different from one another; in fact, there was virtually no common denominator between mid-nineteenth-century France and the country in 1958. The election of Louis-Napoleon Bonaparte by universal suffrage took place in a torn country, with no principle of unchallenged legitimacy and exasperated by the disorders that seemed attendant on democracy. Two years after this election, just after the *coup d'état* in which the President routed his Deputies, Alexis de Tocqueville wrote that 'a Republic without Republicans' was 'a difficult machine to run'. It hardly seems necessary to add that today nobody would envisage invoking a legitimacy to rival that based on universal suffrage, and that the effortless liquidation of the Fourth Republic resulted from the regime's lack of popular support.

Despite certain authoritarian, anti-parliamentary aspects of the Gaullist regime, which give some credence to the Bonapartist comparison, objectively speaking the Fifth Republic appears to be the final phase of a progression, halted for many years, which was restarted abruptly with the arrival of the new order. Proof of this can be adduced from the presidential elections in December 1965, after which General de Gaulle asked, not without a touch of humour, how many dictators had been forced to go through a second ballot. . . . In point of fact, the political machinery so skilfully manipulated by the General to have his Algerian policies ratified has become self-sufficient and now, if need be, might well establish the authority of a successor. All this has taken place as if Gaullism had involuntarily moved on to the lines followed by most modern political systems; at first it was very far removed from these lines, but it is worth remembering that initially it also seemed implausible that the regime would sympathize with the policy of decolonization which it none the less carried out. It is therefore possible to envisage a majority-based political system that, given time, might survive the General – a new system which could make lasting changes in the traditional distribution of power.

Possible future developments are shrouded in uncertainty, due to the discrepancies – almost literally a lack of synchronization – between the various component elements of the political and administrative system. Existing parties and trade-union organizations belong to an earlier age, and are consequently out of phase with the new institutions and procedures that have appeared under the Fifth Republic; as a result, the new mass democracy lacks the appropriate foundations, as it is not based on spontaneously formed structures, but represents an attempt to bring the regime into step with the salient characteristics of industrial society. French society and its Government are thus separated by a sort of gap, one which is camouflaged by Gaullism for the time being, but which will have to be bridged sooner or later.

A majority system as the basis for public life entails certain consequences for the seat of power itself. The May 1968 crisis showed that it had become intolerable that political and administrative authority should be gathered together into the same hands. The reaction of the sector of society at once most volatile and most free from ties – the student population – was more than merely the French version of the Berkeley or West Berlin syndromes, as it showed some specific, new features, some connected with the state of the French educational system (outlined earlier in this book), but most connected to the results of the student rebellion. The movement began in the new Arts Faculty in Nanterre, in the north-west suburbs of Paris, and spread rapidly through large sections of the population – sections basically indifferent to critiques of consumer society, in which on the contrary they were impatient to join more fully – and from there to the upper reaches of the State. The contagious, escalatory nature of the movement has a political significance which cannot be explained away as one more example of revolution French-style.

It is worth considering the following hypothesis: with power being placed in the hands of a majority, the traditional balance, dependent on the existence of a particular type of relationship between representative democracy and the State, was destroyed. In the old system, cooperation between national sovereignty, embodied in the Assembly, and the public service, entrusted to the Administration, made it possible for power to be exercised with moderation. The concept of 'government' corresponded not to the Cabinet–Parliament nexus, but to the executive, i.e. the authoritative bodies entitled to make unilateral, universally applicable decisions (apart, of course, from the Council of State, to which most of these decisions had to be submitted). The executive represented as it were a secular arm in the service of the nation, an organization run by the Administration and directed by the appropriate ministers. The role of the minister was an ambiguous one, since the Cabinet acted both as the higher authority, invested with the confidence of the Assembly and consequently with the principle of democratic legitimacy, and also as the body delegated by Parliament to watch over the doings of the Administration.

At the highest point of this edifice, the keystone was provided by the President of the Republic, in that he kept the balance between the political and administrative systems, which converged in the Council of Ministers over which he presided. But here he acted as an essentially passive magistrate, and his role was without any real political weight. However, now that the President is elected by universal suffrage, the country is run by an executive directly based on the consent of the electors; moreover, ministerial posts are assigned directly by the President instead of, as formerly, by the Assembly. This first stage of concentration of power clearly jeopardizes the precarious balance of recent years. In addition to this, the emergence of a disciplined majority of Deputies devoted to the President has effectively drained the principle of parliamentary control of all its substance, since the existence of this majority depends directly on the very men it is theoretically intended to supervise; in this way the second element which ensured the traditional balance has also disappeared, so that now the President genuinely, not merely symbolically, holds all State and democratic power.

We do not have to look far to see the implications of this change. The Third Republic had ultimately taken the form of a successful attempt to reconcile the democratic ideal and the principle of State authority; this was achieved by stressing the channels through which power in the abstract was transmitted and communicated, although the day-to-day exercise of this power was affected only indirectly, as, while party divisions and government instability served to moderate the consequences of having an anonymous public body wielding power, they did as much to keep alive the tutelary image of this power. The reaffirmation of the principle, dating from the first Revolution, of the Republic 'one and indivisible' was tolerable, and indeed necessary, so long as it applied to a divided, self-contained country, but the new majority-based procedures strengthened the tutelary side of the regime precisely when this was becoming less acceptable to the people, as a result of France's emergence as an industrial society. Precisely when in normal circumstances they should have been increasing, openings for individual initiative and influence were decreasing. The resultant sense of general frustration explains the explosions of May 1968 and the General's choice of 'participation' as the new keyword for the Fifth Republic.

The quest for a new equilibrium entails a sharing of power, allowing for the transformation brought about by the adoption of a majority system and giving greater scope for action to the active components of French society. This has particular significance for the relations between the political sector proper – parties and elected representatives – and the administration. The administration's position took the form it did in order to counterbalance the instability of governments and the boat-rocking competition between the numerous groups whose representatives followed one another into power. The resultant system of flexible pluralism guaranteed civil servants a measure of autonomy which is liable to be severely reduced with the appearance of a solidly established majority power. Once the majority acquires an identity of its own and achieves a degree of stability, it will no doubt come to make its influence felt more strongly in the administration, intervening in the running of departments and directly supervising the most strategically important sectors. In extreme terms, there are two solutions for the administration: it might become completely enclosed and self-contained, on the lines of the British civil service, or, on the other hand, it could become associated with the majority, which would then dispose of key appointments as of right. The role of the State in modern society renders the first solution unlikely, as this would cut across a tendency towards increasing State intervention which is even more marked among young civil servants than among their elders. There remains the second possibility, and certain critics fear that the administration is already moving in this direction as the result of a sort of complicity between the majority leaders and the more ambitious civil servants. Given the absence of any vigorous collective organizations – trade unions or local institutions, for example – the assimilation of the administration's higher grades into the ranks of the majority presents obvious risks.

Administrative centralization could function only providing it was subordinated to a non-partisan conception of the general interest. Similarly, the technocrats enlisted certain elites in support of their development plans largely because their activities were situated on a plane slightly set apart from party conflicts. There is a tacit agreement to keep these instruments out of the struggle for power, so as to meet the universally acknowledged need to preserve as far as possible an area of real objectivity in public life. If we think in abstract terms of the conditions for progress in modern societies, we may conclude that the State's instrumental functions can only increase, as in this way it is possible to satisfy those public needs not met by open market procedures. But if, instead of this technocratic approach, we adopt a more political standpoint, we may equally well claim that the traditional role of the State in the French model stemmed from the parliamentary system's failure to integrate the masses into its functioning; in a sense, political democracy remained marginal and incomplete. With the move towards a government based more broadly among the people, the majority element is bound to come into play more strikingly; it can be argued that, far from attempting to preserve the autonomy of the State, a mass democracy should, on the contrary, bind it more closely to political power. The counterweights to this should be sought in a reorganization of local structures and the expansion of the trade-union network, with a view to lightening the administrative load which, for lack of other active bodies, the State still carries.

But, as we know, the persistent weakness of collective organizations makes them incapable of serving satisfactorily as relays between public and power. One of the main problems facing the future political system in France will be the need to set up a dynamic, effective network of intermediary bodies to replace the individual, clientèle-type relationships that grew up in the first years of the Third Republic; this system still survives, but functions only in a fragmentary, very inadequate way. The need appears all the more vital as the Gaullist taste for a tutelary position, coupled with the regime's allergic reaction to intermediary bodies, has accentuated the archaic nature of the traditional executive, which is now clinging grimly on to its established positions. While Gaullism is directly responsible for the distrust aroused by its secretive, authoritarian methods, it has not created this situation artificially: the modernization of local and regional structures, in particular the amalgamation of communes, would have been necessary in any case and could not have failed to collide with the inertia of old habits. Gaullism has, however, made it more tricky to find a solution, and the regime has failed to take the appropriate steps in so far as it is impossible to direct such measures from Paris without the participation of the social groups involved. Their cooperation presupposes a sharing of authority between the central State and local units, and recognition of the influence of the latter; both must be backed by a large enough consensus of opinion to allow local administrative life to proceed normally at the various operative levels.

Lastly, it is essential that communication between the seat of power and the citizens be ensured on a national scale by some political organization, and this problem has yet to be tackled. In a way, it is a question of how to safeguard the inheritance of Radicalism, as expressed by several UNR leaders, notably M. Louis Terrenoire, who declared in 1961, while Secretary-General of the party: 'We are called on to serve as the kingpins in this vitally important organization round which the democratic life of our nation must resolve. In the past, this role fell to the Radicals. Sociologically Radicalism no longer corresponds to any part of our society or our political life. This vacuum must be filled.'

The Radical legacy is twofold, since the party had played both instrumental and ideological roles. It functioned as a strategically placed cog in the political machine, but it also expressed a coherent set of convictions the absence of which is nowadays acutely felt. Gaullism does not seem to have acquired a real identity of its own to enable it to meet this double need, and so far there are no signs of a successor to Radicalism. The fundamental problem is to know whether it is still possible, in the type of majority system envisaged, to identify a particular political movement with the regime itself, as was the case for Radicalism and the Third Republic. Logically the Radical inheritance should split, to be shared by two formations, but it is by no means absurd

282

to imagine a solution similar to that discovered by the Italian Christian Democrats, who in reality keep their Republic running.

The Future of the Majority System

From the debate surrounding the question whether the regime is moving towards a two-party system or a system with one dominant party, it can be seen that the outcome of current developments is still largely imponderable. The last ten years have seen a series of transformations which might indeed lead to a rationalization of the traditional model, with its distinction between 'government' and 'contestation' parties[2]; on the other hand, they might well reopen the question of this type of deployment of political forces. Both hypotheses are worth examining.

An unusual feature of French political life is that its leaders have always been recruited from the same circles over the last three quarters of a century. There were inevitably a few exceptions to this, but on the whole the regime carried on its way within limits sufficiently circumscribed for these key men never to have been left out of the team in power. Under these conditions, we might say that the Fifth Republic's main innovation was the creation of procedures designed to reveal a majority among the electoral body, and to ensure a permanent expression of this majority in institutional terms. These procedures amplify, simplify and stabilize government majorities, which until then had been narrow and fluctuating, and are now comfortable and lasting. The process was started when the regime's centre of gravity began to drift rightwards, and it swept away most of the old leaders, with obvious consequences for the functioning of the political system, which now centres on the explicit assumption by a majority of responsibility for running the country. (The majority may be a single organization or a group of several: the one condition for a popular mandate is that candidates present a united front.)

However, this development does not imply a corresponding transformation of the opposition, and so it does not automatically

2. See Chapter 3.

lead to the formation of a totally new structure such as a two-party system. The new situation could perfectly well accommodate the time-honoured division, with those in power facing an opposition composed of hostile formations. A very different situation would result from the replacement of this cleavage by a single division into two major streams competing for power; this would split open the exclusive club of government elements, and bring fringe bodies back into the political game. In this connexion, one thinks immediately of the Communist electorate, which hovers between one fifth and one quarter of the total number of voters.

Just before the crisis of May 1968, it seemed that the regime was moving towards a bipolar situation of this type; although this was by no means a two-party system, it did possess the main articulation into two parts. The dissolution and referendum of October 1962 had led the moderates to regroup themselves under the aegis of General de Gaulle; the December 1965 presidential elections persuaded the parties of the Left to make up their differences with a view to taking power. This tendency was reversed by the events that shook the country in May and June 1968, and by the elections which followed. Above all else, spring 1968 showed up the risks attendant on an over-sharp separation of the country into two camps, for the French are not used to a game based on the confrontation of two teams; the difficulty of shaking off old habits and moving from mutual anathema to peaceful competition is so great that unless the circumstances are totally calm, the engagement rapidly degenerates into a state of latent civil war.

The May 1968 crisis also laid bare the contradictory, equivocal aspects of an institutional apparatus which incorporates several competing pathways to the seat of power: the election of the President, which attracted some opposition leaders who were convinced that de Gaulle's days were past, and the legislative elections which were ultimately used to reinstate a majority devoted to the President of the Republic. At this point it would be worth examining the influence of these factors on the future of the majority system.

The term 'majority' is used sometimes to refer to the majority of electors voting for the President of the Republic, sometimes to the majority in Parliament; there is no stable, direct equivalence between these two meanings.

The appointment of the President of the Republic by direct universal suffrage was superimposed on an essentially parliamentary constitution which laid down that the Cabinet remained accountable to the National Assembly. The 'presidential' and 'parliamentary' elements coexist, but in a rather unstable way; although up to now the presidential factors have prevailed, this balance has not yet had to face a swing in the majority which might bring the whole regime back where it started.

Some change of this order is bound to take place sooner or later, perhaps when the National Assembly's term of office expires, or when the President of the Republic's mandate comes up for renewal. The actual timing is not without importance. In the first eventuality, the new parliamentary majority will naturally claim the post of Prime Minister for its own leader, and will expect to control the Government: the replacement of M. Pompidou by M. Couve de Murville in July 1968 gives proof of the rivalry that can grow up between presidential authority, on one hand, and, on the other, the leadership of the Prime Minister, who runs the election campaign and is the recognized head of the parliamentary majority. The discontent of Gaullist Deputies faced with this reassertion of the President's power expressed the fundamental antagonism between parliamentary and presidential machinery. It is even more to be expected that a majority that does not share the President's politics will refuse to countenance the Cabinet's being directed by a President who no longer has the backing of the electorate. In this case the President may indeed dissolve the Assembly and pin his hopes on a trial of strength, but he can do this only once, for after a dissolution a minimum period of one year must elapse before the Deputies can be dismissed again. If the President fails, or if he prefers to accept the verdict of universal suffrage, the result of a swing in the majority at the legislative elections will be a reinforcement of the parliamentary side of the regime, and in particular of the Prime

Minister's preponderance over the President in matters concerning the actual running of the Government.

If, on the other hand, the President's gamble comes off and after a dissolution the new Assembly turns out to be more sympathetic to the Head of State, he will only (even in the most optimistic terms) have staved off the day of reckoning that a change in majority must present for the regime. This could well happen when the presidential mandate comes up for renewal, which brings us to the second possibility.

In this case, the situation is reversed in the presidential elections; it is likely that the new incumbent would retain the position of leadership enjoyed by his predecessor, since by definition he will have the direct personal approbation of the greater part of the electorate. In order to build up a healthy relationship with Parliament (which in these circumstances will certainly want to play a more active part than before) and to stabilize the regime, the new President will definitely have to share his authority, or at least give up the quasi-monarchical posture held by General de Gaulle; it is to be hoped that he will also bring the duration of his mandate into line with that of Deputies, so as to make their renewal dates coincide as closely as possible. Only under these conditions will it be possible to rule out the risk of contradictory decisions by the electorate – a risk inherent in a system based on the election of the President for seven years, while the Deputies serve for four and a half years. The problem is fairly similar to the one raised in the USA by mid-term elections, aggravated by the fact that American congressmen are accustomed to working with a President who does not necessarily belong to their party, whereas the parliamentary sections of the French Constitution enable the Deputies to overthrow the Government.

While it may seem that these hypotheses affect only the juridical side of the regime, in reality they determine all its later development. If we are to understand this fully, we should study the machinery which led to the emergence of the majority, as in this context the ideas of cause and effect are of crucial importance. As the French political scientist Georges Vedel has demonstrated, a parliamentary system along British lines is the translation into institutional form of a particular type of political structure, the most typical of which is the two-party system, whereas a presidential regime is based on a procedure which causes the formation of a majority inside an electoral body naturally split between a number of tendencies. (The American two-party system can be analysed as a two-pronged coalition set up in order to facilitate the election of the President and thereafter gradually stabilized, though it lacks discipline and homogeneity.) The French majority belongs to the second type, as it was produced, to use a mathematical term, by construction. It is a by-product of the presidential system, and as such it is unlikely that it would survive the disappearance of the presidency in its present form. Moreover, it has yet to develop into a lasting coalition, since its component parts are in a state of permanent latent rivalry. It was thought that a few years of discipline might suffice to install a new set of reflexes and make it possible to realize the dream of a real parliamentary regime in France. But the coalitions constituted since 1965 are held together only by the presence of one federator, the majority or opposition leader, according to the case; these two men are the victor in the presidential elections and his main opponent. The parties are thus obliged to group together because of external pressures, any lessening of which would set free centrifugal forces which would endanger the present bipolar situation.

First of all, where the Gaullist majority is concerned, we should not let ourselves be led astray by appearances. On 23 June 1968, 43·65% of votes in the first ballot went to candidates of the new group known as UDR (Union for the Defence of the Republic), which was hastily run up to replace and refurbish the by then rather tired image of the previous 'Union of Democrats for the Fifth Republic' (UDV^{e}R). This is roughly the same percentage obtained by General de Gaulle in the first ballot of the presidential elections on 5 December 1965, but this majority corresponds neither to convictions nor to an organization.

The majority is basically heterogeneous, since circumstances have obliged it to include men brought up in widely differing, if not downright contradictory, political traditions: moderates in the classic mould, liberals, and a few left-wing personalities attached to the General, whose convictions scandalize the numerous authoritarian right-wingers to be found in the Gaullist camp. Indeed, the change of party title at each election could be taken as indicating the purely circumstantial nature of a formation which is less a party than an umbrella organization. The old UNR which had fought in 1958 absorbed the left-wing Gaullists of the UDT in 1962, to become the UNR–UDT; in 1967 it adopted the new title of Union des Démocrates pour la Cinquième République (UDV^{e}R) and in 1968 changed skin once more, becoming the Union de Défense de la République (UDR).

The initials UDR were used as an election label by the orthodox Gaullist group, whereas the independent Republicans headed by M. Giscard d'Estaing decided to maintain their autonomy. Indeed, several of Giscard's group stood in the first ballot against orthodox Gaullists backed by M. Pompidou: an indication of the latent rivalry that can exist between individuals with their eyes on de Gaulle's succession. In this context M. Giscard d'Estaing has never made any bones about envisaging a redistribution of political forces so that they return to their 'natural boundaries'. This should normally lead to a very large moderate group which could provide an alternative to the more authoritarian line liable to attract some Gaullists.

These 'natural boundaries' would include the centrists who, although scattered by the move to a bipolar situation, are still represented in the Assembly; their PDM group, run by M. Jacques Duhamel, who has replaced M. Lecanuet as the centrist leader, includes consular figures such as M. Pleven, and some newcomers who, though occasionally cooperating with the Gaullist movement, have always managed to keep their distance. Both these factions pin their faith on a redistribution of political strength in accordance with the natural tendencies of the French Parliament, i.e. an amalgamation of centre groups, and they hope to act as pivot for this new force.

On the Left, uncertainty is even greater, as the left-wing formations are in a state of crisis. As François Goguel points out, the

Left has shown an overall loss of momentum over the last fifteen years; it maintained an absolute majority among voters until 1956, but this fell to 43·41% in 1958, then, after a slight rise to 43·51% in 1967, dropped again to 41·22% in 1968. This shrinkage of the left-wing electorate expresses the displacement of the regime's centre of gravity occasioned by the Fifth Republic.

The existence of a Communist Party controlling approximately half the left-wing vote represents a burden that can be appreciated fully in periods of crisis, whether the crisis is international or, as in May 1968, domestic. The French Communist Party is attempting to put itself on a steady footing but, contrary to general opinion after the 1967 elections, the party still has a long way to go, especially as the line being prudently followed by M. Waldeck Rochet remains at the mercy of international contingencies, as was evident during the June 1967 Middle East crisis and the tense situation in Central Europe in July and August 1968. Events beyond its control can, and do, easily fling the French Communist Party back into its dark ghetto. But developments within the party are also menaced by the existence of a revolutionary schism. The agitation of pro-Chinese elements and the challenge of the PSU (Parti Socialiste Unifié) are forcing the Communists to take a rather harder line in order to avoid being swamped by competing movements. This schism represents a major factor contributing to the intellectual confusion currently running through the French Left, affecting Communists and non-Communists alike.

The other side of the coin is that the numerical weakening of the Left has tempted some strategically-oriented politicians to try to recruit this lost electorate, and, with this end in sight, to adopt a more directly reformist line. According to their reasoning, instead of pinning their hopes on a union of the entire Left, it might be more realistic to resume contacts with those centrists still uncommitted to Gaullism, as this would seem a natural partnership for a Centre-Left government. Up to now these attempts have been defeated only by Gaullist pressure on the centre electorate and by the constraints of the majority voting system. Up to now, but who can vouch for tomorrow?

'Immutable and Changing'

We now have a clearer view of the link between the constitutional situation and the redistribution of political strength. The problem is not so much one of finding the best way of adapting well-defined, stable structures to the new conditions, but rather one of measuring the interaction of a double-edged institutional apparatus on one hand and, on the other, political forces in search of a state of balance.

These institutional mechanisms can foster a two-way polarization of the decision problem by presenting the question of power to the electorate in the form of two possible choices. On the other hand, they could equally well block this tendency by leaving open the possibility of a third reply. It does seem that propitious conditions for a bipolar system exist at the electoral level, for voters welcomed the opportunity of deciding directly whether to keep on or dismiss the men who govern them, as can be seen from the high voting figures in the various consultations over the last few years. The procedure most suitable for this type of popular decision is, of course, the election of the President, as only the two candidates leading in the first ballot may stand in the second ballot.

But this functional two-way polarization should not be confused with the sociological bipolarization implied by the existence of two permanent competing camps. While this type of situation can function perfectly satisfactorily in societies which have achieved a high degree of consensus and respect for the constitution, confrontations of this order can, negatively, aggravate conflicts in societies that do not fulfil these conditions.[3]

If a binary choice is to be kept open, the presidential mechanisms must function correctly. When these function less effectively by comparison with the parliamentary side of the regime, it is legitimate to suppose that the logical conclusion of this tendency would be the victorious re-emergence of the traditional trend towards a Centre-based management party. However, this would not imply a simple reconstruction of past regimes: through new constitutional rules it would be possible to correct certain flaws

3. As demonstrated by Robert A. Dahl, in *Political Oppositions in Western Democracies*, Yale University Press, 1965.

in the traditional French system (although it would be as well not to set too much store by the efficiency of a parliamentary system streamlined and subjected to rules). The main innovation might grow out of the continuation of a relatively peaceful state of affairs, in which priority would be given to the problems of managing the country. As M. Giscard d'Estaing said, France is a moderate country which has been thrown into dramatic situations; and the country's political malaise can be imputed to the contradiction between the national temperament and the problems to be faced. As things stand now, the idea of the Republic is no longer questioned, and France is learning to live with a more modest international position, more easily since the prestige elements of Gaullism have smoothed the way to exorcizing nostalgia for the days of imperial grandeur.

The outcome of this situation would be an enormous centrist group which would function as a managerial element and could recruit support from as far as the margins of the centre Left. This solution would meet the needs of a mass democracy only in part, but it cannot be ruled out, as an expressed wish to defend the institutions of the Fifth Republic could provide the rallying-point for a political grouping of this type, which would give satisfaction to a number of currents of opinion – and benefit from appreciable backing through the lassitude brought on by reaction to recent struggles.

The other avenue presupposes the continuing key role of the presidential election, and consequently of the President; this implies as a corollary that the Prime Minister's importance would diminish and that the Government would be progressively less accountable to Parliament. The hostility between these two institutions is clearly seen from the dismissal of M. Pompidou. In this situation the two-pole formula would not represent the beginnings of a two-party system, but, rather, a distribution of political forces in terms of the division produced by the second ballot in the presidential elections: the confrontation between the two main candidates would sum up, for public opinion, the real concrete cleavage in terms of which the legislative elections could later be fought. This situation would not be totally unlike that of the USA where, as Nicholas Wahl points out, the two-party system functions only during the election period, otherwise relapsing into a mosaic of groups and formations.

The possibility of a two-way choice can be maintained only if use is made of some external apparatus capable of artificially stimulating the formation of large groups liable to win a majority, since existing groups, if left to their own devices, would never succeed in reconciling a sufficient variety of political traditions and attitudes. Coalitions set up to fight presidential elections would, moreover, be less arbitrarily motivated than those which aim only at winning or defending seats in the Assembly. In short, the main innovation brought about by the election of the President by universal suffrage is that parties now have an incentive to group together with a view to exercising power, and not merely supervising the Government.

This prospect would seem to offer the most hopeful means of reconciling the realities of French political life and the demands of a modern democracy. The various competing political forces could be symbolized as a nebula or, better, a series of constellations gravitating round the two presidential candidates: marginal elements might move from one to the other of the two main bodies. The French 'political families' might in this way be rearranged on an experimental, but by no means arbitrary, basis, since the operation would seek to achieve a state of balance under the control and with the assent of the electors themselves. If this led to a position of stability, it might be the precursor of a more drastically simplified distribution of political strength, as, in the USA, between Republicans and Democrats. But a situation of this kind is still a long way off.

Meanwhile, the presidential system seems to present two specific advantages that are lacking from other possible solutions. First, it seems better fitted to deal with the problem of the Communist Party, which would be integrated into an all-embracing collective organization imposing constraints of its own; the party could no longer wriggle out of these commitments, nor could it continue to take its present line of systematic criticism and non-responsibility, since its own voters would be consulted directly on a question which so far has never been put directly to the French public: to whom are you prepared to give the responsibility for governing you? The extreme left-wing electorate would also be brought back into the political game, without the Communist apparatus being able to use this force for its own ends, whereas it now completely controls the parliamentary extreme Left.

Secondly, a presidential regime implies only a limited (and therefore feasible) reform of the Deputy-centred Republic, since by definition it neutralizes two of the old system's most grievous shortcomings: anonymity and instability. On the other hand, if an effective parliamentary regime is to be set up, it will be necessary to eradicate all established habits and replace them with a new set of reflexes. Since 1959 persistent attempts have been made to introduce a measure of discipline, but they have led only to a state of incipient insurrection since excessive restrictions inevitably carry with them the promise of future reactions in the other direction. A shrub may be pruned, or it may be given a stake to help it grow straight, but nobody can make it grow against the wind. All through the history of France we can trace a constant prevailing wind, which has shaped the political landscape as we know it and swept aside any construction or outgrowth that failed to allow for it. In the end, the success or failure of the undertaking that began in the years from 1958 to 1962 must depend on how far this centuries-old proviso is observed.

Appendix 1 The Influence of the Presidential System

In his article 'Party System and Representation',[1] Seymour Martin Lipset writes:

Few observers have been willing to recognize how comparable are the social bases for multiple parties in France and the United States, and how far the difference between them in political stability is due to varying constitutional structures. The French two-ballot system may be regarded as a functional equivalent to the American primary elections. In both cases, different tendencies may compete in various ways up to the decisive final election. Thus, in most elections of the Third Republic, 'at the first ballot few candidates could obtain an absolute majority, so that at this stage there was no fear of splitting the vote and no deterrent to "splinter parties"; but at the second this fear became as effective as in Britain. Most constituencies then had a straight fight between a candidate of the Right and one of the Left.'[2]

The electoral alliances which, under the Third Republic, gave decisive victories to the Left or Right, would always break down in Parliament; hence the constant reshuffling of Cabinets. The common assumption, that these coalitions were so fragile because they tried to harmonize incompatible views and interests – such as those of the Radicals, as the party of small business, with the workers' philosophy of the Socialists – overlooks the fact that these differences have been no sharper than some within the American parties. The divergences on domestic issues between conservative Southern Democrats and left liberal Northern Democrats, or on foreign affairs between petty-bourgeois Republicans from the provincial mid-west and Republicans from the metropolitan centres of the east, with their close ties to international big business, are fully great. *The American party factions have been held together hardly by the Presidential system. Thus, the changing Congressional majorities on questions which cut across party lines are comparable to the*

1. Published in *Archives Européennes de Sociologie*, 1960, I, 1.
2. Philip Williams, *Politics in Post-War France*, Longmans, 1954, p. 310.

shifts in the Chamber as new issues were taken up. Since in America this cannot change the party in control of the executive, however, there has been continuity of executive action and also a substantial amount of party loyalty in important Congressional votes. It will be interesting to see whether the 'American' elements introduced into the French constitution by General de Gaulle will have comparable effects on the party system.

Bibliographical Note

France is probably the country of the non-English-speaking world which has been best studied by Anglo-Saxon political and social scientists and it is therefore impossible for a short bibliography to do much more than to skim the surface of the works, both general and detailed, which have been concerned with French affairs. Interest in France is unquestionably connected with the peculiar nature of the history and social development of that country, and readers who wish to acquire a more intimate understanding of French affairs would therefore be well-advised to study some of the works in English which have been most concerned with this past, in particular D. W. Brogan's *Development of Modern France* (Hamish Hamilton, 1940) and D. Thomson's *Democracy in France* (Oxford University Press, 1958), both of which are concerned, though the former in much greater detail, with the development of ideologies, political alignments, and underlying socio-economic forces which have shaped the French Republic in the nineteenth and twentieth centuries. Indeed, J. E. Bodley's classic work, *France* (Macmillan, 1898), can still be read with great profit, as the characteristics of French parties and in particular the individualistic nature of the French political leadership are still very apparent despite de Gaulle's rule in the Fifth Republic. For the more recent period of the Fourth Republic, P. M. Williams's *Crisis and Compromise* (Longmans, 1964) is an unparalleled source of information which no one who wishes to specialize in the subject can afford to miss, while those who wish to understand the attitudes, motivations and purposes of de Gaulle should refer to the General's *Memoirs* as well as to A. Werth, *De Gaulle* (Penguin Books, 1965). Finally, the two best introductions to the peculiar social characteristics of the country are perhaps, at two very different levels, H. Lüthy's *The State of France* (Secker & Warburg, 1955; published in France as *À l'heure de son clocher*, and in the USA as *France Against Herself*, Praeger, New York, 1955) and L. Wylie's *Village in the Vaucluse* (Harvard University Press, revised edition 1964): both of these are concerned with the problems of 'older France' and with current rejuvenation in the midst of traditions which die hard.

Studies of the constitutional structure of the country are very numerous, partly because legalism has always been a common French disease and partly because, of course, constitutional structures have repeatedly changed during the last two hundred years. Various British and American political scientists have written on the subject, together with a vast number of French authors. Among the latter, perhaps the best known is M. Duverger, whose *Cinquième République* (Presses Universitaires de France, Paris, 1960) and *La Sixième République et le régime présidentiel* (Fayard, Paris, 1961) should be studied by those concerned with the fairly detailed analysis of texts and the understanding of the approach which French scholars give to these problems. Among the works in English, R. C. Macridis and B. E. Brown, *The De Gaulle Republic* (Dorsey Press, Homewood, Illinois, 1960), and D. Pickles, *The Fifth French Republic* (Methuen, 1960), will be read with great profit.

It is impossible to consider in detail specific studies of French politics and administration. Much of the scholarly work of French political scientists has been devoted to the study of elections, traditionally done on the basis of the painstaking geographical analysis of results in various parts of the country: the masterpiece in the field was written in 1913 by A. Siegfried, *Tableau politique de la France de l'Ouest* (A. Colin, Paris), and, since 1958, every election and referendum has been covered by the French National Political Science Foundation, generally under the editorship of F. Goguel. It is only recently that surveys have begun to be used commonly as a means of understanding the motivations of Frenchmen, but one work in the field, that of P. Fougeyrollas, *La Conscience politique dans la France contemporaine* (Denoel, Paris, 1963), is a most penetrating study of attitudes in the postwar period and of the cleavages which divide Frenchmen among themselves, and in particular those which divide Communists from non-Communists.

British and American scholars have devoted much attention to the study of administrative practices, local and central: this is hardly surprising, in view of the influence which the French civil service has had abroad, both in general, and in the specific context of economic planning. The one general survey of French administration is that of F. Ridley and J. Blondel, *Public Administration in France* (Routledge & Kegan Paul, 1969); more specialized studies are those of B. Chapman,

Bibliographical Note

Introduction to French Local Government (Allen & Unwin, 1953), R. Grégoire, *The French Civil Service* (Brussels International Institute of Administrative Science, 1964), and P. Bauchet, *Economic Planning, the French experience* (Heinemann, 1963). While these studies are mainly concerned with legal and general institutional framework of administration, the social fabric and the social context within which administration action takes place have been analysed by M. Crozier in *The Bureaucratic Phenomenon* (Tavistock Publications, 1964) and the very important relationships between business and administration have been very penetratingly examined by H. Ehrmann in *Organized Business in France* (Princeton University Press, 1957) as well as by A. Shonfield in *Modern Capitalism* (Oxford University Press, 1965). These studies, as well as countless articles and books, have contributed to the rediscovery of France as a modern and profoundly changing society, much of which did account for the 'events' of 1968 and their aftermath. It is clearly too early to hope to see definitive works on *The May Revolution*, let alone on the end of Gaullism, though collections of essays published under this title by Penguin Books, 1969, will at least inform readers on the many strands of the movement. These events, together with the changing character of France in the 1950s and 1960s do assure at least that France will remain for a long time to come a subject of profound interest and controversy.

Glossary

'agreg.': *agrégation*. See p. 205, note

CFDT: Confédération Française Démocratique du Travail – French Democratic Labour Confederation (trade union)

CFTC: Confédération Française des Travailleurs Chrétiens – French Confederation of Christian Workers (trade union: now the continuing minority of the movement which split to produce the CFDT; hence references to 'CFTC maintenue')

CGA: Confédération Générale de l'Agriculture – General Agricultural Federation (trade union)

CGC: Confédération Générale des Cadres – General Federation of Executives (trade union)

CGT: Confédération Générale du Travail – General Confederation of Labour (trade union)

CGT–FO: Confédération Générale du Travail–Force Ouvrière– General Labour Federation–Workers' Power Movement (trade union)

CNIP: Centre National des Indépendants et Paysans – National Independent and Peasant Party (political party)

CNJA: Centre National des Jeunes Agriculteurs – National Young Farmers' Organization (trade union–pressure group)

CNPF: Comité National du Patronat Français – National Committee of French Employers (union-style organization–pressure group)

CODER: Commission de Développement Économique Régional – Regional Economic Development Commission (consultative and study organization created by the State)

ÉNA: École Nationale d'Administration – National School of Administration

ÉNS: École Normale Supérieure (*Écoles normales* are teacher-training establishments; the ÉNS was designed to produce teachers for upper secondary and higher education; recruitment is limited and highly competitive, so that the ÉNS represents one of the pinnacles of the French educational system)

Glossary

FÉN: Fédération de l'Éducation Nationale – National Education Federation (trade union representing staff in the State education system)

FGDS: Fédération de la Gauche Démocrate et Socialiste – Federated Left (Federated Democratic and Socialist Left; political party)

FNRI: Fédération Nationale des Républicains Indépendants – National Federation of Independent Republicans (political party)

FNSEA: Fédération Nationale des Syndicats d'Exploitants Agricoles – National Federation of Farming Unions (trade-union group)

FO: Force Ouvrière – Workers' Power Movement (trade union)

HÉC: École des Hautes Études Commerciales – School of Higher Business Studies

IFOP: Institut Français d'Opinion Publique – French Public Opinion Institute (private opinion-poll organization)

MODEF: Mouvement de Défense des Exploitations Familiales – Family Farm Defence Movement (union-style pressure group)

MRP: Mouvement Républicain Populaire – People's Republic Party (conservative)

ORTF: Office de Radiodiffusion-Télévision Française (French state radio and television organization)

PCF: Parti Communiste Française – French Communist Party

PDM: Progrès et Démocratie Moderne – Modern Democratic Progressives (political party)

PSU: Parti Socialiste Unifié – United Socialist Party

RDA: Rassemblement Démocratique Africain – African Democratic Assembly (political party)

RPF: Rassemblement du Peuple Français – Rally of the French People (United French People's Party; founded by de Gaulle in 1947)

'rue d'Ulm': see ÉNS

SFIO: Section Française de l'Internationale Ouvrière – French Section of the Workers' International (political party)

Société des Agrégés: See p. 205, note

SNCF: Société Nationale des Chemins de Fer Français – French Railways (nationalized)

SOFRES: Société Française des Enquêtes par Sondage (private opinion-poll organization)

UDC: Union de Défense des Commerçants – Union for the Defence of the Small Trader (political party)

UDR: Union pour la Défense de la République – Union for the Defence of the Republic (political party)

UDSR: Union Démocratique et Socialiste de la Résistance – United Democratic and Socialist Resistants (political party)

UDT: Union Démocratique du Travail – Democratic Workers' Federation (political party)

UDV^{e}R: Union des Démocrates pour la Cinquième République – United Democrats for the Fifth Republic (political party)

UNR: Union pour la Nouvelle République – New Republic Party (political party)

X: See p. 159

Index

Index